D0559601

Inside the Mind of the Stakeholder

Also by Ulrich Steger

THE BUSINESS OF SUSTAINABILITY: Building Industry Cases for Corporate Sustainability Mastering Global Corporate Governance (*with Peter Lorange, Fred Neubauer, John Ward and Bill George*)

CORPORATE DIPLOMACY: The Strategy for a Volatile Fragmented Business Environment

THE STRATEGIC DIMENSION OF ENVIRONMENTAL MANAGEMENT: Sustaining the Corporation during The Age of Ecological Discovery (*with Ralph Meima*)

Inside the Mind of the Stakeholder
The Hype Behind Stakeholder Pressure

Edited by
Ulrich Steger

BOWLING GREEN STATE UNIVERSITY
DISCARDED LIBRARY

palgrave
macmillan

IMD
INTERNATIONAL
Real World. Real Learning

EABIS
European Academy
of Business in Society

BOWLING GREEN STATE
UNIVERSITY LIBRARY

© Ulrich Steger 2006

All rights reserved. No reproduction, copy or transmission of this publication may be made without written permission.

No paragraph of this publication may be reproduced, copied or transmitted save with written permission or in accordance with the provisions of the Copyright, Designs and Patents Act 1988, or under the terms of any licence permitting limited copying issued by the Copyright Licensing Agency, 90 Tottenham Court Road, London W1T 4LP.

Any person who does any unauthorized act in relation to this publication may be liable to criminal prosecution and civil claims for damages.

The author has asserted his right to be identified as the author of this work in accordance with the Copyright, Designs and Patents Act 1988.

First published in 2006 by
PALGRAVE MACMILLAN
Houndmills, Basingstoke, Hampshire RG21 6XS and
175 Fifth Avenue, New York, N.Y. 10010
Companies and representatives throughout the world

PALGRAVE MACMILLAN is the global academic imprint of the Palgrave Macmillan division of St. Martin's Press, LLC and of Palgrave Macmillan Ltd. Macmillan® is a registered trademark in the United States, United Kingdom and other countries. Palgrave is a registered trademark in the European Union and other countries.

ISBN-13: 978–0–230–00689–8 hardback
ISBN-10: 0–230–00689–2 hardback

This book is printed on paper suitable for recycling and made from fully managed and sustained forest sources.

A catalogue record for this book is available from the British Library.

Library of Congress Cataloging-in-Publication Data

Inside the mind of the stakeholder : the hype behind stakeholder pressure / edited by Ulrich Steger.
    p. cm.
Includes bibliographical references and index.
Contents: Stakeholders and corporate sustainability – an overview – Stakeholder reports.
ISBN 0–230–00689–2
    1. Corporations – Public relations. 2. Sustainable development.
3. Social responsibility of business. 4. Pressure groups. I. Steger, Ulrich.

HD59.I5577 2006
338.7'4—dc22   2006045373

10 09 08 07 06 05 04 03 02 01
15 14 13 12 11 10 09 08 07 06

Printed and bound in Great Britain by
Antony Rowe Ltd, Chippenham and Eastbourne

Contents

List of Tables

List of Figures

Acknowledgments

The completion of this study owes a lot to the member companies of the Forum for Corporate Sustainability at IMD (see our website at www.imd.ch/csm for details). Their continuous support and their feedback to our presentations at our Forums on October 3 and 4 and November 21 and 22, 2005 were most valuable.

Our Advisory Board, consisting of Daniel Binswanger (Die Weltwoche), Jacqueline Côté (World Business Council for Sustainable Development), Peter Hughes (Philip Morris), Jean-Paul Jeanrenaud (WWF), Vernon Jennings (Novo Nordisk), Christian Kornevall (World Business Council for Sustainable Development), Clarissa Lins (Brazilian Foundation for Sustainable Development), Hans-Peter Meister (IFOK), Joachim Schwalbach (Humboldt-Universität zu Berlin) and Michael Yaziji (IMD), challenged us along the way and kept our research focused and relevant.

And again, we are extremely grateful to Peter Lorange, Jim Ellert, Philip Koehli and the IMD community for their generous material and intellectual support. Without this, we could not have concluded a second major empirical investigation in such a short time.

The research was a real team effort, with a special recognition for Oliver Salzmann in his role as "chief controler," data processor and methodologist and the extraordinary efforts of the PhD students Fabian Baptist, Alexander Nick, Jens Prinzhorn and Simon Tywuschik, who collected an amazing amount of high-quality data across Europe in an extremely short time.

We are also grateful to those who invested their time in this research effort by serving as interview partners or answering our questionnaire. We hope that all find the results worthwhile.

ULRICH STEGER
AILEEN IONESCU-SOMERS
Lausanne, August 2006

List of Abbreviations

ANOVA	Analysis of Variance
BCS	Business Case for (Corporate) Sustainability
CEO	Chief Executive Officer
CS	Corporate Sustainability
CSM	Corporate Sustainability Management
CSR	Corporate Social Responsibility
DJSI	Dow Jones Sustainability Index
EAI	Enhanced Analytics Initiative
EMAS	Eco-Management and Audit Scheme
GRI	Global Reporting Initiative
HGB	Handelsgesetzbuch
IFC	International Finance Corporation
ILO	International Labour Organization
ISO	International Organization for Standardization
M&A	Mergers and Acquisitions
MNC	Multinational Company
NGO	Non-Governmental Organization
OECD	Organization for Economic Co-operation and Development
OFR	Operational Financial Review
P&L	Profit and Loss
REACH	Registration, Evaluation and Authorisation of Chemicals
SA	Social Accountability
SD	Sustainable Development
SRI	Socially Responsible Investment
UNEP FI	United Nations Environment Programme Finance Initiative
WBCSD	Word Business Council for Sustainable Development
WTO	World Trade Organization

Foreword

How can companies engage with all their different stakeholders and respond to all the different, often contradictory expectations? What can be done when stakeholders do not want to dialogue while openness, trust and credibility are becoming an ever more important factor for success? Companies today face the challenge of growing scrutiny in their business environment.

In parallel, stakeholder dialogue is currently entering a new phase. Confrontation is no longer at center stage; dialogue and cooperation are far more self-evident than even a few years ago. Companies and stakeholders have learned to approach one another, to first understand the other side's position and look for common ground. They have created a reliable basis and concentrate on solutions – solutions to challenges that none of them alone can overcome today.

Business models are becoming ever more complex. Our supply chains stretch across continents. Contractual commitments are merely temporary, change is occurring at ever-shorter intervals. Nonetheless, we want to live up to our long-term responsibility. How can one company alone predict the often-unpredictable consequences of its business? Stakeholders can add another perspective here and assess developments differently. In a dialogue, surprising alternatives become possible.

But we are often confronted with a societal dilemma, too. Value concepts clash and the common ground shrinks to a minimum. Managers from the energy industry know all about that. In laborious negotiations politicians, companies and stakeholders try to build frameworks that take into account their controversial standpoints on climate protection, security of supply and economics. Stakeholder dialogue here is a process that will accompany and help us in the long term.

The results of this book give me hope. The studies have shown that talking with one another and learning from one another are becoming increasingly self-evident, that companies and stakeholders are working together to level the playing field. So that fair competition becomes possible and accepted – worldwide.

HARRY ROELS
President and CEO, RWE Group

Notes on the Contributors

Fabian Baptist is researcher for IMD's projects on Corporate Sustainability Management, CSM. In 2005 he graduated in Business Administration at the University of Augsburg with main emphasis on Strategic Management, Environmental Management, Statistics and Informatics. In the same year, he started a PhD in business administration with a focus on stakeholder management of multinational corporations. Fabian Baptist holds a scholarship from the German National Merit Foundation. During his studies, he acquired consultancy experience at Accenture Ltd, Celerant Consulting Ltd and RWE Power Corporation.

Aileen Ionescu-Somers is Program Manager of IMD's research project on Corporate Sustainability Management, CSM. Previously, she was Head of International Projects Unit at the World Wide Fund for Nature (WWF International), and held program management roles with the Africa and Latin America regional programs. She holds a BA, MA, H.Dip. Ed and MSc in Environmental Management and is working on a doctoral thesis in the area of corporate social responsibility in the food and beverage sector.

Alexander Nick is researcher for IMD's research project on Corporate Sustainability Management, CSM. He holds a Masters of Industrial Management from Darmstadt University of Technology and is writing his doctoral thesis on strategic early awareness systems. Since 2002, he has been working as a management consultant and conducted projects in several areas such as strategy and sustainability, corporate foresight, stakeholder dialogues and sustainability reporting. Alexander Nick is a member of the think tank 30 Germany of the Club of Rome.

Jens Prinzhorn is researcher for IMD's research projects on Corporate Sustainability Management, CSM. He holds a BA and MA of European Studies (Politics and Economics) from University of Osnabrueck, Germany, and a Master of Corporate Communication from Bond University, Australia. He is writing his doctoral thesis on the demand for corporate social responsibility through NGOs, Consumer Organisations and Unions toward multinational companies. Since he joined IMD, he has conducted empirical research in several areas such as strategy and sustainability, particularly in stakeholders' perceptions. Jens Prinzhorn is a member of the Foundation of German Business.

Oliver Salzmann is research associate for IMD's research project on Corporate Sustainability Management, CSM. He holds a Masters of Industrial Management from Dresden University of Technology and has recently concluded his doctoral thesis on corporate sustainability management in the energy sector. Since he joined IMD in 2001, he has conducted empirical research in several areas such as private households and sustainable consumption, the business case for corporate sustainability and stakeholders' perceptions and activities with respect to corporate social and environmental responsibility.

Ulrich Steger holds the Alcan Chair of Environmental Management at IMD and is Director of IMD's Forum on Corporate Sustainability Management, CSM. He is Director of Building High Performance Boards and other major partnership programs (e.g. Daimler Chrysler and Allianz Excellence). He also holds an Honorary Professorship for International Management at Technical University Berlin. He was Minister of Economics and Technology in the State of Hesse and a member of the Managing Board of Volkswagen, in charge of environment and traffic matters and the implementation of an environmental strategy within the VW group worldwide. He has published extensively, most recently the book '*The Business of Sustainability*' (Macmillan, 2004).

Simon Tywuschik is a Research Associate at IMD in the Corporate Sustainability Management (CSM) research project. He holds a MSc in International Economics from the International University of Maastricht and is currently writing a PhD on stakeholder and risk management. Since he joined IMD in 2004, he has conducted empirical research on current stakeholder strategies and attended several forums and conferences with respect to this topic.

Executive Summary: Inside the Mind of the Stakeholder

Ulrich Steger

Are we developing a dual culture in business?

Read the finance section of any leading national newspaper and you think: shareholder value is today's mantra and paradigm for companies. They praise themselves on how focused they are on the bottom line and how responsive to every business opportunity – reducing costs and employment permanently. Read the political section and you may be inclined to think: Sustainable development is today's mantra and paradigm. At its peak – the World Economic Forum in Davos – you read how concerned CEOs all over the world are about climate change, poverty, child labor, etc.

Is this "pleasing the gallery" in today's fragmented world, in which you have dozens of audiences and an opportunity to tailor your PR messages accordingly? Is it also happening in a complex, tangled world where contradictions have no limits? Or are we talking about a transition, full of paradoxes, where the old, shareholder-centric thinking is still around, but increasingly substituted by a more enlightened thinking of business responsibility?

We wanted to find out – after all, the main task of empirical research is to discover and present facts that are not easy to discern (... the "truth" will remain elusive anyhow ...). We surveyed the perspectives of very different stakeholders – from capital markets to environmental activists – and examined (see Chapter 2 for more details on research questions and framework):

- How they perceive corporate sustainability, i.e. corporate social and environmental performance in particular.
- How and to what extent they influence it.
- How they select the actions they take to influence companies.

Thus, the study complemented an empirical investigation on the "business case for corporate sustainability" (BCS).[1] Whereas the BCS study took an "inside-out" perspective (surveying managers on how they identified internal and external opportunities to engage in corporate sustainability), the present study takes an "outside-in" approach (surveying stakeholders on how they perceive companies and their activities in corporate sustainability).

Method and samples

We collected the data between May and November 2005 in Europe only. The study design features a mix of qualitative methods (direct semi-structured interviews and content analysis) and quantitative methods (self-completion questionnaires and descriptive/inferential statistics). Thus, we were able to triangulate our results and gain complementary insights into the research field.

We conducted 265 interviews and collected 372 questionnaires in total, across the following nine stakeholders: governments/regulators, unions, NGOs, consumer organizations, financial institutions, corporate customers, corporate suppliers, communities/cities and the media. To obtain essential points of reference and validate our results, we additionally carried out 15 "benchmarking interviews" with managers to examine their views on stakeholders. Our low response rate to the questionnaire (roughly 2–3 per cent) gives some indication of stakeholders' interest in this topic (more on that follows later).

The business case for corporate sustainability

In our previous study (based on more than 1,000 questionnaires and 350 interviews), we looked at nine industries – airlines, automotive, chemical, electricity, financial services, food, oil and gas, pharmaceutical and technology. We found that the business logic for corporate activities in the social and environmental domain (like the issues) vary widely between the industries. However, none of the companies attached more than second-tier importance to social or environmental issues (beyond legal compliance). Most saw the need to monitor and manage the issues professionally, but the issues were not "make it or break it." Since the late nineteenth century, companies learned to use technology and business processes to cope with social regulations and (for nearly four decades) environmental standards. For the last two decades, they have also learned to communicate better to their public audiences on the issues.

The study showed that the ignorance and reluctance of key stakeholders (such as customers and financial markets) with regard to corporate sustainability was a significant barrier. Without changes in that "department," companies tended to stick with their incremental approach to improve social and environmental performance rather than develop radically innovative business models and products: "Laggards are punished, but innovators are not rewarded" was the bottom line of our evidence.

As Figure ES.1 shows, internal barriers to corporate sustainability (mindset, organizational culture, processes and tools) took a greater share than external barriers. It is obvious that both are interdependent: Internal capacities would most likely be built if external pressures were more significant. Until today, the main pressure comes from individual incidents damaging brand value and reputation (in fact the number of

Figure ES.1 Barriers to corporate sustainability

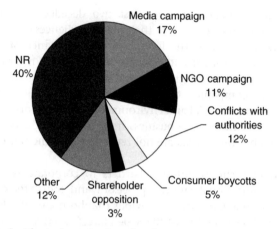

Media campaign
17%

NR
40%

NGO campaign
11%

Conflicts with
authorities
12%

Other
12%

Shareholder
opposition
3%

Consumer boycotts
5%

Figure ES.2   Incidents damaging brand and reputation

incidents that make headlines has drastically declined since Brent Spar in 1995) (Figure ES.2).

Given the marginality of the business case for corporate sustainability, few companies took the trouble to build it systematically. Some companies were reluctant due to the difficulty of monetizing the "external effects" (often the less active companies). The more active companies attempted to establish a link between social and environmental issues and their core business strategy, which can be – due to the lack of interest from primary stakeholders – very challenging.

What did we find inside the minds of stakeholders?

General findings. The more demanding stakeholders are about social and environmental issues, the more irrelevant they are for companies. NGOs and consumer organizations are most demanding, but they are also not companies' primary stakeholders. They themselves admit that they do not have the leverage to push the companies toward more sustainable business models and products. In turn, companies envy NGOs, as they are much better – because they are more credible – political campaigners.

Overall, regulatory compliance is the most important factor for stakeholders, and it is – in Europe – very common. For a company, this clearly means that corporate sustainability management essentially boils down to minimizing the downside potential (being compliant, avoiding incidents). In contrast to the often-used rhetoric, it hardly involves innovation.

Given the relatively high social and environmental standards in Europe, most stakeholders see little room beyond the incremental progress that is part of "normal" business life. Nevertheless, one should not underestimate the impact of gradual, but steady improvements (as long as they are not overcompensated by other effects).

One issue of specific concern appears to be the lower social and environmental standards in emerging markets, especially Southeast Asia, and the impact on the competitiveness of Europe-based manufacturing and services. A variety of stakeholders and industries, therefore, are calling for a "level playing field" (but are uncertain about how this can be achieved).

Transparency and accountability are two general, broader trends that are clearly important. Corporate sustainability has clearly profited from them – as one can easily see in the rapidly growing number of reports. Nevertheless, some cynics maintain that corporate behavior today has not changed significantly, it has merely been documented and "sold." We conclude that companies have learned their key lessons in the past. They not only learned to manage most social and environmental issues more systematically, but to communicate better (with their stakeholders about their arguments). It is no accident that the big PR disasters, which continue to be quoted time and again in today's academic literature, happened a decade or more ago (e.g. Shell's Brent Spar or Nike's child labor).

Stakeholders clearly focus their attention on the big US or European companies and their social and environmental performance. This is not self-evident per se, considering that:

- Small and medium-sized companies produce between two-thirds and three-quarters of the nations' GNP, and can often be linked to similar social and environmental issues.
- Big (often state-owned) companies from emerging markets are more ruthless in their behavior (e.g. natural resource extraction, dealing with dictators). They are also rarely in the spotlight.

The reason for this is a self-feeding information cycle: Media believe that only "household names" are of interest to the broader public, which leads NGOs (and sustainability analysts) to focus on those companies. The public recognizes them ("oh, it's Nestlé again ..."), which is also due to media coverage.

Overall, financial markets and media are seen as the most influential stakeholders. Most stakeholders (communities, governments and unions in particular) see themselves as more influential than the other stakeholders see them. While this can be expected, it is a dilemma that (1) those stakeholders with less stakes in corporate sustainability (corporate customers, suppliers and financial institutions) have the best tools to assess corporate social and environmental performance and that (2) they use them more systematically (as they are mostly businesses used to this kind of approach).

If there is any significant current risk for companies, it is the increasing opportunism of the different players: antagonistic players can come together in a certain context and for a specific issue (e.g. when conservative politicians jump on the union- or NGO-driven bandwagon and call for a boycott of a company that is closing a plant). Alliances are formed and gain momentum before the company has really noticed. (A recent example is the plant closure in Nuernberg by Electrolux.)

Overall confrontation may become "outdated." With the exception of some parts of the NGO community who stick to their classical advocacy and political lobbying, everybody is looking for dialogue, cooperation and joint projects with companies as the way forward. If this continues, a boring world will be ahead of us. Memories of the gladiator-style battles of the "good old days" will fade …

What we learned about individual stakeholders. Despite their heterogeneity in some areas, we managed to capture stakeholders' approaches to corporate sustainability accurately. In the following, we will briefly describe the nine groups surveyed – respectively providing an illustrative quote:

Financial institutions obviously exert tremendous influence on companies nowadays. This applies in particular to the financial mainstream (the niche around socially responsible investing and corporate sustainability ratings and indices is growing but still rather insignificant) that is not a strong driver for corporate sustainability.

As long as financial market institutions are opportunists and not strategists, the financial market will not be a strong driver for corporate sustainability.

> The economic logic and business advantages of corporate sustainability are not strong enough. Assessment of corporate social and environmental performance occurs, but it is not part of the mainstream analyses. Hence, the overall significant risks and opportunities associated with financial institutions' role as stakeholders are limited. Their activities are limited and intended to increase accountability and transparency as well as engagement and dialogue.

Most *cities and communities* are basically – in their constant struggle to maintain employment – being "blackmailed" by companies:

> We do not apply any criteria [beyond compliance] because our challenge is to promote the region of our city to companies. There is strong competition between communities across Europe. We only win those "battles" if we do not ask for more than what the regulators want.

In particular, small communities have very little capacity and responsibility to assess and influence corporate behavior individually. They often rely on personal contacts and the chamber of commerce. They are satisfied with widespread regulatory compliance, and hardly dare to raise social and environmental standards. They aim to engage with companies and hope to be seen as partners that are (more) serious.

Governments and regulators are also primarily concerned about employment levels and thus regional competitiveness. In this situation, higher social and environmental standards are largely "taboo," and they fall back on an enabling approach to corporate sustainability.

> Governments do not have enough money [...]. Therefore, we have to mobilize companies to meet their responsibilities and to be more active in CSR.

Governments provide and promote standards and guidelines (also to create more transparency), establish award schemes and adopt softer (more negotiated agreements) and less bureaucratic legislation. In light of their weakening bargaining power (against the big multinationals in particular) they have also (more or less desperately and opportunistically) tried to target the reputation of companies that have decided to relocate or lay-off significant parts of their workforce.

NGOs are driven by a great variety of social and environmental issues: They mainly aim for more corporate transparency and accountability, particularly in developing countries. We detected a certain frustration about the skill of companies in managing NGOs and their campaigns more and more proficiently (a lot of talks and dialogues without real changes on the ground).

> In the early days, we could not get to the factory gates; today they serve us tea and cookies.

This is why the NGO community has increasingly engaged with companies (cooperation and partnerships) – however, not without a sometimes-heated debate about whether "flirting with the enemy" is the right thing to do. It appears that a combined "carrot and stick" approach often works because companies see the upside (gaining more credibility and expertise through engagement) next to the downside of ignoring the campaigning NGO.

Consumer organizations were somewhat "happy" that companies (particularly those that have branded goods and are close to the consumer) are at least doing a bit. They also pointed beyond the big western multinationals to the challenges in emerging economies and among small and medium-sized companies.

> We need to get to the tier below big companies and also away from the dialogue on big companies in Western Europe. There are huge companies in India and China that are not focused as key players of the CSR debate. I don't think that these can fall off the radar screen for much longer.

Most significantly, consumer organizations lack resources because their activities are largely based on their own product-related research. We see an interesting new development through bilateral activities between different national consumer organizations, as they provide an opportunity for more accurate and powerful assessment of corporate behavior and products.

Media are quite a special group of stakeholders, since their mission is to disseminate information that is novel and relevant to their target audiences:

> Our program is to reflect adequately the topics that are currently most important to society. Unemployment, business relocation and sustainability are such topics; we try to address the worries and questions of our audience.

Corporate sustainability plays a significant role only in niche media and publications. Journalists primarily assess corporate performance through desktop research (other media, internet) and their own investigations (through personal contacts with third parties). Their approach is quite intuitive and targeted at corporate reputation and implicitly customer loyalty. They often criticize corporate sustainability management as a PR tool and window-dressing.

Corporate suppliers and customers are in several ways different from each other. Corporate customers have a clear business case to make their suppliers to comply with certain social and environmental standards. In developing countries, those standards most often go beyond domestic regulations

> For "beyond compliance," we want suppliers to be comparable to the level used in our own production plants. For the moment, it is not exactly the same. And in some countries, it is not possible to come even close ...

In contrast, corporate suppliers often do not "dare" to bother their customers with corporate sustainability, unless there is a clear need for product responsibility and risk management, e.g. hazardous chemicals.

> There is no room for CSR – my job is to manage, run and grow the business. From day-to-day, other than aspects of good management, I do not have space for these issues.

Obviously, there is a clear preference for long-term relationships. Performance assessment largely occurs through internal audits (corporate customers) and key account management (corporate suppliers – although social and environmental have little relevance), overall it is clearly more systematic among corporate customers. To manage their risks and protect their brands, corporate customers and suppliers tend to "use" engagement (e.g. cooperation, partnerships), guidelines and standards as well as regulation.

Unions' attitudes toward corporate sustainability reflect their weakening bargaining power in Europe and their great concern about employment and job security. Only a very few take an active and holistic approach to it; some even see it as a corporate attempt to forestall legislation:

> We have a nuanced view on CSR: It is neither inherently bad, nor good. And, it is not a substitute for regulation and collective bargaining.

Thus, it is obvious that assessment of corporate performance is largely unsystematic and based on networks, corporate reports and the media/internet. They criticize a reactive compliance-oriented approach by companies and consider corporate sustainability management largely a PR exercise with few changes "on the ground." They aim to influence companies through engagement, political lobbying and praising and blaming in the public arena. In light of weakened regional competitiveness in Europe, they call for a more universal application of social and environmental standards by companies around the globe.

Four clusters of stakeholders. Based on our evidence, we clustered the nine stakeholders into three groups (plus media): challengers, bystanders and incrementalists. They can be profiled as follows:

1. The *challengers* include NGOs and consumer organizations. Their demands for corporate sustainability are by far the most specific (related to certain issues or products) and highest. Hence, it is not surprising that their activities – along with those of the media – are met with opposition from companies. Among other things, they call for more proactive corporate behavior, foremost in developing countries, and more transparency and accountability. Their strategy to this end is essentially two-pronged: It includes both engaging with companies as well as a more confrontational approach through political lobbying, praising and blaming. In some areas, they have also taken quasi-regulatory functions through the provision of labels, standards and guidelines.

2. The *bystanders*, governments/regulators, cities/communities and unions, are largely concerned about regional competitiveness and employment. Corporate sustainability is of minor importance because social and environmental standards are already high in Europe. Hence, those stakeholders are "standing by" and some are (unions in particular) even skeptical because they feel that corporate sustainability clashes with their primary mission (compromising regional competitiveness, forestalling legislation).

3. The *incrementalists* are all corporate stakeholders, i.e. corporate customers, corporate suppliers and financial institutions. They are primarily concerned about their competitiveness and, hence, a level playing field. Since social and environmental issues only have marginal relevance to their core business models, corporate sustainability is essentially part of risk management to protect brand value and reputation. Since companies have learned to manage issues and reputation more systematically, incrementalists see little need to go beyond quasi-regulation and engagement when it comes to influencing companies.

Despite the great differences between the four groups of stakeholders, they exhibit two very interesting commonalities: First, they are equally (more or less) satisfied with corporate regulatory compliance, companies' willingness to engage and dialogue, and their transparency and accountability. This clearly reflects: (1) the significance of Europe's high social and environmental standards; and (2) companies' new openness (in comparison with the early 1990s) to stakeholders. Second, all four groups are equally effective (or ineffective) at engaging and changing companies, which we attribute to the strong bargaining power of companies and/or overall limited pressure to engage more strongly in corporate sustainability.

A glance at the crystal ball

Our research clearly provides a snapshot of the status quo. Nobody should assume that this remains stable, for several reasons:

- The issue of job erosion might be tackled by (protectionist) government intervention. The first wave of "anti-globalization" campaigning had little impact, but created a ratchet effect of awareness. A second wave – fuelled by continuously higher unemployment – may have deeper political implications, especially if it coincides with any dramatic worsening of the (energy) security situation.
- NGOs will surely find new ways of effective campaigning and will meet a new generation of corporate executives (outside the investment banks) with potentially different values.
- Global companies are currently at the peak of their power – but will they stay there? After all, there is no natural propensity for a global market economy. It is currently accepted – after the collapse of communism – as the better-performing alternative. But with fading memories and a decaying social fabric, the tide might turn again.

Currently, companies do not need to worry. However, will this comfortable position eventually lead to complacency and to the downfall of corporate dominance? After all, one of the few "iron laws" appears to be that one can only maintain power, if one uses it responsibly.

Note

1 U. Steger (ed.), *The Business of Sustainability* (Basingstoke: Palgrave Macmillan, 2004).

Part I

Stakeholders and Corporate Sustainability: An Overview

1
The Hype Behind Stakeholder Pressure

Ulrich Steger

The pressure on companies to report on these issues cannot be ignored... It comes not just from activists but also from investors, accounting bodies and governments. The Japanese government has published environmental reporting guidelines, and France requires public companies to provide social and environmental information in their financial reports.[1]

A number of studies have indicated that the environmental disclosure of corporations is still at a very low level even though they are faced with increasing pressures from diverse stakeholder groups, including governmental agencies, to address environmental concerns.[2]

How concerned are CEOs of global companies about receiving pressure from their stakeholders to behave in a more socially and environmentally responsible manner? Ask McKinsey what CEOs were talking about beyond their daily operations in 2005, and you will find the following answers:[3]

1. Asia's continuing emergence and the implications, especially offshoring.
2. Maintaining growth.
3. Energy prices and supply.
4. Aging population and underfunded pensions.

Topics 3 and 4 have some relation to sustainable development (SD). However, are they really driven by companies' stakeholders or do they reflect CEOs' natural concern about potential impacts on the (financial) bottom line?

The hype in the rhetoric of political and academic communities dealing with corporate sustainability management (CSM) or corporate social responsibility (CSR) was already noticeable when we looked into the "Business Case for Corporate Sustainability" (BCS). However, it became even more significant when we tried to go "inside the mind of stakeholders." Simply put, there is no empirical evidence for what is the mantra of many statements on the increasing pressure for CSM/CSR. In fact, we detected a very patchy picture, reflecting cyclical dynamics of pressure and shifting issues. In light of globalization and Europe's currently constant struggle for competitiveness, a decrease of stakeholder pressure seems at least as plausible as an increase.

However, our main research rationale was not to reject unproven claims in the CSM/CSR debate. It was to complement the "inside-out" perspective of our previous BCS study[4] with an "outside-in" perspective from stakeholders. After all, the sustainability efforts of companies would only be of limited success if not appreciated by their stakeholders. Our previous study clearly showed that many managers in global companies perceive the support of stakeholders for sustainable development as less than enthusiastic.

As Figures 1.1 and 1.2 show, both general managers and sustainability officers (i.e. managers responsible for driving the corporate sustainability agenda – of some sort – in their companies) consider external stakeholders to be

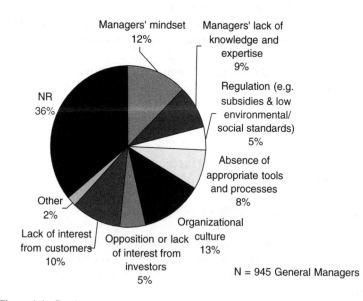

Figure 1.1 Barriers to corporate sustainability management – as perceived by general managers

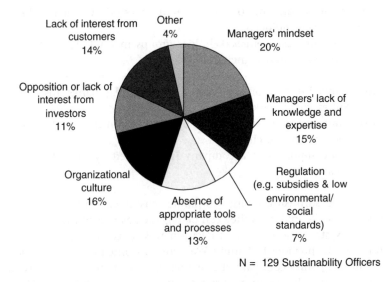

Figure 1.2 Barriers to corporate sustainability management – as perceived by sustainability officers

a significant barrier to corporate sustainability management. Our evidence showed that stakeholders' opposition and lack of interest ultimately rule out any first-mover advantage. Nevertheless, corporate sustainability is professionally managed because no one wants to be seen as a laggard.

In the following sections, we will complement (and validate) these findings by examining:

- How important CS/CSR is to stakeholders.
- How they assess and influence corporate behavior.
- How effective they are.

Obviously, the results will be relevant to both companies and stakeholders. Like companies, stakeholders can be very different from each other. An aggregation of any sort would most probably "average out" the most interesting findings. How do you ensure a differentiated and meaningful analysis and avoid overwhelming complexity? Global companies have thousands of (local) stakeholders of which headquarters are largely unaware. Some of them are part of the business system (we call them transactional stakeholders); others are outside of the business system, but nevertheless relevant for companies because they can influence the economic performance of companies (in this study, we refer to them as contextual stakeholders).

We chose nine different stakeholder groups in total. The group of transactional stakeholders includes:

1. All financial institutions or "capital markets" (e.g. banks, insurance companies, stock markets).
2. Corporate customers (represented by managers in the supply chain, i.e. procurement, purchasing).
3. Corporate suppliers of a company (represented by marketing and sales managers).

It might be surprising to list (corporate) customers and suppliers as important stakeholders as they can be regarded as part of the extended business system. However, this decision was based on an interesting finding of the previous BCS study: We were confronted with the paradox that all companies complained that their customers were not ready to honor sustainability performance in the products and services they buy. However, they exhibit a similar pattern in their behavior as customers.

Our set of contextual stakeholders is comprised of:

1. Communities/cities.
2. Non-governmental organizations (NGOs), mostly environmental and social pressure groups.
3. Consumer organizations, a special kind of NGO with a focus on consumer interests.
4. Unions.
5. Government agencies/regulators (not the lawmaker themselves).

Media represent a special kind of stakeholder. They were included due to their significant role in moderating and amplifying the perceptions of other stakeholders.

The book is divided into two parts. In Part I, we provide a holistic and aggregated view of our evidence. After this brief introduction, we describe our research design and method in Chapter 2. Chapter 3 provides initial background on dynamics between companies and their stakeholders. In section 3.1, we review significant trends that have emerged over the last decades and how they have affected both companies and their stakeholders.

The following two sections are an essential part of our research design, as they provide the reader with a more holistic perspective on the research topic. It seemed appropriate to complement our stakeholder data with recent empirical evidence collected from managers:

- In section 3.2, we recap our previous study on the business case[5] and elaborate on how managers at that time (2002–2003) viewed the importance of corporate sustainability, their stakeholders and the key drivers and barriers to corporate sustainability.
- Section 3.3 features the findings of 15 interviews with managers, carried out in the summer of 2005, to have an up-to-date view on how they see their stakeholders.

In section 3.4, we discuss stakeholders' transmission belts (their means of influencing companies) in more detail. This will allow the reader to have a more detailed and comparative look at stakeholders' actions and their effectiveness in influencing companies.

Chapter 4 presents the consolidated findings from the research. We assign nine stakeholder groups into three stakeholder clusters with similar strategies and attitudes. Furthermore, we discuss the specific role of media as an amplifier in more detail. In sections 4.1.1 to 4.1.4, we elaborate on the clusters' and media's missions, processes and tools, actions and their effectiveness and discuss nuances within the clusters.

In section 4.2, we analyze similarities and patterns across the clusters. In section 4.3, we highlight significant future trends, which emerged from our research, and their impact on companies. We will come back to assess critically the claim of increasing stakeholder pressure and highlight our key findings in Chapter 5.

Part II of our book documents the findings of the nine individual stakeholder groups in detail. We elaborated on corporate customers and suppliers in the same section to avoid too much repetition. These stakeholder reports are descriptive in nature and focus on the individual stakeholder in detail: their background, their approach to corporate sustainability, their incentives and motives, processes and tools, criteria used for actions, expectations, their current stakeholder strategies (actions and their effectiveness, determinants of the effectiveness) and future trends.

Notes

1   Allen White, GRI Secretariat Director, quoted in the *Financial Times*, 28 March 2002.

2 Robert Dixon, Gehan A. Mousa and Anne Woodhead, "The Role of Environmental Initiatives in Encouraging Companies to Engage in Environmental Reporting," *European Management Journal*, Dec. 2005, vol. 23 issue 6, pp. 702–16.

3 *McKinsey Quarterly*, Online Special Topics, 27 December 2005.

4 U. Steger (ed.), *The Business of Sustainability* (Basingstoke: Palgrave Macmillan, 2004).

5 Ibid.

2
Getting into the Minds of Stakeholders: Framework and Methodology

Oliver Salzmann

In this chapter, we will briefly elaborate on the rationale and technicalities such as the framework, method and the sample of our study.

Rationale

We designed the study as a follow-up to previous empirical research on corporate sustainability management (CSM) and its business case.[1] In this previous study, we defined CSM as a strategic profit-driven approach to resolve or mitigate environmental and social issues,[2] explicitly to demarcate it from a potential "philanthropic aura." At that time, we surveyed more than 1,000 managers in nine different industries across the globe (mainly in the USA, Western Europe and Japan). Our respondents unanimously complained about the prevalent ignorance and indifference of most of their stakeholders with regard to corporate sustainability initiatives, and hence about the rather weak and elusive business case for corporate sustainability. It appeared obvious that we test these findings, this time, by surveying stakeholders and their interest in and demand for CSM.

Framework

The study examined the extent to which stakeholders actually perceived corporate sustainability management and how they aimed to influence it. We focused primarily on the outcomes of corporate sustainability management, i.e. various dimensions of corporate social and environmental performance that are visible and, hence, assessible to the stakeholder, for example, transparency and accountability, the use of environmental management systems, targets, social and environmental effects of the supply chain, production and products. In the context of this study, notions such as corporate social responsibility, corporate citizenship (also if used in an interviewee's quote) should be understood as synonyms to corporate sustainability management.

If we were to ascertain that superior corporate social and environmental performance is rewarded by stakeholders through improved brand value, access to capital or fewer controls by regulators – leading to better corporate financial performance – we could claim that a business case for corporate sustainability exists. So the study is rooted in:

- Strategic legitimacy theory: This suggests that legitimacy is to a certain extent controllable by managers. It is seen as a resource that organizations want to obtain through corporate activities such as communication, social and environmental initiatives, etc.[3]
- Stakeholder theory: According to stakeholder theory, corporations have relationships with many constituent groups that affect and are

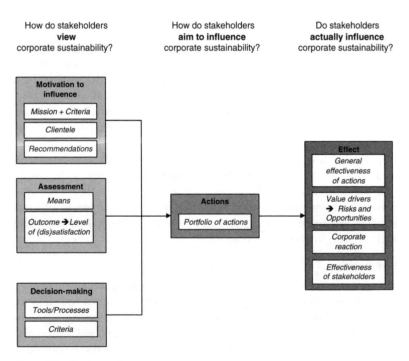

Figure 2.1   Framework

affected by its decisions. Those relationships affect corporate processes and outcomes.[4]

The study's framework is depicted in Figure 2.1. It features three main fields of analysis:

1. Stakeholders' view of corporate sustainability: How important is it in light of their own mission and stakeholders? What do they recommend companies should do about corporate sustainability? How do they assess corporate social and environmental performance (own investigations, media, third party audits, etc.), and what is the outcome of that assessment – are they satisfied or not, and, if so, to what extent? Finally, how do they make their decisions?

2. Stakeholders' actions: Do they actually take actions to influence corporate sustainability management and what is their focus: campaigning, lobbying, regulating, labeling/certification, etc.?

3. Stakeholders' influence on companies: Which actions are considered especially effective? Which corporate value drivers are affected by stakeholders' actions (reputation and brand value, access-to-capital, innovation etc.)? How do companies react to stakeholders' actions – do they ignore them, cooperate, change? Finally, how effective do stakeholder groups perceive themselves to be relative to others?

Focus

In the BCS study, we had selected the most exposed and hence relevant industries (i.e. those with the biggest social and/or environmental footprints) in Europe, the USA and Japan. This time – due to the greater heterogeneity of stakeholders (after all – even companies in different industries are more alike than, for example, unions and private banks), – we had to adopt a more narrow focus: We surveyed a range of the nine most important stakeholders for companies (see Figure 2.2).

We differentiated between five regions: (1) Germany/Austria/ Switzerland; (2) France/Belgium; (3) Spain/Portugal; (4) Nordic countries; and the Netherlands and (5) Great Britain/Ireland.

Method and samples

We collected the data between May and November 2005 in Europe only. Hereby, we deviated from the BCS study (which included North America and Japan) for the following reasons:

- Many stakeholders are still dominantly nationally organized. If we had gone beyond Europe, the substantial heterogeneity in our sample would have increased further.

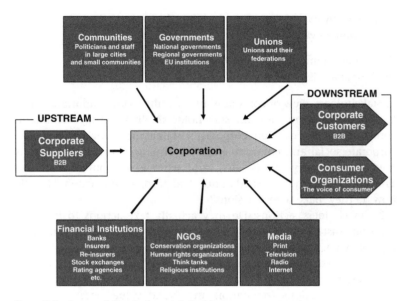

Figure 2.2   Scope of the study – stakeholder groups surveyed

- As IMD is a business school with a focus on companies, we expected it to be more difficult to access the stakeholder population. A European focus allowed us to concentrate our resources.

The study featured a mixed methods design including semi-structured interviews and a self-completion questionnaire to complement each other and triangulate our results (see Appendixes). We conducted 280 interviews and collected 372 questionnaires in total. They were analyzed through content analysis and standard statistical tools (chi square tests, ANOVAs, factor analysis) respectively. Unless indicated otherwise, results we report on are statistically significant at a 5 per cent level.

Table 2.1 describes the number of interviews conducted per stakeholder and region as well as the details of our interviewees' positions. As Figure 2.3 shows, our interview sample has an intended bias toward NGOs and governments. The geographical distribution of interviews depicted in Figure 2.4 shows a significant bias toward Germany, Switzerland and Austria. This is primarily due to convenience sampling.

We not only interviewed nine stakeholder groups referred to above, but also conducted 15 benchmarking interviews (5 per cent of all interviews) with managers in companies to validate our results. This was

Table 2.1 Samples per stakeholder and region – interviews

Stakeholder	Interviewees conducted	Interviewees' position/role	DE/CH/AT	UK/IRL	PT/ESP	Nordic/NL	FRA/BEL	Other
Governments	47	Head, deputy head, policy advisor, press officer	17	4	6	4	9	7
NGOs	48	Head, deputy head, department heads of campaigning and business liaisons, policy advisor, press officer	18	13	5	10	2	0
Consumer organizations	15	CEOs, department heads and deputy	5	3	0	4	3	0
Communities	18	Mayors, city managers, directors and department heads in local authorities/regulators	12	1	1	3	1	0
Financial institutions	37	CEO, board member, analyst, director, general manager, vice president	24	5	2	4	0	2
Media	32	Editors, senior editor, freelance journalists	12	8	4	4	4	0

Continued

Table 2.1 Continued

Stakeholder	Interviewees conducted	Interviewees' position/role:	DE/CH/AT	UK/IRL	PT/ESP	Nordic/NL	FRA/BEL	Other
Unions	20	Heads, deputy heads, policy advisors, press officers, department heads, directors	8	2	1	6	3	0
Corporate customers	32	Departments heads in supply chain management, procurement, contracting and or purchasing	18	2	0	10	2	0
Corporate suppliers	16	Departments heads in marketing and sales	4	4	0	7	1	0
Benchmarking interviews	15	Sustainability officers, department heads of stakeholders relations, issues management or communications	7	2	0	4	2	0
Total	280		125	44	19	56	27	9

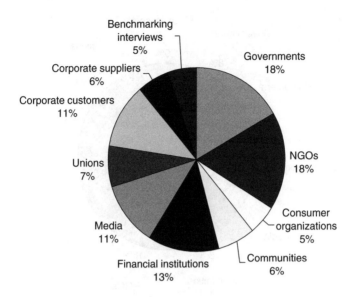

Figure 2.3 Interview sample – stakeholder groups

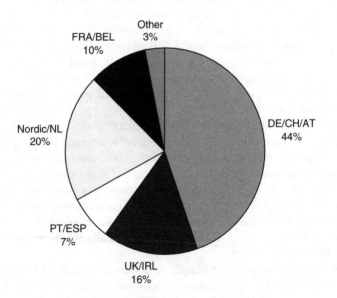

Figure 2.4 Interview sample – regions

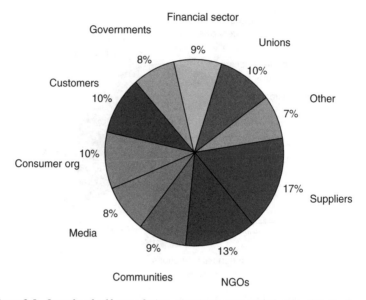

Figure 2.5 Sample of self-completion questionnaires: stakeholder distribution

important in detecting any possible self-representation bias (i.e., stakeholders considering themselves more influential than they actually are).

We had hoped for a sample size of 80–100 questionnaires per stakeholder, which turned out to be impossible to achieve. We mailed the questionnaire to more than 16,000 addresses (most of them personalized) and followed up by fax where possible. Even if one takes into account that organizations are often "bombarded" with questionnaires on various topics, our response rate on mailed questionnaires of less than 2 per cent clearly indicates that at this present time most stakeholders have little interest in corporate sustainability. This is also why we had to rely on convenience sampling more strongly than expected.

In terms of representation of stakeholders, our sample is almost equally distributed (see Figure 2.5). There is a slight overrepresentation of corporate suppliers, i.e. managers in marketing, sales and distribution, which we also attribute primarily to convenience sampling. We also received a relatively high number of questionnaires from NGOs. This was to be expected, as NGOs are traditionally strong in the area of corporate sustainability.

As Figure 2.6 shows, our sample of quantitative data (obtained from the self-completion questionnaire) is biased toward Germany, Austria and Switzerland, followed by the Nordic countries and the Netherlands.

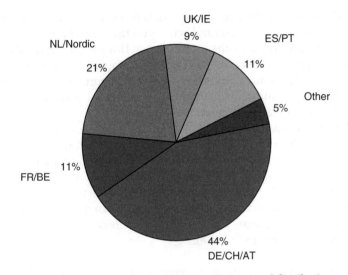

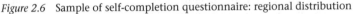

Figure 2.6 Sample of self-completion questionnaire: regional distribution

The remaining regions – France and Belgium, the UK and Ireland as well as Spain and Portugal – account for almost a third of our sample in total.

As mentioned above, our study relies to a significant extent on convenience sampling – in particular for questionnaires, i.e. we asked our interviewees and other key contacts to circulate questionnaires within their organizations. Overall, the resulting bias is less problematic, as we collected data from respondents who actually have something to say about our research topic.

Nevertheless, some words of caution are due:

1. Our data are necessarily subject to selection bias (people who are not interested in this topic choose not to respond), self-representation and social-desirability bias (those who respond tend to paint an overly positive picture of themselves and their organizations). Also, in light of our low response rate to the questionnaire, this can only suggest that reality is actually more sobering than our data suggest; i.e. more hype, less substance.

2. It is important to note that our measurement is largely based on stakeholders' self-perception. This is a perfectly legitimate and very effective form of measurement for most of our questions: our respondents act upon their perception (perception is reality). However, measurements of stakeholders' effectiveness call for further elaboration in this regard: stakeholder perception is a safe contextual measure for

stakeholders' mission and actions (stakeholders certainly adjust their mission, assessment criteria and actions on the basis of how effective or ineffective they consider themselves to be). However, it is less reliable at measuring stakeholders' actual effects on companies, i.e. value drivers and corporate reactions. In this respect, it is important to interpret our results carefully and benchmark them accordingly, e.g. with the data we obtained from managers in our previous study.

3. The heterogeneity of stakeholder groups also depends on the country under consideration. This applies to some more than it does to others. For example, some communities are very actively carrying out a local Agenda 21 process (part of the Rio Declaration, which deals with sustainable development on a local and regional level); others are not. Similarly, some unions are more responsive to sustainability issues than others are and integrate them into their strategy. The same applies to corporate suppliers and customers.

Despite the heterogeneity in our sample, we are confident that we have identified the key patterns in our data, for two reasons in particular: First, we were able to triangulate our findings through both interviews and statistical analysis. Second, while interpreting our data within and across the individual stakeholder groups, we achieved strong interpersonal consensus in our research team and the advisory council.

Notes

1 U. Steger (ed.), *The Business of Sustainability* (Basingstoke: Palgrave Macmillan, 2004).
2 O. Salzmann, "Corporate Sustainability Management in the Energy Sector," Dissertation forthcoming, p. 2.
3 B. E. Ashforth and B. Gibbs, "The Double-Edge of Organizational Legitimation," *Organizational Science*, I (1990) 177–94; J. Dowling, and J. Pfeffer, "Organizational Legitimacy: Societal Values and Organizational Behavior," *Pacific Sociological Review* XVIII (1975) 122–36.
4 R. E. Freeman, *Strategic Management: A Stakeholder Approach* (Boston: Pitman, 1984).

3
Stakeholder Dynamics

This chapter will set the scene for the subsequent chapters of the book. In it we will explore the dynamics of the stakeholder environment.

First, we will discuss the major trends that have affected both companies and their stakeholders in recent history. Second, we will present some of the most relevant empirical results of our previous study on the business case for corporate sustainability (BCS) (see section 3.2).[1] In section 3.3, we will then convey some conclusions from our series of interviews mainly conducted with sustainability managers in companies. These interviews were conducted to cross-validate our evidence. We will conclude this chapter with a discussion of stakeholders' transmission belts, i.e. their approaches and means of influencing companies (see section 3.4).

3.1   Companies and their stakeholders: recent trends in their interaction

Oliver Salzmann

To provide an adequate context for our empirical analysis, we will briefly review the most recent trends that have set the stage for interactions between companies and their stakeholders.

Globalizing economy

Over the last decade in particular, corporate value chains have become increasingly global. This gives companies in most industries significant flexibility in selecting and switching locations. To deliver satisfactory shareholder value and boost their profits, many companies have restructured and merged, others have outsourced or relocated. As a result, they have benefited from less costly business environments, primarily in developing or emerging countries, which have had several significant implications:

- Companies in general, and large multinational corporations in particular, have gained considerable bargaining power over their stakeholders.
- To a certain extent, governments and companies have engaged in a "race to the bottom" by competing for and exploiting lower social and environmental standards. This makes it difficult for sustainability leaders to maintain their relatively high environmental and social standards when competing with less scrupulous competitors.
- This trend has triggered significant opposition from NGOs, to which companies have reacted by managing and auditing the social and environmental performance of the suppliers over which they have sufficient power.
- Value chains have become increasingly complex. Many companies have hundreds, if not thousands, of suppliers (often small and medium-sized) that are difficult to manage. Also, as part of globalization, the "extended enterprise" has emerged and includes various arrangements such as outsourcing, partnerships, joint ventures and preferred suppliers. The importance of corporate stakeholders, i.e. suppliers and customers, has increased substantially. They now expect companies to exert influence along their value chain to mitigate or resolve social and environmental issues that occur beyond their factory gates.
- Resource-intensive western lifestyles and products and brands (as they protect against "commoditization" and lead to more customer loyalty) have proliferated. This kind of global consumerism leads to: (1) growing vulnerability of brands; and (2) larger environmental footprints.[2]
- Unions have lost a considerable amount of their bargaining power due to their inability to prevent major job losses. In an attempt to fight this downward spiral, they have started establishing international networks, undertaking significant restructuring and cutting costs.

Governance in a struggle

In recent decades, governance has been primarily driven by globalization and shifts in bargaining power between corporations and national, regional or local governments. Until the 1980s, governance was influenced almost exclusively by national governments. Since then the boundaries between international, national, regional and local governance have become increasingly blurred.

National governments are gradually moving away from a command-and-control approach. This approach was somewhat effective in reducing air and water pollution (acid rain, pollution of rivers) in the 1980s, but it has proven to be costly on a macro level. Also, in light of globalization and deregulation, governments have moved toward more market-based policies, such as emissions trading, and negotiated agreements to mitigate emerging issues.

It is argued that the importance of communities – relative to national governments – has actually increased because local governments are able to adapt more quickly to the changing demands of companies and because they are more aware of local issues. In Europe in particular, the influence over governance is shifting toward supranational authorities: the European Commission and European Parliament have significant influence on environmental legislation in Europe, as REACH and the European Emissions Trading System show. International treaties such as the Kyoto and Montreal Protocols, which came into force in 1989 and 2005 respectively, also reflect this cautious new trend of handling global issues at the supranational level.

Overall, global governance has clearly become more complicated. Technological innovation has accelerated, primarily due to new information technologies. New knowledge-based, service-oriented industries have resulted in enormous structural changes in labor markets.

The complexity and dynamics of today's business world has also led to a struggle in *corporate* governance (e.g. Enron, WorldCom), which resulted in companies and governments introducing codes of conduct and regulations.

Financial institutions – the paradigm of shareholder value

Since the mid-1990s, several significant events have affected financial institutions and markets – for example, the emerging market crisis in Asia, the creation and burst of the dot.com bubble and scandals relating to bad corporate governance and accounting fraud. The growing importance of financial institutions as stakeholders and the strong focus on shareholder value have become major factors in determining how companies operate.

The focus of mainstream financial institutions on short-term financial performance results in them neglecting social and environmental considerations. However, recent developments, such as the Carbon Disclosure Project and the adoption of the Equator Principles, point to a tentative tendency by the financial sector to be more socially and environmentally responsive.

Institutional investors such as hedge and pension funds have gained considerably in importance. Whereas hedge funds have a "hard-nosed" investment approach, pension funds, driven by recent pension fund legislation, are adopting a more proactive approach by taking environmental and social criteria increasingly into consideration. In some instances, this has also meant support for or the introduction of a corresponding shareholder resolution. As these examples reveal, corporate sustainability in the global business environment has developed into a niche – not more but no less either.

Advocacy and transparency

As companies have become more global and their power over national governments has increased, they have also become more complacent. In addition, because intergovernmental organizations were largely proving to be ineffective due to their affiliation with national governments, NGOs and a more vigilant civil society have emerged. On certain issues, such as human rights and conservation, organizations such as Greenpeace, WWF, Friends of the Earth and Amnesty International "took over" – to a certain extent – the autonomy of governments.

Since NGOs tend to focus on a single issue (or a cluster of similar issues), they are able to mobilize and articulate the demands of wide audiences (across different countries). Modern information technology and the internet provide them with effective tools to find and disseminate relevant information. Scrutiny from the media further increases the risk of companies being "caught in the act." In today's "goldfish bowl," transparent world there is no place for companies to hide.

When stakeholders, particularly consumers, buy into NGO campaigns, this can have a significant effect on whole industries (e.g. the Greenpeace campaign against Shell's disposal of Brent Spar or the pressure exerted on Nike to stop sourcing from Asian sweatshops). In general, gaining buy-in is not easy, but occasionally it peaks, depending on several moderating factors such as the emotional appeal of the issue, corporate visibility and attitude. Over the past decades, the share of consumers who are environmentally aware has certainly increased. Nevertheless, actual consumer behavior has changed very little else because of the lack of labeling, which keeps the consumer uninformed.

However, greater transparency through the activities of public pressure groups and consumer organizations has affected corporate behavior in developed – and, increasingly, in developing – countries. For example, Nike now publishes a list of its suppliers on the internet. Nevertheless, civil society and the media have provided few rewards for sustainability leaders over the years. Instead, society tends to punish laggards rather than to reward sustainability leaders: companies are more likely to be blamed for incidents or their ignorance or resistance to change, than to be praised for taking a more proactive stance.

3.2 Stakeholders' contribution to the business case for corporate sustainability: how managers see it

Oliver Salzmann

In the following, we will briefly revisit empirical evidence collected in our previous study on the business case for sustainability[3] to provide the reader with an important reference point for the subsequent sections of this book. Among other things, we will discuss managers' views of the importance of social and environmental issues, corporate sustainability in general, stakeholders and their business case.

Importance of corporate sustainability and sustainable development

Our data showed that overall corporate sustainability holds relatively little importance among general managers: roughly 40 per cent were not at all, a little or only fairly familiar with the concept of sustainable development. In general, sustainability officers revealed higher levels of awareness and greater expectations with regard to their companies' sustainability management: It is most likely that this also reflects the wishful thinking or expedient optimism of "standard bearers."

Issue significance

None of the social and environmental issues could be considered to be "make it or break it" issues. They generally lacked strategic importance, the only exception being the food and beverage industry where no resources mean no business (e.g. water shortage, overfishing). Furthermore, the universe of social and environmental issues is huge and extremely fragmented, which made it difficult to track and comprehend emerging problems: We were only able to cluster 350 responses into 225 distinct categories of social, environmental and economic challenges.

Role of stakeholders

The results of two surveys, one with general managers and the other with sustainability officers, on the role of stakeholders in the area of corporate sustainability were largely in line with each other: public pressure groups (NGOs) were considered the most proactive, consumers the least proactive. We also noted that managers see industry as being roughly as (if not more) effective as governments in contributing to sustainable development (see Figure 3.1 and Figure 3.2).[4]

Our interviewees' perceptions of individual stakeholders can be summarized as follows:

- Shareholders and financial institutions play a strong deterring role, primarily due to their focus on short-term profits. Certain developments (e.g. Equator Principles, Carbon Disclosure Project and support for social and environmental shareholder resolutions by institutional investors) could point to a more proactive role in the future.
- Customers are primarily interested in getting the lowest price (or best quality–price ratios) and exhibit little willingness to pay or switch to another product in exchange for a sustainability premium.
- The role of regulators and governments is clearly contingent upon the location and industry under consideration. They are more proactive

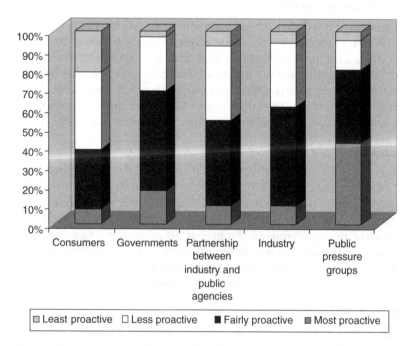

Figure 3.1 Current role of stakeholders in terms of corporate sustainability management – seen by general managers

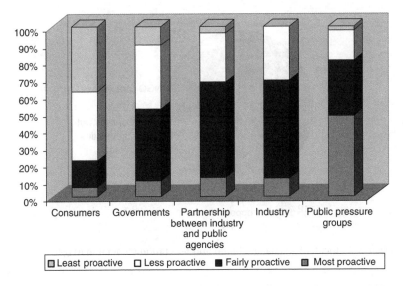

Figure 3.2 Current role of stakeholders in terms of corporate sustainability management (sustainability officers)

in developed countries as well as in the food and beverage and energy industries (due to regulations on food safety and climate change respectively).

• NGOs (civil society) exhibit the greatest demand for corporate sustainability. In developing countries, they have taken on the role of watchdogs to compensate for the social and environmental disregard of most domestic governments.

Causes of damage to brand value and reputation

Sixty per cent of our respondents acknowledged that their company had experienced an incident in the last three years that had affected brand value and reputation (see Figure 3.3). These incidents were primarily triggered by the media (17 per cent), authorities (12 per cent) and NGOs (11 per cent). In the case of media and NGOs, this reflects the ability of both to raise public awareness. It should be noted that their actions are only effective if companies' primary (or transactional) stakeholders, such as customers, governments and financial institutions, buy into them, i.e. respectively decide to switch products, change legislation or cut off access-to-capital. The 12 per cent share of authorities most likely hints at governments' and authorities' ad hoc buy-in to media and NGO

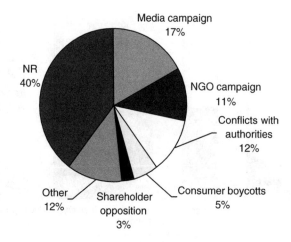

Figure 3.3   Incidents damaging brand and reputation (general managers)

actions, as well as conflicts due to environmental incidents and major layoffs.

However, a vast majority of managers reported that incidents hardly affected brand value and reputation. This does not mean that the damage cannot be significant. Our interviews for the BCS research clearly suggested that certain campaigns (e.g. Brent Spar, STOP ESSO) had a clear impact on companies.

Main barriers to corporate sustainability initiatives

Managers' perceptions of the key barriers to corporate sustainability management were most telling: As both Figures 3.4 and 3.5 show, our respondents clearly pointed to internal barriers (mindset, lack of knowledge/expertise, tools and processes, culture) more often than external barriers (regulation, lack of interest or opposition from customers and investors).

Also in line with our interviews, we concluded that external stakeholders – despite their disregard or opposition – do not significantly deter corporate sustainability management. In most cases, companies aim for incremental innovation to be able to interpret their current business models in more responsible ways (radically new business models make little sense in this situation). This incremental approach does not meet any external resistance, as it does not overstretch "stakeholders' imagination" (in fact in most cases, it may remain unnoticed). Instead, it is primarily deterred by insufficient internal awareness and capacity.

Managers' mindset
12%

Managers' lack of
knowledge/
expertise
9%

NR
36%

Regulation (e.g.
subsidies & low
environmental/
social standing)
5%

Absence of
appropriate tools
and processes
8%

Other
2%

Organizational
culture
13%

Lack of interest
from customers
10%

Opposition or lack
of interest from
investors
5%

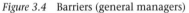

Figure 3.4 Barriers (general managers)

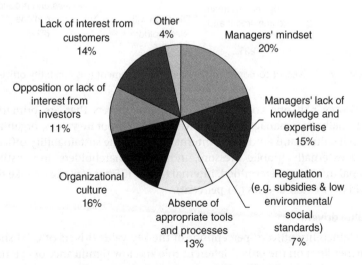

Lack of interest from
customers
14%

Other
4%

Managers' mindset
20%

Opposition or lack of
interest from
investors
11%

Managers' lack of
knowledge and
expertise
15%

Organizational
culture
16%

Regulation
(e.g. subsidies & low
environmental/
social
standards)
7%

Absence of
appropriate tools
and processes
13%

Figure 3.5 Barriers (sustainability officers)

Drivers of corporate sustainability management

Sustainability officers' perceptions of the key drivers of CSM underlined the importance of internal rather than external factors. Many of the drivers displayed in Figure 3.6 reflect an interconnectedness of companies and their environment – their strengths are contingent on whether a company or industry decides to embrace or look for new opportunities in its business environment, e.g. increased competition, new business opportunities, product and process innovation and stakeholder dialogue.

Figure 3.6 Drivers of corporate sustainability management (sustainability officers)

However, if one compares the shares of drivers that are primarily internally (top management and leadership, corporate values, organizational culture and autonomy/internal scope of the sustainability officer) and externally (public pressure, individual shareholders and institutional investors) determined, internal factors (35 per cent) again take the lead over external ones (24 per cent).

Value drivers

Sustainability officers' perceptions of the key value drivers of CSM shed further light on the rather deterrent role and low significance of external stakeholders (see Figure 3.7).

Figure 3.7 Value drivers (sustainability officers)

- Financial institutions scarcely ever use access-to-capital as a lever to promote corporate sustainability.
- The share of value drivers having primarily internal effects is significant: Attraction and retention of talent (16 per cent), cost reductions (14 per cent) and innovation (8 per cent) account for 38 per cent in total.
- The 23 per cent share of brand value and reputation largely reflect the minimization of downside potential: stakeholders do not tend to reward superior performance but tend to punish laggards for social and environmental incidents and reactive attitudes.
- The same applies to risk management (17 per cent) and the license-to-operate (18 per cent). Both items largely reflect little outside pressure and upside potential, particularly in developed countries, since companies are already in compliance with high social and environmental standards.

3.3 Views of managers about their stakeholder environment: an update

Aileen Ionescu-Somers

Our study focused on the perceptions of stakeholders about the environmental and social performance of companies and their influence over this. However, we also decided to ask managers how they perceive the dynamics of the different stakeholder groups included in the study. In this section, we draw some conclusions on a series of benchmarking interviews carried out with managers during our study. In these interviews (15 interviews carried out with a range of sustainability officers in a diversity of companies participating in our study), it was possible to update and further benchmark the information we gleaned from our BCS research data with a more recent account from the managers themselves. The approach we took was simply to ask the interviewees for their current views on the current evolution of each stakeholder group, and whether there were any salient issues that they felt influenced their role as socially and environmentally responsible companies.

One general comment emerged from these interviews: overall, there appears to be a strong movement among global companies toward stakeholder dialogue and engagement with NGOs or in public–private partnerships. Managers of global companies in Europe today appear to have more or less accepted that a strategic stakeholder approach to resolving social and environmental issues of economic relevance to them is part of a "new norm." This general viewpoint shapes the managerial perspective of stakeholders as can be seen from the following sections.

Non-governmental organizations (NGOs)

We begin with managers' perspective on the non-governmental organizations (NGOs). The reader will note that this is the longest section, and it reflects the reality of the benchmarking interviews; managers had a lot to say about NGOs and much less about communities and unions, for example. The subject of NGOs is one that tends to get managers talking; all interviewees had a point of view to offer on this subject. In fact, during both the BCS project and the benchmarking interviews, one often got the impression that with some managers, the subject of NGOs was quite a "hobby horse."

Since the first NGO/corporate partnerships, such as the Unilever/ WWF/Marine Stewardship Council, were launched in 1999, there have been increasing numbers of cases of other so-called "win–win" partnerships, if not quite as innovative. Engaging or dialoguing with NGOs has become a new trend at global companies. Many companies have jumped "on the bandwagon" to the extent that NGOs' resources are increasingly becoming overstretched, as it is simply not possible to respond to all corporate requests. Gone are the times when NGOs scarcely heard from corporations unless a charitable donation was on its way. Not that corporate donations have disappeared altogether; far from it. However, there is a whole new area of "win–win" activity where NGOs such as the Rainforest Alliance and Greenpeace have gone into an entirely new set of relationships.

In our benchmarking interviews with managers, it was clear that they view relationships with NGOs as improving overall, sometimes as a result of these closer bonds. The increasing number of platforms where NGOs and companies get together has also opened the way to more trust between the NGOs and companies. In typically pragmatic manner, managers tend to distinguish between the NGOs that they can work with, and those that refuse to even dialogue with them. The dialoguing organizations tend to be those that are viewed as more streamlined, strategic and professional. The others are viewed with skepticism and even a degree of cynicism. In addition, managers recognized that NGOs were very different from corporate entities. Those that have worked alongside NGOs accept, for example, that different branches of the same NGO can be either more collaborative or more confrontational with their company. This may depend on the country in which they operate and the nature of the issue being addressed.

Company managers complain that NGOs can be extremely one-dimensional when it comes to situating complex social and environmental problems in the global macroeconomic context. The single-issue, radical activist organizations are viewed as having an "all or nothing" approach; this loses some NGOs a great deal of credibility within business organizations, particularly those that view and portray companies as no more than "the enemy." In these circumstances, managers tend to feel that companies are much maligned. They say that companies nowadays do not get enough public recognition for the very important economic and "quality of life enhancing" factors (e.g. jobs, wealth, etc.).

Some managers see the more influential and professional parts of the NGO movement as evolving toward becoming more moderate and "grounded in reality." As NGOs gain a better understanding of corporate challenges (and companies now manage the relationships between companies and NGOs better), managers are optimistic that NGO pressure has been "contained" and is unlikely to increase significantly in the future. Managers appreciate the learning that they have gleaned from their first experiences of working more closely with NGOs and feel that there is plenty of scope for more learning. Their view is that NGOs have probably also benefited from their direct interface with companies. Broadly, managers at global companies appear to have recognized that many of the sustainability issues (such as climate change or sustainable agriculture) cannot be appropriately dealt with by one party alone, and that coalitions and meaningful partnerships will change the goalposts much more effectively than a "lone ranger" approach.

Several managers regarded Greenpeace, for example, as having lost its "raison d'être" to a certain extent – managers feel that confrontational campaigning is less effective today since companies are increasingly willing to come to the negotiating table and communicate directly with NGOs.

> I do not think that you can group all NGOs together – there are two basic groups. One group that is trying to solve problems and another group stuck in an "awareness-raising phase." Some are locked into an old product, and the market place has moved on.

Managers we spoke with felt that traditionally confrontational NGOs are in need of developing new strategies to deal with new social and environmental realities. They pointed out that the general public in Europe, having had their awareness built over some 20 to 30 years, is now waiting to hear about solutions. Certain NGOs are simply not meeting public expectations from this point of view. This is viewed by managers as a potentially dangerous situation for sustainable development, as the public quickly becomes disenchanted and loses interest if awareness is raised and no solutions are on the horizon:

> People want facts and solid information; they don't want people to give a "spin" about a theoretical lobby.

NGOs are perceived by managers as pursuing increasingly political agendas by, for example, increasing their lobbying pressures at the EU:

> A lot of the success of NGOs depends on their ability to mobilize regulators and the media. A number of NGOs with offices located in Brussels bear witness to this.

While managers perceived NGOs as being particularly successful in lobbying for new legislation, some felt strongly that there needed to be a better balance of representation between companies and NGOs on key platforms. The current balance was perceived in the minds of these managers as in favor of NGOs. This sometimes led to unreasonable or irrational legislation, which sometimes made little sense and resulted in competitive disadvantages for Europe vis-à-vis the rest of the world. We were surprised that managers did not view companies as overly bent on political lobbying – many felt that this tended to be an American rather than a European trend. NGOs complain on the other hand that large companies throw around their political weight to a very large extent. This was, we felt, an interesting divergence in opinion.

Increasingly, companies are finding that it is effective to work at a grassroots level with smaller and local NGOs; although one manager pointed out that it was important to be sure that local groups are adequately representative – otherwise companies can run the risk of alienating community stakeholders.

While managers tend to be critical about NGOs, and are cynical about some of them, they appear to accept and recognize an important role that NGOs play in today's society. They feel that NGOs are essential to ensuring that sustainable development remains on key agendas: as one manager put it, "It stops us from becoming complacent."

Global companies have been subject to increasing amounts of scrutiny over time. In light of this "goldfish bowl transparency" they face, they feel there is an absence of similar scrutiny of NGOs. Managers feel that NGOs are not transparent and, given their declared high expectations from companies, they should put more pressure on themselves to become transparent.

Corporate customers and suppliers

Managers' view of their own influence, as customers and suppliers on corporate environmental and social performance, is reflected in Part II, Chapter 12 of this book. In this chapter, we present the views of supply chain and marketing and sales managers on the influence of the corporate customer and supplier over social and environmental performance of other companies. Here we limit ourselves to a few comments.

It is interesting that the bargaining power in companies is largely held by the corporate customer; pressure goes up the supply chain, not down, and efforts by corporate customers to influence suppliers are not balanced by corporate suppliers' influence over customers. Companies are in a process of continuous improvement and there will be incremental progress over time, with no "giant steps" as pressure is not being strongly exerted on suppliers by customers, and certainly not by the end consumer. Rather than seek regulatory solutions (about which a satisfactory outcome is difficult to ensure), the corporate customer tends to opt for internal standards under his direct control, leading to a huge array of differing standards and guidelines, and resulting in suppliers struggling to be responsive. Overall, managers clearly see themselves in a dynamic environment of change and are conscious of the power of global corporations to instigate change. Many of the managers of global companies we spoke to were proud of the steps taken to bring up the standards of suppliers in Asian countries. However, managers remained perplexed at the scope of the challenge ahead given the sheer complexity of the supply chain complexity and the number of suppliers to deal with in an increasingly "difficult to read" business environment.

Regulators/governments

Managers at every global company have a certain innate respect for and sometimes almost a perceptible fear of "the regulators." It is an essential prerequisite for doing business that a global company be in compliance with regulation. And why would it not be? Not to be "in compliance" places organizations in danger of losing their license to operate within a very short period of time, with massive bottom-line impacts. The regulators assure a "level playing field" and, as such, resolve some of the competitive advantage dilemmas that hinder and delay action on "beyond compliance" sustainable development initiatives. In spite of this, most global companies appear to prefer voluntary standards rather than legislation when it comes to sustainable development. According to our interviewees, the reason hinges on the degree of unreasonable legislation that they have been confronted with in the past. Managers in the chemical industry expressed a degree of frustration with the levels of what they perceive as unnecessary or inharmonious legislation in Europe (particularly referring to the "REACH" program).

> We run risks of having an overregulated environment. Our experience with regulation is not so positive. If regulation is focused on setting targets and reaching targets, this is better than regulation that controls and prescribes everything. When that happens, useful regulation gets lost in a mire of useless regulations. In my view, 20 to 35 per cent of what companies do in terms of legislation is not necessary.

They appeared particularly harassed in this respect. However, they were not the only interviewees who felt that the dangers of unreasonable legislation were enough to prompt them to work hard to stave off just about any additional legislation. Regulators are generally perceived by managers as being overly reactive. As politicians are elected for short timeframes, their focus is on making an impact in the short term; managers do not view this as being positive for sustainable development as a whole, which requires a much longer-term perspective.

Politicians are opportunistic, not "sustainable" people – they put sustainability on the agenda just to get votes, that's all.

Much of what global companies do for sustainable development beyond compliance is related to staving off regulation and, as such, the regulators continue to exert influence beyond regulation. In spite of these efforts to stave off regulation, most managers expect regulation to continue its gradual incremental increase in Europe; in fact, managers appeared to have a resigned acceptance of this fact:

Regulatory bodies have no choice but to be more regulatory. First, they have to justify their existence and to do so they have to generate bureaucracy. Second, the condition of the environment is worsening all the time.

Reasonable or unreasonable, regulators in Europe have long succeeded in putting high levels of environmental and social regulation into place that have gone a long way to resolving many of the immediate problems of, for example, local industry pollution or exploitation of workers in European countries. However, in our discussions with managers, we discovered that manufacturing bases are moving out of Europe to developing countries more or less wholesale. As a result, there are increasing dilemmas and risks for global companies when environmental or social regulations are either nonexistent in these countries or not applied (as appears to be the case in China and India, for example). As a result, there is a new and emerging focus on how emerging economies are tackling the complex social and environmental issues. Managers perceive a very large gap in terms of global environmental and social regulations. A manager told us:

It would be good to have more global regulation, but for the moment, it is mostly single national regulation that stops the level playing field. National regulation is good for dealing with national problems. But the issues are global issues that cannot be regulated on a national level. There is no global governance in place.

However, managers fully expect that there will be more calls for changes in regulation and control in developing countries. Global companies are likely to play a strong role in the "leveling of the global playing field" in this respect, and to some degree, this aligns with governments in establishing new game plans.

Some managers that we spoke with also feared a wave of deregulation in Europe owing partly to global competitive tensions between developed and developing nations. One manager said:

> It will be interesting to see what is done about China; there is pressure on jobs in Europe. Ultimately, social and environmental criteria may even be used as a trade barrier with quotas and claims of low labor standards and low environmental standards. There is already some noise being made. This is likely to be more significant in the future.

Investment community and financial service organizations

Our study on the business case (we elaborated on the key findings in section 3.2) indicated that for today's corporation focused on shareholder value, the investment community is of utmost importance. Also, in our benchmarking interviews with managers, it was apparent that executives perceive their heaviest pressure to be making a profit in an increasingly competitive global business environment:

> By not fulfilling our role of profit, we are reneging on our primary social responsibility. For our company, the principle stakeholder, the investor, is currently not being treated well. This is a pressure that we in companies traditionally understand.

When asked about the approaches of investors to sustainability, we inevitably came up with responses from managers that illustrated the minimal interest of the financial services sector and the investment community in social and environmental issues. Nevertheless, managers we spoke to demonstrate a high level of awareness of indexes such as the Dow Jones Sustainability Index and an increasing interest from the investment community in sustainable investments. Nevertheless, managers will admit that these developments still only have a marginal effect on their activities. Our conclusion from interviews with managers is that corporations keep a close eye on developments in this regard, but do not consider that there is a dominant investor focus on corporate sustainability yet; these activities remain largely marginal for the moment. However, branded companies do not want to lose their Dow Jones Sustainability Index status once gained; several managers stated that it was very important to their company to retain the listing on the index, presumably because of the reputation and brand image consequences of losing this label.

Consumer organizations

Ah... consumers. What manager can afford not to think about what essentially constitutes their markets? The nature of market forces and the influence of consumer behavior upon them is the focus of so many activities within companies that one would think that companies could easily state that they know their consumers "like the back of their hands." However, in talking to managers one cannot help but get the sense that their behavior remains a mystery to them. The mystery is echoed in the many surveys carried out across the globe that identify consumers as increasingly concerned with social and environmental criteria. Yet these surveys also report that consumers do not act on these beliefs by following up their thoughts with actions and "putting their money where their mouths are." People like to think of themselves as benevolent creatures, thoughtful of others and the planet's well-being; however, when it comes to dipping into their pockets to do so ... well, that's another matter. Of course, managers are more than aware of this inconsistency and will even exploit it either consciously or subconsciously. Their view of the consumer is reflected in the following comments:

> Demand for sustainability from consumers depends on the category of product. However, 95 percent of consumers are not oriented towards sustainability. Consumers react because of press reports. Most consumers are not concerned with social and environmental issues unless the issues are specifically related to them personally.
>
> The consumer is just not interested in these issues generally. We sometimes carry out phone marketing to see whether they have views on these aspects. They never do.

Consumer organizations represent the myriad of consumers out there that also have a myriad of concerns. As the representing bodies for the seemingly all-powerful consumer, one might expect that companies would perceive consumer organizations as a formidable challenge. Also, since they represent the more or less 6 billion people on the planet, one might expect to hear tell of consumer organizations in discussions about stakeholders with companies quite regularly. However, this is not the case. The consumer organization is actually rarely brought up by managers as a stakeholder that greatly affects their sustainability actions. However, consumer organizations tend to be subsumed by managers in the NGO category. In fact, in our survey, respondents that were managers in the supply chain and in marketing/sales inevitably scored consumer organizations in the same way as they did NGOs.

In general, the managers we spoke to did not appear to view consumer organizations as a particular threat. They saw consumer organizations as sometimes working at cross-purposes. For example, they found it contradictory that consumer organizations focus on lowering prices for consumers, while they also placed an (albeit weak) emphasis on the importance of a sustainability agenda. They saw that consumer organizations were gradually increasing their pressure on the social and environmental agendas of companies, but the pressure, in the view of most managers, remained weak. Few of the managers we interviewed were aware of any direct efforts within their organizations to collaborate or work in liaison with consumer organizations, although they recognized that there might be potential for such efforts.

Unions

Companies working in a global environment generally recognize the importance of a corporate sustainability agenda to attract and retain the most talented employees. In Nordic countries, in particular, sustainability is recognized as a "draw" for top-quality staff.

While unions are not seen as broadly representative of employees as a whole, they are nevertheless perceived by managers as conveyers of messages from important employee groups. However, we found that managers perceive unions as having lost much of the influence that they had in, say, the 1970s. At present, the role of unions seems to be under some scrutiny:

> In Denmark, there is very little union activity in our sector; conditions are very similar everywhere. The question is what is the union's role in the future?

In sectors where there is more "union presence," unions are seen as being only in the initial stages of finding themselves a new role in the current business environment. Most managers see unions as still being concerned with mainly saving and protecting jobs, a stance that is increasingly seen as unproductive in the current global economic reality. Interestingly, managers appeared to feel that unions needed to move very quickly to define their new role on tomorrow's business stage. Managers commented:

> Job creation and sustainability implementation do not go hand-in-hand. There is a danger that in the current economic climate, with the transfer of many jobs to Asia, unions will become defensive. However, there is an opportunity here for them to help find something

new for Europe. After all, the move is unavoidable, so it is best for the unions to work with others to build something new.

However, one may also ask whether the current threats to European jobs through outsourcing may get the unions more concerned with the "leveling of the playing field" on a global level as a way of staving off the immediate impacts. This would clearly have implications for sustainable development:

> Maybe trade unions in the future should move away from being individualistic-type organizations. Trade unions cannot make the argument anymore that jobs must be protected "per se." They have to step one argument above that and look at the economic needs and what is competitive. That will give support to jobs.

Managers felt that unions could take on a needed new role in tomorrow's society, and that perhaps engaging more fully on social and environmental issues may be one of the factors that could give strength and credibility to their new role:

> In the next five to ten years, I see that there will be an evolution. Trade unions will be much more engaged in understanding business decision-making. Currently, trade unions don't stamp their feet like before; they are getting more involved in business planning. It is happening and it is positive. It feels like a more mature relationship and it makes more sense.

> Unions are moving toward more constructive collaborative arrangements. In our country, unions were a huge contributing factor to the improvement of our economy.

Media

Managers make no secret of the fact that they regard the media with even more skepticism than the "renegade" NGOs referred to earlier in this chapter. Managers generally portray the media as a chameleon that changes its views depending on the audience to which they play. Their perception of the media is inevitably grim as is reflected in the following comment:

> The media have a bad news–good news working principle. Good news does not have the entertainment value; the public interest is the driver for news picking. Sustainability topics are not set in the media;

the rule of the game is that the more exciting and dramatic topics are more important.

The media are the strongest drivers in society. What makes the media effective? Attack is always more successful than defense. It is much easier to criticize than to defend.

Managers, like the rest of the public, have observed radical changes in the media over the last 5 to 10 years and have come to expect different and ever-changing demands as a result. Dominance of electronic media has fundamentally changed the expected engagement of companies in providing information practically on a 24-hour basis. The corporate multinational is constantly on its guard and most have built up sophisticated media tracking systems to be "ahead of the posse" and to be able to second-guess how the media is presenting or is likely to present their public image. Public affairs and media teams at multinationals have grown over the last few years to cope with a media body that is increasingly more difficult to manage. Staffs with media responsibilities have to be increasingly more professional as they deal with the intricacies of maintaining a public image that must not impact the brand at any cost. However, one director of communications pointed out the following:

> The discussion about just about any subject is more polarized than it used to be. For example, the fact is that genetically modified crops are neither Frankenfood nor a solution to world poverty. They are something in between. But the media maintains a polarization in the GM debate. The middle ground just simply does not sell newspapers.

The same manager felt that more polarized debates are also a result of the decline of print media:

> The electronic media squeezes out debate even more and the opportunity for debate is even less than before. Industries need to watch how to react.

Certainly, it is far more difficult to deal with issues, particularly complex social and environmental issues, when the many facets of an argument are on the table. The information society, bombarded with facts and half-facts right, left and center, tends to be drawn by easily understood messages and the media caters to that. Social and environmental issues do not lend themselves to simplicity.

However, as compared to the 1980s and 1990s, some managers stated that they observed less NGO pressure on the media than before regarding social and environmental issues.

Communities/local authorities

As obtaining community buy-in to their projects is fundamental to corporations retaining their "license to operate," managers regard local communities as key supportive stakeholders. This is reflected in the many corporate philanthropic efforts around community involvement, which, in the view of managers, obtain their companies considerable "brownie points" with local communities. Few global, branded companies do not have an array of community programs to which to point.

> We recently made an inventory of our community programs. I contacted our 84 production sites to find out how many community projects we were engaged in. The result was that there are more than 2.5 community projects per production site, although we have no strategic focus on this kind of work.

One good secondary effect of these programs as perceived by managers is that a relationship with local authorities has built up over time and has led to more mature and much less confrontational relationships between corporations and communities:

> Communities have become more influential and more mature. They want to be more involved in decision-making.

However, given the evidence presented in Chapter 7, we question whether communities have similar views. On the contrary, communities appear to be a little "at sea" when confronted with global companies with hard core, high profile CEOs that they rarely see, let alone meet. This is different from the reciprocal relationships with smaller and medium-sized companies that pervaded the business context of local communities in the past.

The issues that companies have with communities often concern physical assets, job creation, local noise or air pollution and transport issues. However, managers perceive local authorities as mainly driven by economic arguments and foremost in most community leaders' minds is the prospect of job reductions, particularly since the wave of outsourcing to Asia and Eastern Europe has gathered momentum. One manager identified the strong effects of the changing times on community leaders, and he put this in the context of social and environmental issues:

> We are all reconciling ourselves to shorter terms of employment and less permanent employees; fewer "jobs for life." Nowadays, local authorities are looking less for long-term employment and more for germinating start-ups and creative industries. These are not bigger employers, but there is a law of diminishing returns; doing this demands resources and there is no time to engage more in sustainability matters.

However, that said, it was clear that once local authorities "got hold" of an issue, they did not easily let it go. Some managers felt that local authorities are sometimes very difficult to influence. We concluded that it depended on the bargaining power of the industries concerned; where water and power supply companies are concerned, the threat of switching location was less prevalent, and, therefore, this increased the bargaining potential of local authorities. Also, in situations where a local authority is affected by a corporation (through truck transport, for example), with little economic gain for themselves, it is difficult to engage them in discussion and communities rally forces to lobby for legislation and create political issues.

3.4   Transmission belts: how stakeholders influence companies

Oliver Salzmann and Simon Tywuschik

In this section, we investigate how stakeholder groups are channeling their interests, i.e. how they make decisions either in favor of or against certain actions to influence companies, and how effective they perceive themselves to be in affecting corporate behavior.

3.4.1   Definition and framework

We define transmission belts as activities stakeholders carry out in order to influence corporate behavior. In this study, we distinguish between the following transmission belts:

1. Regulation.
2. Political lobbying.
3. Quasi-regulatory actions (e.g. guidelines and certification schemes).

4. Engagement.
5. Actions at annual meeting, e.g. shareholder activism.
6. Praising and blaming in the public arena.
7. Direct actions.

Our findings are based on both interviews and questionnaires and embedded in the framework depicted in Figure 3.8. The framework features all stakeholders surveyed in this study and their individual transmission belts.

Based on how stakeholders influence companies, we differentiated between transactional and contextual stakeholders. (To clarify, this systemization is only based on stakeholders' selection of transmission belts – the stakeholder clusters presented in section 4.1 take into account more factors such as mission, assessment of corporate performance, bargaining power and effectiveness.):

- Corporate customers, corporate suppliers, communities, governments, consumers and financial institutions from companies' transactional environment. They closely interact with companies through direct

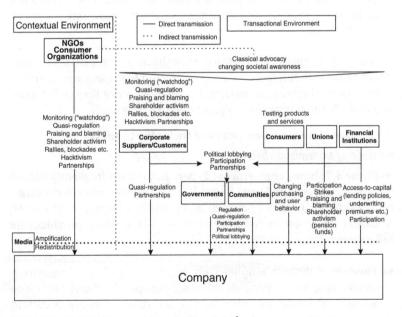

Figure 3.8 Stakeholders and transmission belts[5]

transactions (labor, materials, capital, etc.). Unions could be seen as both transactional and contextual stakeholders, as they engage in transactions with companies (e.g. indirect influence through collective bargaining) and impact the wider business environment through political lobbying. N.B. employees – also an important transactional stakeholder, as they directly influence companies when making their individual, managerial decisions – are not surveyed, since the focus of this study was on external stakeholders.

- NGOs, consumer organizations and the media are contextual stakeholders. They have no (or few) transactional relationships with companies but set the wider framework (public awareness, societal and political pressure), in which companies operate.

Furthermore, we distinguish between two ways that stakeholders use to transmit their interests to companies:

- Direct transmission occurs through activities that directly affect companies, e.g. through consumer boycotting of certain products, unions mobilizing strikes, governments introducing new legislation.
- Indirect transmission occurs through stakeholders who influence other stakeholders who then use their own means of influencing companies. Indirect transmission occurs through one or more intermediaries.

Media play a special role, since they have – compared to other stakeholders – no full-blown agenda or mission to influence companies. Nevertheless, they are an important gatekeeper, since they redistribute and amplify the transmission signals of other stakeholders.

3.4.2 Use of transmission belts and their effectiveness

Portfolio of transmission belts

As Figure 3.9 shows, engagement (20 per cent) is most frequently named by our respondents, followed by guidelines and standards (16 per cent), regulation/legislation (15 per cent) and political lobbying (13 per cent). A clearer view on overall priorities of stakeholders provides the following:

- There is a distinct emphasis on regulation and quasi-regulation (accounting for 41 per cent in total), particularly if one takes into account that political lobbying (13 per cent) primarily occurs to influence regulatory actions.

- Roughly, the remaining half of the portfolio is characterized by engagement (20 per cent) and direct non-regulatory actions (22 per cent).

It is essential to interpret the shares displayed above in the context of complementary evidence obtained from our interviewees. The role of regulation and political lobbying (for regulation or quasi-regulation) should not be overestimated. Stakeholders who are actually in a position to regulate (i.e. governments and unions) often refrain from doing so to avoid undermining regional competitiveness, i.e. there is even a certain willingness to de- or re-regulate ("better" regulation since it is more effective, less bureaucratic, easier to enforce). Hence, overall pressure from social and environmental regulation is limited because of widespread regulatory compliance in Europe.

To a certain extent, quasi-regulation is substituting real regulation. It is not only used by NGOs, but also by corporate customers (making their suppliers adhere to certain standards – particularly in developing countries) and governments and financial institutions (e.g. social and environmental guidelines for project financing).

The significant share of engagement reflects companies' strong bargaining power in a global economy (hence, there is little room for tightening legislation). It also shows that both companies and their stakeholders are willing to engage. Companies have learned that

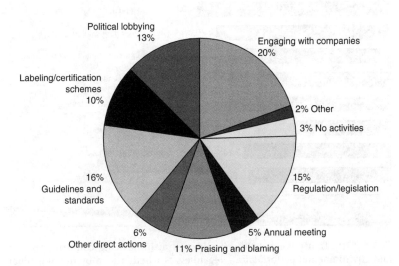

Figure 3.9 Portfolio of transmission belts (all stakeholders)

ignoring stakeholders can be a dangerous game and stakeholders (and NGOs) have realized that engagement is, in some cases, the only, and in many cases, the most effective way to influence companies – if it is complemented with other direct actions that exert pressure on companies (e.g. shareholder resolutions, rallies and other campaigning activities). Today, engagement is often the first step in influencing companies. It is also supported by the stakeholders' clientele, which applies to NGOs, governments and unions in particular.

Finally, the low share of no actions shows that most stakeholders take a stake in the social and environmental performance of companies' and attempt to influence it one way or the other.

Effectiveness of transmission belts

As one would expect, the respondents' perception of the effectiveness of transmission belts broadly mirrors the overall portfolio of belts used (see Figure 3.10). Regulation/legislation and engagement are considered most effective, followed by quasi-regulatory actions and praising and blaming that have roughly the same effectiveness.

As effective as regulation/legislation may be, our interviewees, across the board, showed it is difficult to implement and defend as it is seen as undermining regional competitiveness. This situation (which is also

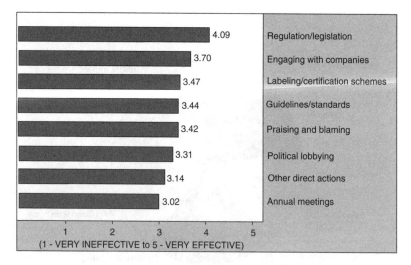

Figure 3.10 Transmission belts' effectiveness at influencing companies' social and environmental performance – regardless of whether used by the individual stakeholder or not (total sample)

characterized by the increasing bargaining power of companies) and the greater openness of companies to dialogue and engagement explain the high effectiveness of engagement as the "second-best" alternative.

3.4.3 Transmission belts: a cross-stakeholder comparison

In this section, we will focus on the individual transmission belts. We will provide a cross-stakeholder analysis of the use of transmission belts and their effectiveness, based on both quantitative data (chi square tests, ANOVAs) and our interviews. Rather than reporting on every single percentage share and mean value, we will concentrate on the most important and interesting findings.

As shown in Figure 3.10, the share of "no activities at all" was low in the total sample, most likely due to self-representation and a social-desirability bias. We detect significant differences across individual stakeholders: The share of no activities was highest among the media and financial institutions: 37 per cent of media respondents and 23 per cent of respondents from financial institutions reported that their organizations took no actions to influence the social and environmental performance of companies. This illustrates for those two stakeholders in particular that corporate sustainability remains a niche. Following, we will elaborate in more detail on the actions taken.

Regulation

Regulation can be distinguished into three types: economic, social and functional.

- *Economic regulation* modifies market mechanisms by affecting the processes between supply and demand. These modifications may be the result of a market that may work inefficiently due to a certain market structure (monopoly, duopoly) or be distorted by externalities or lock-in costs. Given this setting, government enters the stage by regulating key market parameters such as prices, quantity, market entry conditions or quality requirements.
- *Social and environmental regulation* aims to influence certain social and environmental aspects regarding the economic activity and behavior, such as pollution control, workplace safety and health, consumer protection and equal employment opportunity. In general, it is applied industry-wide.
- *Functional regulation* refers to certain activities (e.g. production) and functions of corporations that should be modified, such as labor

practices, competition or taxation. A recent policy adopted in the EU makes it obligatory for corporations to issue sustainability reports.

All three types of regulation are able to influence corporate social and environmental performance as they internalize the so-called externalities (i.e. effects of economic activities that are not reflected in market prices). However, our interviewees pointed to a certain backlash, i.e. new regulation has become more and more difficult to introduce. In fact, it is often criticized as a barrier to economic growth and competitiveness.

Our quantitative data show statistically significant differences across the stakeholders in terms of their use of regulation/legislation:

- Not surprisingly, governments and unions strongly emphasize regulation: More than 58 per cent of the union respondents and 67 per cent of the government respondents report the use of this transmission belt. The high share among unions reflects the importance of collective agreements with the corporate sector.
- In contrast, media and financial institutions hardly engage in regulatory activities (both at roughly 16 per cent). In terms of media, this result is self-explanatory; the low share among financial institutions suggests that their activities are largely unrelated to social and environmental regulation, most likely due to widespread corporate regulatory compliance.
- In all other stakeholders groups, between 42 and 52 per cent of our respondents mention regulation as a transmission belt, which underlines – despite the mentioned backlash – the significant importance of regulation.

We also detected statistically significant differences across the stakeholders in terms of how they perceive the effectiveness of regulations. Among all stakeholders, corporate suppliers, corporate customers and communities consider regulations most effective; media, consumer organizations and governments consider them least effective. It appears that stakeholders who are most strongly affected by regulation – in terms of corporate or regional competitiveness – are more satisfied; this suggests regulatory compliance is widespread and easy to achieve, and the "bar should not be raised." By contrast, the media and consumer organizations appear to see a greater need for more regulation. The low effectiveness of regulation among governments (this is surprising since they are discounting their own role) reflects their limited bargaining power in light of globalization and the need for regional competitiveness. In comparison with the other stakeholders mentioned above, NGOs' score of the effectiveness of regulations is neither high nor low. This could be partly due to the great diversity in this group. Nevertheless, we can conclude that NGOs are clearly not overwhelmed by regulatory effects for two reasons: (1) They are familiar with companies' current pressure for cost competitiveness. (2) Regulation in many developing countries is ineffective due to dysfunctional enforcement.

Political lobbying

Political lobbying aims to influence current and future policies, i.e. legislation and its enforcement. It can take place at different levels, ranging from the local (city, community, district), to the regional (federal states), national (country) or intergovernmental level. Stakeholders use formal and informal means to communicate opinions and their own interests and, hence, influence the legislation. Formal means refer to certain phases in the political decision-making process where stakeholders can formally submit their opinions (e.g. through public hearings). Informal means refer to active lobbying outside the formal democratic process through inter-organizational (political institutions) and interpersonal linkages (political decision-makers). While formal means are available to any stakeholder to the same degree, the access to informal means can vary considerable between stakeholder, depending on factors such as access to political leadership, compatibility between organizational mission statements and the political/institutional agenda.

The use of political lobbying varies significantly across the stakeholders, this difference being statistically significant:

- Political lobbying is most popular among unions (83 per cent of the respondents), NGOs (74 per cent) and consumer organizations (60 per cent). This very strongly aligns with our findings from the interviews and points to the stakeholders' strong emphasis on changing "the rules of the game" – in addition to targeting companies directly.
- Roughly one-third of our respondents in the corporate supplier and customer sample reported that they engage in political lobbying to influence the social or environmental performance of their customers and suppliers. This share appears to be the result of a self-representation bias, since our interviews with particularly corporate suppliers (e.g. marketing and sales managers) indicated that they use hardly any means at all to influence their customer – "We are lucky to have customers, we are not driving them away." We suggest that this form of lobbying for "good" legislation (as NGO interviewees would like to see more from sustainability leaders) is the exception rather than the rule.

Perceptions of the effectiveness of lobbying also differ significantly across stakeholders. Most importantly, we observed that it is considered:

- Most effective among unions and communities. This aligns with the significance our interviewees attached to this transmission belt, most likely because they have the necessary bargaining power to deal with companies directly.
- Least effective among governments, which most likely reflects (1) governments' resistance against political lobbying from other stakeholders and the challenges governments face when lobbying for their national policies on a local, regional and supranational level.

Quasi-regulatory actions

Quasi-regulatory activities are in most cases multilateral in nature and result in the creation of a set of non-regulatory rules or guidelines, e.g. labeling and certification schemes such as SA 8000 and ISO 14000, guidelines and principles (e.g. Equator Principles established and signed by several financial institutions to guide their project-financing activities in developing countries), labels, etc. If adopted by a certain critical mass of companies, quasi-regulation virtually sets industry standards, creating a pull for laggards to catch up.

Again, stakeholders differ in terms of how often they use these transmission belts (both guidelines/standards and labeling/certification), the differences being statistically significant. Overall, the picture is very conclusive (and interesting), since respondents from corporate customers and suppliers most frequently report the use of quasi-regulation, followed by respondents from NGOs/consumer organizations and communities:

- It is self-evident why companies would prefer quasi-regulation to "real" regulation; nevertheless, it is somewhat surprising that they lead the total sample of stakeholders in this respect. Although there is a clear business case for quasi-regulation (it is simply good management improving safety and quality), we suggest that this almost overwhelming "vote" for certification, standards and guidelines at least partly reflects our sample bias toward corporate suppliers and customers leading in sustainability.
- The high importance of quasi-regulation for NGOs/consumer organizations is obvious, since they are strongly involved in its creation and maintenance, e.g. product labels, guidelines on human rights by Amnesty International.

- Community respondents indicate frequent use of guidelines and standards. This most likely shows the use of such softer transmission belts as a substitute for regulation.
- The introduction of a level playing field is perceived to be good for companies.

The difference between stakeholders' perception of the effectiveness of quasi-regulation is only statistically significant for standards and guidelines. Their effectiveness is considered highest with corporate customers and suppliers, which is in line with our findings on the frequency of use presented above. Guidelines and standards score the third highest effectiveness in financial institutions. This is plausible since (1) the bargaining power of creditors can be substantial, and (2) social and environmental guidelines are in fact – next to engagement – the two major means of influencing corporate behavior.

Engagement

Direct engagement includes partnerships and dialogues with companies. Stakeholder dialogues are platforms where corporations and stakeholders exchange on issues regularly or on an ad hoc basis. In contrast, partnerships can be very close, as the conservation partnership between WWF and Lafarge[6] has shown.

There is a statistically significant difference in the use of engagement across stakeholders. It is most commonly used by NGOs/consumer organizations, corporate suppliers and customers, unions and communities. Also based on our interviews, we concluded that:

- NGOs and consumer organizations increasingly consider engagement through partnerships, coaching activities and dialogue as valid and effective transmission belts, particularly since companies are more willing to engage. Since both parties know what is at stake, engagement is more pragmatic (less ideology and fundamentalism) and thus more effective. Nevertheless, this trend was criticized by several interviewees suggesting that by convening rather than campaigning, NGOs are merely being used and managed by the companies.
- Corporate suppliers and customers see a clear upside in various forms: forestalled legislation, new expertise and increased goodwill among stakeholders.
- Unions and communities engage primarily because they lack bargaining power for other means.

Stakeholders also differ in terms of how they perceive the effectiveness of engagement – again the difference being statistically significant.

Engagement is seen as most effective by corporate customers and suppliers (again this underlines the clear upside engagement has for companies), NGOs (also in line with findings presented above) and communities. This underpins our findings that communities consider engagement the second-best transmission belt (since regulation is under the current pressure for regional competitiveness hardly realizable).

It is remarkable that governments consider engagement less effective than any other stakeholder does. We conclude that local and individual engagement with companies – as it occurs at the communal level – is clearly more effective (due to more personal relationships and mutual understanding for each other's local needs). At the national or EU level, governments and the corporate sector engage at a more abstract level through industry associations (that often tend to stand for the lowest common denominator) and lobbyists. Hence, obtaining quick and significant results is clearly more difficult.

Direct actions at annual meetings – shareholder activism

There are several ways of exerting influence on companies at annual meetings, e.g. introducing shareholder resolutions, supporting it (by using voting power), demonstrating in front of the venue, even probing for an answer to a tricky question.

As shown above, this transmission belt is relatively new (compared to campaigning and regulation) and obviously limited in several ways: It only concerns publicly listed companies and parties that attend their annual meetings, or choose to demonstrate in front of the building. This is clearly reflected in our data, which again point to statistically significant differences across the stakeholders. Overall, it plays a minor role, but it is most often used by NGOs (34 per cent of our respondents report such actions), corporate customers (a surprising 19 per cent), unions (19 per cent) and financial institutions (13 per cent).

The still relatively low share among respondents from financial institutions shows the sector still sees corporate sustainability as a niche. The fact that guidelines and standards are more often applied than any other actions at annual meetings furthermore suggests that financial institutions do not want to expose themselves as "social or environmental activists" when "Wall Street" is present. Stakeholders do not exhibit any significant differences in terms of how they perceive the effectiveness of taking direct actions at annual meetings. This most likely also reflects respondents' lack of familiarity with this transmission belt.

Praising and blaming in the public arena

Means of praising and blaming include reports (on environmental and social issues and corporate behavior), award schemes and ceremonies as well as launching PR campaigns (large-scale advertisements complemented with rallies, etc.). Obviously, praising and blaming can also be a byproduct of other (direct) actions such as boycotts. This is because such actions can trigger media attention. Media then "codifies" corporate behavior as positive ("praising") or negative ("blaming") and then redistributes and/or amplifies messages to the public.

The use of praising and blaming differs across stakeholders in a statistically significant way. As one would expect, it is most common for NGOs and unions (in both samples, 70 and 78 per cent of our respondents respectively indicated the use of praising and blaming), followed by consumer organizations (60 per cent), the media (50 per cent). The 46 per cent share for governments is also somewhat remarkable, since it may also reflect a growing willingness on the part of politicians to name and shame companies publicly (and opportunistically – since they find it difficult to regulate them) primarily for their decisions to relocate, outsource and reduce their workforce.

The effectiveness of praising and blaming is perceived differently across the stakeholders. Mean differences are statistically significant. Our data show that respondents from NGOs, communities, consumer organizations and unions consider praising and blaming more effective compared to the remaining stakeholders. Here we detect one particularly interesting pattern: The remaining stakeholders are either companies or governments; hence, they are relatively powerful stakeholders. In contrast, NGOs/consumer organizations, unions and communities have very limited bargaining power. Hence, we conclude that praising and blaming is particularly effective if a small "David-like" institution takes on a big "Goliath-like institution."[7]

Direct actions

Direct actions include transmission belts such as product boycotts, blockades, etc. They also include any kind of corporate action taken to impose certain standards on suppliers and customers. A rather new and emerging form of direct actions is "hacktivism." (For recent examples, see the HV archive at www.thehacktivist.com.) This kind of "electronic disobedience" involves hacking company websites, launching worms and viruses, "denial of service" attacks, etc.

As these actions are characteristic of certain stakeholders, it is not surprising that their frequency of use differs significantly (again this difference being statistically significant). They are most commonly used by corporate customers (exerting influence on their suppliers), unions, NGOs and consumer organizations. In terms of unions, NGOs and consumer organizations, we ascertain a certain congruence with praising and blaming, as they are often closely connected. In terms of their effectiveness, other direct actions do hardly differ across stakeholders surveyed, most likely since a plethora of possible actions (with varying effectiveness) could be taken under this heading.

3.4.4   What determines stakeholders' selection of transmission belts?

We also examined what factors most strongly determine stakeholders' decisions to select one transmission belt over another. As Figure 3.11 shows, across the entire sample, three factors – characteristics of the company or sector targeted, the severity of the problems under consideration and the demand of the individual stakeholders' clientele/customers – are of roughly equal importance as differences are "averaged out."

However, a closer look across the individual groups reveals statistically significant differences on the following items in Figure 3.11.

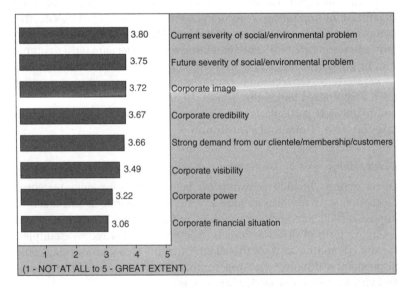

3.80	Current severity of social/environmental problem
3.75	Future severity of social/environmental problem
3.72	Corporate image
3.67	Corporate credibility
3.66	Strong demand from our clientele/membership/customers
3.49	Corporate visibility
3.22	Corporate power
3.06	Corporate financial situation

1   2   3   4   5
(1 - NOT AT ALL to 5 - GREAT EXTENT)

Figure 3.11   Extent to which criteria determine actions to influence companies (total sample)

Severity of problems

The current problems are most important to NGOs, unions and consumer organizations, which reflects the fact that all three stakeholders are clearly issue-driven. Corporate suppliers, financial institutions and corporate customers attached the least importance to current issue significance. We attribute this to the little impact current issues generally have on core business models.

It should be mentioned that stakeholders do not differ in terms of the importance of future issues. Overall, their importance moves closely with that of current issues (hence, similar conclusions apply), with one exception: In our data obtained from the media, the importance diverges. The fact that current issues are more important than future ones points to the short-term focus of media.

Corporate image

Individual corporate image (primarily this boils down to open and proactive vs closed and defensive corporate attitudes) matters most to corporate suppliers, corporate customers and communities. Image can be used as a relatively reliable proxy, since all three stakeholder groups are either locally present and/or have transactional relationships with the company under consideration. In the case of small communities in particular, it may also be a second-best criteria, as they lack capacity for more sophisticated decision-making processes. Corporate image is least important to NGOs, consumer organizations and the media. This reflects their clear issue focus. As an interviewee from a human rights organization said:

> Human rights are non-negotiable. As an NGO in this domain, you simply cannot make compromises. You have to table the issue, even if it occurred in a best-practice company.

In addition, the data also clearly showed – in line with our interviews – that a good image does not really protect a company. In some cases, it actually may make it more vulnerable, as NGOs become pickier and smell "window-dressing."

Corporate credibility

Corporate credibility (in contrast to corporate image, credibility is essentially about whether a company does what it says it does) is most important to communities, corporate suppliers and corporate customers, which underpins the previous finding. It has lowest importance among respondents from governments, consumer organizations and unions. This result is also in line with the greater concern expressed about current social and environmental problems by consumer organizations and unions. We attribute the low importance in the government group to their more macro-level, national perspective, in which the credibility of individual companies has little meaning.

Strong demand from clientele

Corporate suppliers, consumer organizations and unions attach the greatest importance to the demands of their clientele and customers. The result is self-evident for corporate suppliers ("the customer is the king"). With regard to consumer organizations and unions, it reflects the importance of their readership and membership respectively. Respondents from financial institutions, governments and NGOs consider the demands of their clientele – compared to other groups – least important. In the case of governments and financial institutions, this clearly reflects their clientele's disregard for corporate sustainability (issues such as employment and shareholder value are respectively more important). The low importance in the NGO sample again reflects issue-driven missions and actions. This does not mean that they ignore their clientele, i.e. contributors and members, but that their clientele is largely interested because of issues that are detected and owned by the individual NGO.

Corporate visibility

Corporate visibility is most important to corporate suppliers and customers, which reflects the rather pragmatic and risk-based approach of companies: Obviously, the more visible the company (e.g. in terms of size, risks associated with certain kind of activities such as extractives, chemicals) they supply or they buy from, the more exposed the supplier or customer is. The lowest importance of corporate visibility among financial institutions, NGOs and consumer organizations underlines the issue focus of the latter two, and a somewhat risk-inelastic approach of financial institutions. We conclude that risk primarily moves along the supply chain and rarely "jumps over" to creditors.

Corporate power

This particular item essentially measures the importance of bargaining power. It is plausible that communities and unions attach great importance to this factor, since they both lack the necessary bargaining power. The similarly high importance of corporate power among corporate customers points to bargaining power as the ultimate precondition to make the supplier engage and adopt social and environmental standards. Our data point to a lower importance of corporate power among governments, financial institutions and corporate suppliers. Obviously, corporate suppliers primarily aim to serve their customers; they do not fully use their bargaining power. Power of individual companies is of minor importance to governments, since they deal – on a national level – more often with industry associations. Finally, we attribute the low importance of corporate power in financial institutions to several reasons: (1) Creditors generally have a very strong bargaining position; corporate image and credibility are factors that are more important; (2) Certain actions such as rating procedures and due diligence in project appraisals are simply carried out by default – independently from bargaining processes.

Corporate financial situation

Companies in severe financial situations make rather bad targets, since they are "wounded" already – jobs could be on the line. This pattern is clearly reflected in our data, since communities, financial institutions and the media attach the greatest importance to individual corporate financial situations. In line with the findings mentioned above, responses from NGOs and consumer organizations underpin issue-driven actions, as they attach – jointly with governments – the lowest importance to corporate financial situations. The low importance of corporate financial situations among governments is somewhat surprising in light of the current need to maintain and increase employment levels. We suggest that they have accepted a kind of economic necessity, and beyond that, they are largely issue-driven.

Conclusion

It is difficult to detect one, most or several more significant determinants of decision-making, if one looks at the total sample. However, a cross-stakeholder analysis reveals several interesting findings. We conclude the following:

- Issues most strongly determine decision-making by NGOs, consumer organizations and unions, since they are – ultimately – the reason for their existence.
- Corporate visibility, credibility and image represent a set of corporate characteristics that describe risk and uncertainty associated with the company under consideration. This set is most important to corporate

suppliers, customers and communities, i.e. stakeholders that are immediately and continuously (through transactions, use of resources and infrastructure) affected by the company.

- Corporate (bargaining) power most strongly determines decisions of those stakeholders that most strongly rely on it (corporate customers to impose standards) or even lack it (communities and unions).
- Overall, corporate financial situations are a weak factor, but it tends to be more relevant to those stakeholders that have a large vested interest in the financial health of the company under consideration, i.e. communities (as they need income through taxes), financial institutions (as they want secure loans and rising shares) and also the media: A scandal in a company that is already struggling financially makes a worse target than "catching a rising corporate star in the act."
- The demands of clientele, members and customers are a particularly strong factor for those stakeholders that have a very clearly defined set of customers, members, etc. This applies to consumer organizations (consumers), unions (employees and members) and corporate suppliers (their customers).

3.4.5   Synopsis

Our analysis of transmission belts – their use and their effectiveness – revealed various significant differences across stakeholders. Hence, it is impossible to identify one dominant and most effective action to influence corporate performance. The selection of transmission belt is contingent on several factors, including, most importantly:

- *Bargaining power and resources*: Stakeholders that hold relatively little bargaining power (NGOs, consumer organizations and communities in particular) focus more strongly on political lobbying (as an attempt to address governments rather than the more powerful corporations), praising and blaming (benefiting from the "David–Goliath Syndrome") and other direct actions, e.g. boycotts, blockades (also to leverage possible media coverage).
- *Mission*: We see that stakeholders whose mission is only weakly linked to corporate sustainability – or not at all (namely financial institutions and the media) – take less actions to influence companies.
- *Characteristics of the corporate counterpart* (e.g. visibility, credibility and image). They are most important to stakeholders that are most directly affected by the counterpart, i.e. corporate suppliers, customers and communities.

We conclude that regulatory compliance is widespread in Europe, and regulatory pressure is rather weak. Since this is unlikely to change in the near future, due to the imperative of regional competitiveness, stakeholders are "betting on different horses":

1. *Political lobbying* to change the rules of the game, i.e. taking on governments as a different "opponent." Corporate suppliers and customers have done little in this respect so far (to raise the bar for their customers and suppliers respectively), most likely because cost pressure is high, win–win potential (e.g. increased efficiency and safety) is underestimated and – maybe most importantly – they would rather go for quasi-regulation to maintain their freedom.
2. *Quasi-regulation*: This is most often achieved through multi-stakeholder initiatives, mostly welcomed by companies as it most likely prevents regulation and is often supported by NGOs and consumer organizations. Widespread application of such guidelines, standards and labels could be seen as de facto regulation. However, this requires the use of complementary transmission belts building up necessary pressure (praising and blaming, other direct actions).
3. *Engagement*: Engagement is most frequent and effective at the local level. It often goes hand-in-hand with the creation of quasi-regulation and has become increasingly accepted in the NGO community – despite ongoing significant dissent (even in the engaging NGO). The increased popularity of engagement appears to result from a steep learning curve the partners (in particular companies and NGOs) have been on over the last two decades: Engagement has become more effective.
4. *Praising and blaming*: This transmission belt is an essential complement to engagement and quasi-regulation as it creates the so-often needed pressure and, hence, the incentive to cooperate. It reflects not only classical advocacy of NGOs and unions, but also a "new advocacy" of governments and communities, on which they fall back since their traditional area of responsibility (regulation and enforcement) is of little use in global economic "racing to the bottom." However, praising and blaming only works if the target company cares about its brand value and reputation.
5. *Other direct actions* (such as imposing certain standards or triggering consumer boycotts). Some are taken at shareholder meetings, even if this approach is rather new and has marginal importance because the majority of shareholders have a clear focus on short-term financials.

Notes

1   U. Steger (ed.), *The Business of Sustainability* (Basingstoke: Palgrave Macmillan, 2004).
2   U. Steger, *Corporate Diplomacy* (London: Wiley, 2003).
3   U. Steger (ed.), *The Business of Sustainability* (Basingstoke: Palgrave Macmillan, 2004).
4   Ibid., p. 21.
5   U. Steger, *Corporate Diplomacy* (London: Wiley, 2003).
6   U. Steger, O. Salzmann, O. and A. Ionescu-Somers, *Flirting with the Enemy: the WWF/Lafarge conservation Partnership* (Lausanne: International Institute for Management Development, 2003).
7   U. Steger, *Corporate Diplomacy* (London: Wiley, 2003), p. 82.

4
Stakeholders and Corporate Sustainability

4.1 Four distinct stakeholder clusters

Ulrich Steger

An initial analysis of both our quantitative and qualitative data quickly revealed that a full-blown analysis across all nine stakeholders would have made little sense. By grouping the individual stakeholders into three clusters plus media (see Figure 4.1), we adopted a more effective approach to discuss similarities, commonalities and patterns, as it is clearly more meaningful to:

- Discuss the key patterns across the clusters.
- Provide a more nuanced analysis across *individual* stakeholders *within* the clusters.

Following is a brief introduction of the clusters. More detailed analyses will follow in sections 4.1.1 to 4.1.3.

The first cluster is called "challengers" (gray box), and is comprised of consumer organizations and NGOs. The cluster is relatively heterogeneous if one looks at the thousands of issues NGOs target individually. However, it features institutions that all have very specific and – compared to the other two clusters and media – distinct (and often very idealistic) demands of companies.

The "incrementalists" (black boxes) are transactional stakeholders. They want to do business with companies and are businesses themselves: the financial institutions as well as the customers and suppliers of corporations. Corporate sustainability is part of the overall business relationship, but not a dominant part in most cases. Any demands with regard to sustainability will be clearly balanced against other business goals. The incrementalists do not want to have risky or even

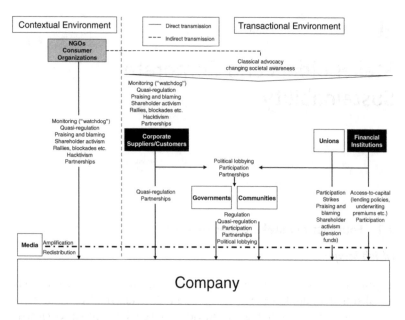

Figure 4.1   Stakeholder clusters

unpredictable outcomes. They tend to see the business case for improving (eco-)efficiency and health and safety performance, but are not ready to sacrifice their own business interest for progress in the sustainability area (i.e. as a customer, accept higher prices for more sustainable products or services). They also oppose social and environmental regulation, if it compromises their competitiveness.

The "bystanders" represent the political-societal "establishment" among our nine stakeholders: This cluster includes governments and regulators, communities and cities, and unions. We included unions for three reasons:

- First, in many European countries they are closely linked to the political system (e.g. through members of parliament, political affiliation with Labor/Social Democratic Parties, etc.), significantly closer than NGOs.
- Second, unions have a strong preference for regulation. In fact, collective agreements could be considered as such.
- Third, in most cases they are similarly reluctant to take corporate sustainability onboard, as it is seen as a corporate effort to forestall legislation.

The cluster's key characteristic is its main concern about economic growth and employment. Corporate sustainability is a second-tier issue and half-heartedly supported as long as there is a positive, cost-free side effect of job creation and competitiveness.

The media take a unique position in this study: their purpose is not to influence companies but to disseminate information. For them, sustainability and corporate behavior are an area of interest – even if clearly a niche. Thus, media are drivers and implementers of transparency to a certain extent. They support other stakeholders in evaluating and influencing corporate performance.

Since the individual stakeholder groups are not homogeneous, neither are the clusters. Hence, we will also discuss the most important and statistically significant differences between individual stakeholders within the respective cluster. The next sections – 4.1.1 to 4.1.4 – will show that we have not lost "our sight in the forest" but have successfully focused on the most relevant patterns of the clusters' interactions with companies. In doing so, we recognize that real life is even more pluralistic and that there are exceptions to every rule. Obviously, no empirical research can relieve companies from the need to analyze the very specifics of their situation, the issue at hand and the characteristics of individual stakeholders they have to deal with.

The sections 4.1.1 to 4.1.3 are structured in a similar way. They begin with a description of the clusters' mission and expectations. We then elaborate briefly on the origin of their mission by examining drivers for the organizations' activities (issues, clientele) and the resulting criteria they use to assess and influence companies. We then describe processes and tools used for assessing and influencing corporate social and environmental performance. We conclude the sections by portraying actions to influence companies (i.e. transmission belts) and their effectiveness.

The structure of section 4.1.4 is different, as it focuses on only one stakeholder, namely the media. We provide a bird's eye view of the media (typology, framework, the importance of corporate sustainability, etc.) here, since a detailed presentation of our empirical evidence is presented in Chapter 11.

4.1.1 Governments, unions and communities: bystanders in corporate sustainability

Fabian Baptist

Mission and expectations with regard to corporate sustainability

Mission. Currently, the mission of bystanders is primarily characterized by not intending to intervene strongly and actively in the corporate sustainability arena. Governments, cities and communities and a few leading unions try to stimulate a rather voluntary approach to corporate sustainability (CS) solely through engagement and cooperation. Most unions lack a proactive approach and ignore corporate sustainability to a large extent. The primary focus of bystanders is on employment and economic growth, which they see as a sort of prerequisite for corporate sustainability. Predominantly, because of the current lack of economic growth and employment, bystanders are forced not to confront corporations with high demands for corporate sustainability management so as not to worsen regional, national and international competitiveness.

The primary focus of governments, as well as cities and communities, is on programs linked to the main goals of the new Lisbon strategy on employment and growth (2005). Hence, the provision of jobs and income is considered the most important element of corporate sustainability, in many instances the only one that is seriously discussed, given the high environmental standards in Europe. Nevertheless, governments on various levels, such as the European, national and regional level, *publicly* place corporate sustainability high on their political agenda, which can be largely seen as window-dressing. In this context, some governments try softly to promote corporate sustainability by (1) setting the right framework and incentives for companies to engage in social and environmental projects. Furthermore, governments intend to (2) act as a meeting place for different stakeholders and corporations and to (3) be a facilitator by encouraging research on CS and by promoting best practice in CS.

Our research suggests that a comprehensive understanding of corporate sustainability is still rare in cities and communities, the exception being interviewees specializing in this field (a few experts dealing with local Agenda 21 processes). Regional competitiveness and employment dominate the political agenda, while the importance of environmental issues is contingent on local conditions such as economic activity, tourism and biophysical constraints.

In terms of unions, two major positions on CS can be identified. The first position is that unions partly perceive CS as a threat. Voluntary CS is considered a corporate means to strengthen corporate bargaining and to prevent regulation through voluntary activities, which goes hand-in-hand with a "race to the bottom." However, a few leading unions have tried to take advantage of the rise of CS by connecting CS with their traditional area of competence. Topics such as wages, work–life balance, working time, freedom of association and gender mainstreaming can be linked to CS and thus can be brought to the corporate agenda in a new form.

Expectations and satisfaction with corporate social and environmental performance. Apart from being "in compliance with regulation," the overall satisfaction of bystanders with corporate environmental and social performance seems to be moderate. This is illustrated in Figure 4.2, which shows a mean level of satisfaction of 2.7 and 3.4 for the majority of the items. Considering this, it seems to be surprising that bystanders want to bring CS to corporate agendas mainly through a "soft voluntary approach." We attribute this to a strong need for competitiveness and decreasing bargaining power in light of globalization and ongoing corporate restructuring.

Relatively low satisfaction with three items is of particular interest: supply chain under corporate influence, social effects in developing countries and environmental effects in developing countries. Apparently, bystanders think that multinational corporations (MNCs) should evaluate the implications of their activities in developing countries more thoroughly. The expectation for greater corporate responsibility in developing countries also reflects the desire of unions and European governments for a more level playing field between developed and developing countries. From an idealistic and a pragmatic point of view, unions want higher social standards in developing countries with low social and environmental standards, which would lead to less international competition.

In terms of satisfaction levels, we found the following differences within the cluster: cities and communities are significantly more satisfied with regulatory compliance than governments and unions. We conclude that governments and regional authorities exhibit lower satisfaction levels

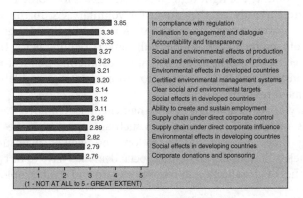

3.85	In compliance with regulation
3.38	Inclination to engagement and dialogue
3.35	Accountability and transparency
3.27	Social and environmental effects of production
3.23	Social and environmental effects of products
3.21	Environmental effects in developed countries
3.20	Certified environmental management systems
3.14	Clear social and environmental targets
3.12	Social effects in developed countries
3.11	Ability to create and sustain employment
2.96	Supply chain under direct corporate control
2.89	Supply chain under direct corporate influence
2.82	Environmental effects in developing countries
2.79	Social effects in developing countries
2.76	Corporate donations and sponsoring

1   2   3   4   5
(1 - NOT AT ALL to 5 - GREAT EXTENT)

Figure 4.2 Satisfaction with corporate social and environmental performance (bystanders)

since they have a greater responsibility and more capacity to monitor and enforce legal compliance than small communities in particular. Unions might be relatively less satisfied due to some cases of cancelled collective labor agreements.

Drivers of and criteria for corporate sustainability

Drivers. In general, we found that bystander subgroups (unions, governments and cities and communities) are mainly driven by globalization and their clientele/voters. Governments as well as cities and communities have to serve the needs of a highly fragmented clientele (e.g. companies, employees, residents etc.). The same applies to federations of unions who are dealing with various affiliated unions of different sizes, industries, etc. In contrast, individual unions' clientele are rather homogeneous.

In the era of globalization, regional, national and international competitiveness is essential. Therefore, governments as well as cities and communities do not want to weaken competitiveness through high social and environmental standards. At the same time, governments as well as cities and communities have received mandates to address possible environmental problems and increase the levels of social welfare. In this context, governments as well as cities and communities consider voluntary CS as the right tool to promote. Nevertheless, they emphasized that the resulting discretion of corporations to address issues (or not) must not lead to a social and environmental "race to the bottom." If this were the case, governments would have to force corporations to address social and environmental issues by appropriate regulations. It seems to be interesting that national governments have increasing difficulty finding the right regulatory instruments for borderless MNCs, which are currently another driver for voluntary CS. In this context, national governments have opted for multinational agreements (e.g. Kyoto protocol, the double hull tankers requirement). However, their effectiveness so far is limited, since conflicting political interests and industry lobbying have led to little ambitious regulation and enforcement remains difficult.

The key driver of unions is clearly their clientele. Employees and work councils are concerned about topics such as wages, work–life balance, working time, freedom of association and gender mainstreaming. Nevertheless, unions are aware that social demands have to be appropriate at times of globalization in order to sustain and create employment.

Criteria. The interviews with bystanders revealed several important assessment criteria. These criteria are used on the macro- (i.e. national, regional or sector) level or micro-level (focusing on individual companies).

Unions, as well as cities and communities, assess companies predominantly on the micro-level. Unions try to evaluate corporate performance through works councils, whereas cities and communities rely on personal contacts and third parties (e.g. the chamber of commerce) for company-specific information.

Governments largely rely on macro-level assessment: they assess social and environmental performance through sustainability indicators. Based on these indicators, governments know the areas of sustainability into which they should put more effort. The sustainability indicators such as energy productivity, climate protection, education and safety at work also serve as a benchmark for companies.

The quantitative data (see Figure 4.3) highlight the importance of the criteria when assessing companies. Considering that bystanders lack a clear agenda on corporate sustainability, the somewhat high mean scores for corporate sustainability criteria are a little surprising.

Apart from corporate donations and sponsoring, the items listed in Figure 4.3 are above 3.5. This illustrates a call for genuine corporate sustainability activities in terms of an improved corporate behavior rather than corporate giving.

The social and environmental effects in developing countries are considered significantly more important by governments and unions than

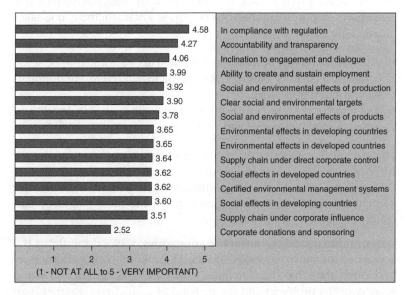

Figure 4.3 Importance of criteria for assessing corporate social and environmental performance (bystanders)

by cities and communities, these differences being statistically significant. This finding underpins the local focus of cities and communities, whereas unions and governments are also interested in the corporate social and environmental performance in developing countries. The more international perspective of governments and unions is also underpinned by their stronger interest in international guidelines and conventions (OECD guidelines, UN Global Compact, ILO conventions).

Processes and tools used in relation to corporate sustainability

Assessment processes and tools. The qualitative data show that overall *systematic* assessment of corporate environmental and social performance rarely takes place. On the macro-level, national governments mainly use sustainability indicators for yearly (rather than continuous) assessments. Cities and communities stated that they only use personal contacts and third parties to get an impression of the social and environmental performance of companies. Some unions use standards (OECD guidelines or ILO conventions) as checklists for the assessment of corporate performance outside their home country.

Figure 4.4 illustrates a wide and balanced portfolio of bystanders' assessment means, which is led by their own investigations (17 per cent), followed by opinion surveys, media and corporate reports (all at 14 per cent). Overall data are in line with bystanders' tentative (sometimes-skeptical) approach to corporate sustainability, if one takes into account that:

- Their own investigations are, as suggested above, limited to personal contacts, regulators' controls or – on the macro level – environmental and social indicators.
- The remaining three key means are also more or less pragmatic and low-cost means of assessment.

The statistical analysis of the quantitative data shows that unions use corporate reports and opinion surveys significantly more frequently than governments and cities and communities. Both means of assessment, particularly employee surveys, appear to be the most pragmatic and readily available methods for unions.

Determining actions to influence companies. When determining the actions to influence corporate social and environmental performance, bystanders state that they are mainly driven by the current and future severity of the problems and the demand of their clientele rather than corporate characteristics. In light of the limited bargaining power of

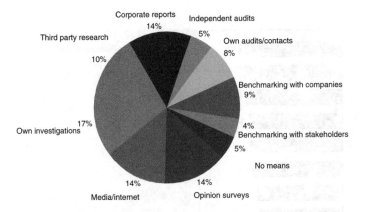

Figure 4.4 Means of assessing corporate social and environmental performance (bystanders)

bystanders, this result is somewhat counterintuitive; one would have expected more opportunistic behavior based on the financial situation and power of companies. However, the putative contradiction dissolves "quickly" if one takes into account that employment and economic growth are current key issues of bystanders.

We note that bystanders largely lack systematic processes to determine actions to influence companies. They primarily base their decisions on past experiences, which also can be traced back to the overwhelming complexity of assessing and influencing CS in a holistic way.

The quantitative data shows that decisions are made largely on the basis of issues rather than corporate characteristics (see Figure. 4.5). Despite this predominantly issue-driven attitude, some bystanders indicate opportunistic behavior, contingent upon corporate characteristics (corporate image, corporate financial situation, etc.) This applies to unions in particular due to their close ties with companies (through members and works councils).

Furthermore, we ascertain that governments are significantly less focused on corporate characteristics than unions and cities and communities. This appears to reflect governments' primary focus on the macro level where (individual) corporate characteristics are less relevant.

Actions and their effectiveness to influence corporate sustainability

Portfolio of actions. The portfolio of bystanders' actions aimed at amending and influencing corporate social and environmental performance is

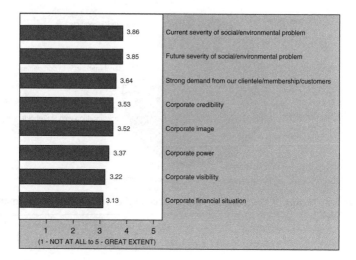

Figure 4.5 Extent to which criteria determine stakeholder actions to influence companies (bystanders)

extensive and diverse. It features three key categories:

1. Enabling actions.
2. Collaborative actions.
3. Adversarial actions.

1. Enabling actions. Bystanders aim to enable CS through awareness building (dialogue, presentations and personal contacts). This strategy is primarily applied by governments, and through incentives such as award schemes. Several ministries stressed the importance of standards for CS actions to make corporate performance more transparent. Since regulation is usually met with resistance from the corporate sector, quasi-regulatory actions (labeling, guidelines, certification, etc.) have taken an increasingly significant role. Standards serve corporations as an orientation for changing processes and products.

2. Collaborative actions. Bystanders stated that they are primarily interested in cooperating with companies. Unions and especially works councils try to improve the working conditions of the employees through partnerships and dialogues. The strategy employed by governments as well as cities and communities based on collaboration and participation ranges from public–private partnerships via offering workshops to participating in stakeholder dialogues.

3. Adversarial actions. Bystanders consider adversarial actions as the very last "resort." Governments and communities have the mandate to influence corporations through laws and ordinances. Politicians have also increasingly voiced public criticism against certain corporate actions (e.g. in reaction to planned mass layoffs after announcing record profits, as in the recent of case Deutsche Bank). In the case of mass dismissal or disagreement in bargaining, unions obviously take the lead in direct and/or indirect confrontation against the corresponding corporation. These actions range from strikes to public criticism – sometimes they also collaborate with other stakeholders such as NGOs.

Our quantitative data (see Figure 4.6) point to a still significant share of adversarial actions: Political lobbying (13 per cent), praising and blaming in the public arena (16 per cent) and regulation (18 per cent) account for 47 per cent in total. Nevertheless, their importance should not be overestimated, since social and environmental regulations are unlikely to be tightened, and lobbying as well as praising and blaming have been a rather desperate and largely ineffective means of influence in the past.

Further, the statistical analysis of the data shows that unions use the strategy of praising and blaming, direct actions and lobbying more often than governments and cities and communities. This plausibly illustrates

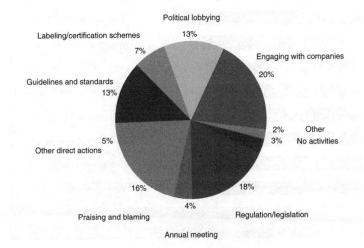

Figure 4.6   Portfolio of actions to influence companies' social and environmental performance (bystanders)

that overall unions take a more confrontational stance through lobbying, strikes and demonstrations.

Overall, we detect a strong role of enabling and collaborative actions, which clearly illustrates that bystanders are driven by globalization and regional competitiveness. They lack the bargaining power for a more confrontational stance.

Effectiveness of actions and determinants. Bystanders view the "hard instrument" of issuing regulation as the most effective strategy – provided stringent enforcement can be ensured – because it allows for a high level of control. However, as effective (and hence desirable) it may be, our interviewees also acknowledged that it is hardly feasible in light of current social and environmental standards, the need for regional competitiveness and enforcement costs. In several instances, they even saw a need to deregulate.

Apart from regulation, bystanders see engagement, praising and blaming and labeling and certification schemes as very effective ways to influence corporate environmental and social performance (see Figure 4.7). Furthermore, we ascertain that governments assess engagement, praising and blaming and regulation as less effective than unions and cities and communities. This most likely reflects the problems associated with regulation discussed above, but also suggests that public criticism and

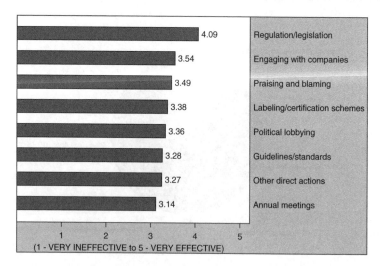

Figure 4.7 Perceived effectiveness of actions in influencing companies' social and environmental performance regardless of whether used or not (bystanders)

engagement is less successful at the national level: several governmental interviewees stated that cooperation with corporations is problematic since corporations do not like to communicate about successful partnerships with public authorities especially on a national level. Corporations do not want to give the impression that they might publicly lobby for their interests through partnerships. We also suggest that cooperation on the national level is less effective since negotiation with (mostly) industry associations is often reduced to the lowest common denominator.

Governments, cities and communities and unions emphasized that the effectiveness of the actions is contingent upon various factors that make it difficult to select the right action. The effectiveness of the action depends strongly on:

- The bargaining power of the stakeholder who is carrying out the action (resources, networks).
- The corporation that should be affected through actions (corporate image, financial situation).
- Situational factors, such as public awareness.

Predominantly, the latter factor often means leveraging the effectiveness of the action when there is public awareness. They clearly see the opportunity to jump on the bandwagon in order to address certain issues, as the recent discussion about hedge funds in Germany shows.

Influence of stakeholder groups. For the most part, bystanders perceive all stakeholders as influential in the sustainability arena. This is clearly illustrated in Figure 4.8 where all listed stakeholders have a mean score between 3.1 and 4.2. They see the media and financial institutions as having the greatest power to change corporate behavior. In the interviews, bystanders emphasized that financial institutions play a crucial role in fostering corporate sustainability due to their tremendous influence on companies as a business stakeholder. The strong influence of media is also very plausible, given their capacity to shape public perception and thus set agendas.

Despite the regulatory power of governments, bystanders do not see governments as significantly more influential than customers, NGOs or consumer organizations. Again, this clearly illustrates the difficulty of influencing companies (large multinationals in particular) today through national legislation and policies. Unions are perceived as more influential than communities, probably due to unions' possible direct influence on employees.

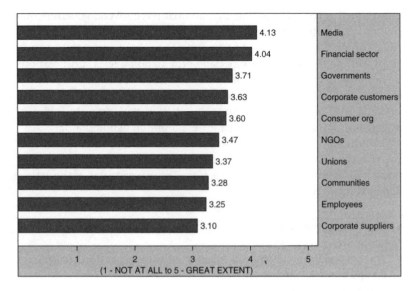

Figure 4.8   Extent to which stakeholders are able to influence corporate behavior (bystanders)

Resulting corporate risks and opportunities. The "portfolio of actions" section shows that bystanders predominantly intend to enable voluntary corporate sustainability efforts. This makes it clear that currently bystanders do not intervene strongly in the sustainability arena because of the imperatives of growth, employment and competitiveness. Nevertheless, it cannot be concluded that through bystanders' actions, opportunities are more prevalent than risks. Adversarial actions taken by bystanders, e.g. "blaming in the public" can have a great influence on brand value and reputation.

This is also illustrated in Figure 4.9, which shows that bystanders view themselves as having a slightly stronger effect on companies' reputations than on their license to operate, i.e. acceptance of project launch and growth, strictness of regulators' controls and tightening regulation. We conclude that, in light of globalization and declining bargaining power, bystanders are not only focused on companies' license to operate but also on other intangibles such as brand and reputation.

Our analysis further shows that governments perceive their influence on "frequency of strikes" and "access to and retention of talent" as significantly lower than unions. Both findings reflect that unions can have a direct impact on single corporations and particularly on their employees through works councils.

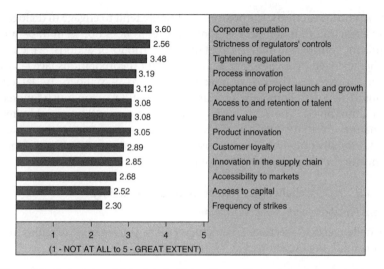

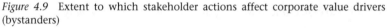

Figure 4.9 Extent to which stakeholder actions affect corporate value drivers (bystanders)

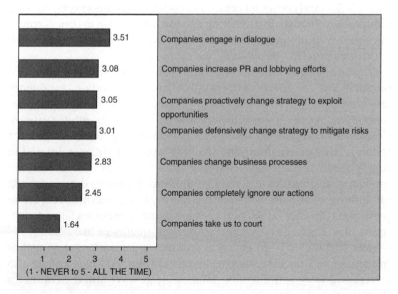

Figure 4.10 Frequency of corporate reactions to stakeholder action (bystanders)

Corporate reactions. Corporations primarily tend to engage in dialogue as a reaction to bystanders' actions. This result does not seem to be surprising considering that (1) bystanders' portfolio of actions, which is characterized by a voluntary approach, and (2) corporations face – to a certain extent – the risk of adversarial actions. Bystanders are largely unsatisfied with corporate responses, as they still feel too much ignored or uninvolved. The remaining corporate reactions (PR and lobbying, changes in strategy and processes, etc.) occur less frequently, which additionally underpins bystanders' limited bargaining power and minor mission in terms of corporate sustainability (see Figure 4.10).

4.1.2   NGOs: challengers for corporate sustainability
Jens Prinzhorn and Oliver Salzmann

Challengers (see section 4.1) include NGOs, think tanks, religious and consumer organizations.

Mission and expectations with regard to corporate sustainability

Challengers' missions reflect a strong interest in and demand for corporate sustainability management. Their missions are usually very clearly articulated and do not span the entire range of social and environmental issues, but reflect a strategic focus on a single issue or a cluster of similar issues. NGOs and consumer organizations have a common goal: creating transparency through disseminating relevant information to their clientele. Beyond this commonality, we detect various nuances within the cluster, which clearly reflect its diversity and scope.

Consumer organizations were more concerned with the effects of products, and the effects of the supply chain under corporate influence and control respectively. This most likely reflects consumer organizations' clear focus on consumer products and consumption patterns. Consumer organizations state measurable facts (e.g. results of product testing) rather than naming and shaming laggard companies. Interest in supply chain management is strong since it significantly determines product characteristics (e.g. use of child/forced labor in the production of clothing or the use of hazardous substances). Health effects are of particular relevance, as they, in contrast to many other social and environmental effects, directly affect consumers' quality of life.

Most NGOs clearly go beyond consumer organizations' key goal of transparency. They campaign against companies, and increasingly also engage and work with them on solutions (e.g. WWF and the Forum for the Future).

All in all, we could detect significant strategic synergies and complementary target audiences in this cluster. This is also reflected in coalitions and alliances between NGOs on certain issues (e.g. climate change) and activities (e.g. political lobbying).

Both our questionnaire and interviews showed a very homogeneous profile of satisfaction levels and expectations. Interviewees acknowledged significant progress (particularly in the environmental domain) in the industrialized world, also in light of existing regulatory and quasi-regulatory standards. However, they also pointed out that there was still a long way to go, since corporate sustainability was still limited to:

- Incremental changes to business models (they ascertained an (almost) complete lack of sustainable models)
- Pilot ("lighthouse") projects and public relations.

Based on their experiences in several stakeholder dialogues, some NGOs were dissatisfied with corporate efforts to integrate sustainability into the core business. Furthermore, they criticized the fact that companies tried to keep them busy with stakeholder dialogues. They felt as though they were being "managed."

As Figure 4.11 illustrates, our respondents were most satisfied with regulatory compliance (in Europe), the use of environmental management

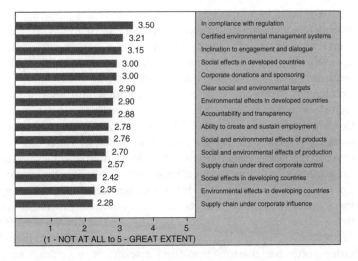

Value	Category
3.50	In compliance with regulation
3.21	Certified environmental management systems
3.15	Inclination to engagement and dialogue
3.00	Social effects in developed countries
3.00	Corporate donations and sponsoring
2.90	Clear social and environmental targets
2.90	Environmental effects in developed countries
2.88	Accountability and transparency
2.78	Ability to create and sustain employment
2.76	Social and environmental effects of products
2.70	Social and environmental effects of production
2.57	Supply chain under direct corporate control
2.42	Social effects in developing countries
2.35	Environmental effects in developing countries
2.28	Supply chain under corporate influence

1   2   3   4   5
(1 - NOT AT ALL to 5 - GREAT EXTENT)

Figure 4.11 Satisfaction with corporate social and environmental performance (bystanders)

systems, and companies' (sometimes-overwhelming) inclination to engagement and dialogue. They were clearly more critical about companies' behavior in developing countries, their supply chain management and the resulting social effects. Overall, we ascertain a clear change in the focus of challengers from environmental issues in the 1980s to an increasingly global perspective and strong advocacy on corporate behavior in developing countries today.

Drivers of and criteria for corporate sustainability

Challengers' agendas are clearly driven by their memberships, i.e. donors and contributors, and governance structures. Depending on the size of the organizations, those governance structures can be quite complex. Furthermore, challengers were also pulled toward a participatory role by companies and other stakeholders, e.g. in High Level Groups at the EU, discussion boards of the UN Global Compact initiative, and ISO advisory boards.

Challengers' assessment of corporate performance is orientated toward existing standards and regulation as well as compliance with certified management systems. It also reflects a general call for the proactive, beyond-compliance behavior of companies, in developing countries in particular where regulation and/or enforcement are inadequate ("responsibility comes with power"). Our interviewees pointed to the following key areas of corporate performance:

- Transparency: Challengers view corporate transparency as well as product transparency – beyond compliance – as key criteria when assessing corporate performance. In this context, they also call for more *consistent* labeling of products and services.
- Challengers increasingly focus on developing countries and supply chain management, since this is where the major issues (labor conditions, pollution, etc.) remain. We found NGOs, which are already working closely with companies, to be in audit functions. They develop their own guidelines oriented along international standards.
- Consumer organizations have a strong interest in effective monitoring to ensure the quality of products and services. So far, they largely focus on environmental effects and occupational health and safety issues of products, which reflect a factual-based way of assessment (in many cases scientific). However, there is a new trend toward incorporating softer social issues into their assessment, e.g. based on the forthcoming ISO 26000 (available by 2008).

We ascertain that overall NGOs shifted their focus more to issues in developing countries and built an international network, whereas consumer organizations – despite their more recent interest in developing countries and supply chains – remain largely rooted in their national context.

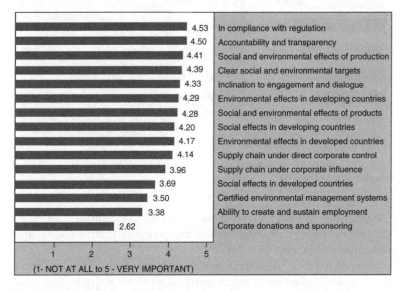

Value	Criterion
4.53	In compliance with regulation
4.50	Accountability and transparency
4.41	Social and environmental effects of production
4.39	Clear social and environmental targets
4.33	Inclination to engagement and dialogue
4.29	Environmental effects in developing countries
4.28	Social and environmental effects of products
4.20	Social effects in developing countries
4.17	Environmental effects in developed countries
4.14	Supply chain under direct corporate control
3.96	Supply chain under corporate influence
3.69	Social effects in developed countries
3.50	Certified environmental management systems
3.38	Ability to create and sustain employment
2.62	Corporate donations and sponsoring

(1- NOT AT ALL to 5 - VERY IMPORTANT)

Figure 4.12 Importance of criteria for assessing corporate social and environmental performance (challengers)

Our quantitative data (see Figure 4.12) point to a wide range of important criteria for corporate sustainability (the first 10 items have mean values between 4.14 and 4.53), which underlines the number and diversity of organizations in this cluster. It is plausible that corporate philanthropy, employment, environmental management systems and social effects in developed countries are less important, since they are either non-differentiating (corporate giving and EMS are indeed largely inaccurate indicators of performance) or typically "occupied" by other stakeholders and their clientele (e.g. employment).

Operational decision-making (to take certain actions rather than others) is primarily determined by issue significance and demands from clientele. It is plausible that corporate characteristics (see Figure 4.13) are less important, since challengers are – as mentioned above – issue-driven.

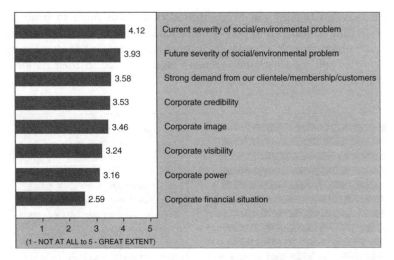

Figure 4.13   Extent to which criteria determine stakeholder actions to influence companies (challengers)

However, our interviews also showed that an opportunistic approach focusing on particularly well known and powerful brands and companies could also be very effective.

We also detected significant internal criteria: Human and financial resources were often very limited (partly due to very restrictive fundraising policies). Several organizations felt an overwhelmingly high demand to contribute to roundtables or cooperate with companies. To use their resources as effectively as possible, challengers tend to select initiatives carefully, especially in terms of partnerships, since they are particularly resource-intensive.

Processes and tools used in relation to corporate sustainability

Challengers' portfolio of assessment tools is rather balanced, which reflects the cluster's diversity. Low-cost assessment tools like the media/internet and corporate reports account for almost 30 per cent, which we attribute to the lack of resources mentioned above (see Figure 4.14).

Most organizations lack a sophisticated approach to assess corporate performance. However, more powerful and resourceful NGOs and consumer organizations are more systematic: They exchange information with rating agencies, use tools to survey their memberships' interests and needs, etc. They also collect information about corporate failures and wrongdoings.

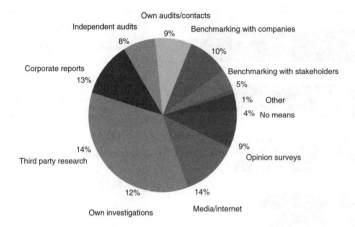

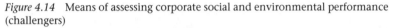

Figure 4.14 Means of assessing corporate social and environmental performance (challengers)

Overall, assessment clearly reflects:

- Organizations' missions, i.e. issue-driven in the case of NGOs, product-driven in the case of consumer organizations. Hence, direct assessment of individual companies occurs only rarely (e.g. through websites such as corporatewatch.org that tracks the behavior of industries and individual companies) but is in the pipeline. For instance, Germanwatch developed a tool to assess the sustainability performances of leading German DAX companies.
- An orientation toward existing international standards (OECD guidelines, ISO standards) that make assessment of companies more transparent and measurable.

Interviewees also reported that personal contacts helped to significantly lower their reservations about top-level management (roundtables organized by third parties, foundations or politicians and stakeholder dialogues initiated by industry federations or companies). We also ascertained a tendency toward more scientific research to build up reputation and knowledge.

Decision-making processes were largely pragmatic and based on previous experiences (see also Figure 4.15). Systematic processes were only used by a minority of organizations' interviewed, mostly big multinational NGOs that carry out a "due diligence" process before engaging with companies.

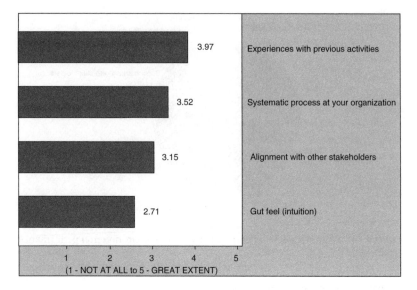

Figure 4.15   Extent to which processes/tools determine actions to influence companies (challengers)

As our interviewees suggested, more diligence is required prior to engagement, since the organization's credibility, as a "demander," is more at risk because it is "flirting with the enemy."

Actions and their effectiveness to influence corporate sustainability

In line with the qualitative data, we detected four dominating activities (see Figure 4.16):

- Engagement and cooperation through partnerships (19 per cent).
- Confrontation (classical advocacy in the form of direct action against companies, new kinds of internet-based activism – "hacktivism"): Direct actions and praising and blaming account for 22 per cent in total. This rather adversarial approach is also complemented with a softer kind of advocacy through transparency (disseminating information about corporate behavior and products).
- Political lobbying (17 per cent).
- A quasi-regulatory approach, e.g. through the provision of labeling and certification schemes (10 per cent) as well as guidelines and standards (11 per cent).

We note that – in some instances – several of those approaches are "applied" within the same organization. Since this requires more

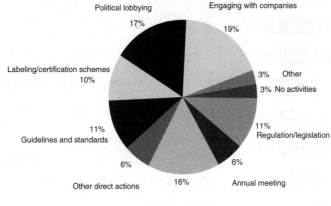

Figure 4.16   Portfolio of actions to influence companies' social and environmental performance (challengers)

resources than usual, it is most likely to occur in the larger NGOs. This two-pronged approach (advocacy through campaigning and convening through partnerships) tends to be associated with conflicts between the advocates of the two – within the individual organization and the NGO community. To reconcile both strands, the convening arm:

• Is very selective and cautious about choosing their corporate partners.
• Aims to demonstrate transparency and effectiveness in its partnerships through clear and ambitious targets.
• Sometimes salomonically points to the fundraising effects of the partnerships (if they are significant).

Despite this agreement, overall our interviewees suggested that a simultaneous "carrot" (cooperative) and "stick" (confrontational) approach appears highly effective in some cases, since it combines downside potential (bad press, boycotts, etc.) with upside potential (innovation, greater credibility).

We also detected ambivalence toward instruments such as roundtables or stakeholder dialogues. Although interviewees acknowledged that companies are increasingly open to engage in dialogue, they also complained about a lack of corporate willingness to really listen and change. This pattern in corporate reactions is also reflected in our quantitative data (see Figure 4.17). Our respondents acknowledged companies' openness but also relatively frequently noted defensive corporate attitudes

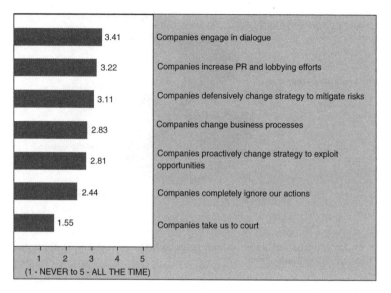

Figure 4.17   Frequency of corporate reactions to stakeholder action (challengers)

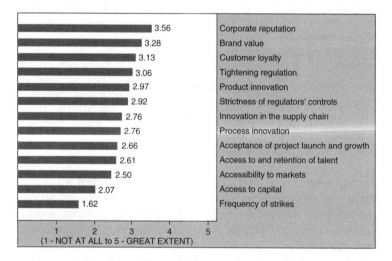

Figure 4.18   Extent to which stakeholder actions affect corporate value drivers (challengers)

reflected in PR campaigns and defensive, incremental changes in strategies and processes.

As one could expect, challengers primarily target corporate brands, reputation and customer loyalty through their actions (see Figure 4.18).

However, in line with our interviews, we point to a significant (and growing) interest in and effect on companies' license-to-operate, i.e. regulators' controls and regulation (through political lobbying) and innovation (through partnerships and greater transparency).

4.1.3 Suppliers, customers and financial institutions: incrementalists in corporate sustainability

Alexander Nick

The incrementalist cluster is composed of financial market institutions, corporate customers and corporate suppliers. Within our study, these three stakeholders are also business stakeholders; the others are "non-business" stakeholders.

Business stakeholders are primarily concerned about competitiveness and creating a level playing field. They are relatively satisfied with corporate social and environmental performance and less interested in it than non-business stakeholders are. Nevertheless, we observed a rising awareness of incrementalists in corporate sustainability. This is primarily a result of them being scrutinized for the social and environmental effects across their entire value chain, e.g. banks for their role as investors and creditors, industry for social and environmental issues caused by their suppliers and customers.

On the following pages, we elaborate on the mission, drivers and actions of incrementalists in more detail.

Sustainability mission of incrementalists

Depending on the business group in question, environmental and social issues are assessed from different angles. While corporate customers and corporate suppliers focus on the supply chain and therefore only focus on a relatively well-defined area, financial market institutions have a broader view on companies as a whole and their performance on the capital markets.

It is not surprising that as business stakeholders, incrementalists tend to follow an economic logic. After all, they are part of the economic system. For companies, incrementalists are transactional stakeholders (as elaborated on in section 3.4) and they thus receive considerable management attention. At the end of the day, corporate success largely depends upon how the relationships with customers, suppliers and the financial market are managed. Contrary to the challenge of managing the non-business environment, companies have a long history of dealing with incrementalists and have developed a strong expertise in this area. Again, this is not surprising, as this result reflects a business-as-usual scenario. The principal question is whether companies are also prepared to manage the social and environmental expectations of the incrementalists. To do so, they first have to learn and understand them.

The sustainability mission of financial institutions, corporate customers and corporate suppliers is not very strong. This group is content with incremental progress in sustainability – slowly, but surely – and this is why we employ the term incrementalist to describe them. The goal of financial institutions is to provide information and to create transparency. Corporate customers aim to ensure appropriate environmental and social behavior on the part of their suppliers. As the power is mostly with the buyer, stakeholders on the sales side are most concerned with their business and do not address the corporate sustainability of their customers proactively.

Incentives and drivers to address sustainability

In general, we found that incrementalists, as corporate stakeholders, do not have a strong corporate sustainability agenda. The business of companies is to increase profits, and companies are successful because they stick to this goal and focus on what matters. For incrementalists, sustainability only becomes important if social and environmental issues become material. This tends to be more so for corporate customers as they experience increased public pressure in their operations. Environmental and social concerns are on the table: environmental destruction up the value chain or child labor in supplying factories. NGOs and media tend to target well-known branded companies. Managers in exposed industries in particular are familiar with the campaigns against Nike and Shell. To protect their corporate reputation and brand image, they have put appropriate management systems into place and started to exert influence beyond their "factory gates." The financial community is also under scrutiny, especially due to their project financing activities in developing countries. To protect their reputation, banks have come up with a self-commitment to take care of environmental and social impacts while financing big projects (known as the Equator Principles).

By taking a closer look at the incentives of incrementalists to influence corporate social and environmental performance, we can identify two major categories of motives:

- Motives based on the protection of their corporate value, i.e. minimizing downside potential.
- Motives anchored in the enhancement of their corporate value, i.e. building upside potential.

However, incrementalists mostly focus on the former argument. Material social and environmental issues are incorporated into risk management with the aim of protecting the reputation and brand image of the company. Successfully building upside potential is currently much more challenging. For corporate stakeholders, it is not easy to prove that they can generate value through corporate sustainability management. The disinterest and ignorance of their own clientele is seen as one of the prime reasons, as they are driven by a focus on economic performance, shareholder value and short-term profits.

Criteria and processes to assess the social and environmental performance of companies

As the incentives are not very salient, social and environmental criteria have not become an integral part of the business decision-making mechanism. Nevertheless, we observed that in some industries incrementalists have started to assess corporations in terms of their social and environmental performance. In order to carry out these assessments, incrementalists have developed sophisticated decision-making tools and processes, which by far surpass the standards of processes developed by non-business stakeholders. They introduced these processes with the same professionalism and efficiency as other management processes. Thereby, they build on the experience and know-how existing in the company.

Figure 4.19 illustrates the relative importance of the assessment criteria used by incrementalists to evaluate companies' sustainability performance. It is remarkable that nearly all items have an importance score above 3. Only corporate donations and sponsoring scores below 3. This result speaks for itself, since incrementalists do not care for activities that only benefit society and that are handled by PR departments. Being in compliance with regulation is viewed as having the greatest importance. This reflects the findings from our interviews that incrementalists can be satisfied if companies act within legal frameworks with the exception of corporate customers acting in developing countries. Accountability and transparency also scores relatively high (above 4), which aligns with the mission and expectations of incrementalists discussed above.

Moreover, incrementalists believe that the regulatory burden should not be increased. Economic pressure and new threats from emerging economies in Asia (in particular, China and India) are issues of concern to them. In this context, another unsolved problem is the management of the supply chain in Eastern Europe and in Asian countries. These countries

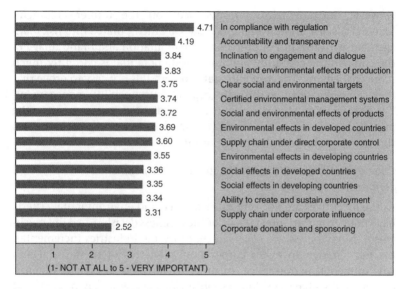

Figure 4.19   Importance of criteria for assessing corporate social and environmental performance (incrementalists)

are competitive for various economic reasons, but also because their social and environmental regulation is less strict and/or less strongly enforced. When we discussed our research findings with managers at IMD, it became obvious that companies in Western Europe are still struggling with this development. One manager put it as follows: "To be successful in the future, you either need to be good or bad." With this perspective, corporate sustainability can also become a competitive advantage for those companies who are able to differentiate themselves through social and environmental standards, provided stakeholders start rewarding companies for superior social and environmental performance, i.e. provide some real first-mover-advantage (rather than penalizing weak performance).

Actions and their effectiveness to influence companies' social and environmental performance

Taking into account the above findings, we can also reach the conclusion that activities from incrementalists are primarily determined by corporate characteristics. Here again, the name we chose for this group proves to be appropriate: We observed that the activities of financial institutions, corporate customers and suppliers aim for *incremental* social and environmental progress. To put it in a nutshell, as one asset manager told us: "Financial markets will not change the world."

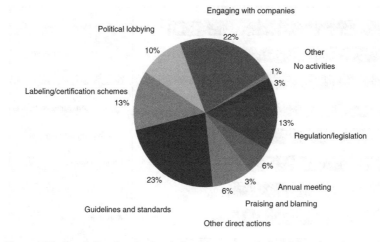

Engaging with companies

Political lobbying

22%

10%

Other

No activities

1%

3%

Labeling/certification schemes

13%

13%

Regulation/legislation

6%

23%

3%

Annual meeting

6%

Praising and blaming

Guidelines and standards

Other direct actions

Figure 4.20   Portfolio of actions to influence companies' social and environmental performance (incrementalists)

Figure 4.20 shows incrementalists' portfolio of actions. Main activities are in the field of quasi-regulatory actions such as the development of guidelines, standards and labeling schemes (36 per cent). Engaging with dialogues is another important strategy for incrementalists. Direct activities like praising and blaming or other direct actions contribute only to a minor part to the portfolio of actions.

For incrementalists to be successful with their activities, it is essential to integrate them into their core business. If certain organizational and systemic barriers (lack of corporate culture, tools and systems, stakeholders' indifference, etc.) are not too high, companies are able to formulate sound business logic for their actions. Since this is still rarely the case, incrementalists are engaged in awareness building, dialogue and research activities. They also investigate the possibility of leveraging their activities through coalition building.

In addition, the effectiveness of the actions also depends on contextual factors, e.g. the regulatory environment. Last but not least, some of our interviewees stated that we cannot get away from the fact that environmental and social disasters are a strong lever for raising awareness of the need for a sustainable business model within incrementalists and companies. The increasing costs of damages give companies a strong incentive to act.

Figure 4.21 shows incrementalists' view of the relative effectiveness of actions aimed at influencing companies' sustainability performance. Here regulation/legislation receives clearly the highest mean value of

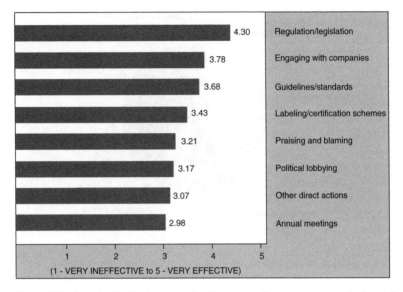

Figure 4.21   Perceived effectiveness of actions in influencing companies' social and environmental performance – regardless of whether used by the individual stakeholder or not (incrementalists)

4.3. This is a bit counterintuitive in light of companies' typical aversion to regulation. Obviously, this primarily applies to situations in which they are targeted by regulation themselves. In contrast, incrementalists appear to appreciate regulation (and stringent enforcement), if it keeps other companies (suppliers, customers, debtors, etc.) "in check," since it makes the business environment more stable.

The provision of guidelines and standards and the engagement with companies are also perceived to be more effective activities. In comparison with non-business stakeholders, business stakeholders consider campaigning activities like boycotts, imposing standards and praising and blaming activities to be less effective. Activities like boycotts and praising and blaming are mostly undertaken by NGOs that do not have other levers to influence corporate actions. Imposing standards is perceived as lowering the competitiveness of companies.

When comparing incrementalists within their own cluster, we found the following nuances: financial institutions rely more on the effectiveness of actions at annual meetings, while corporate customers and suppliers focus more strongly on guidelines and standards, as they work as quasi-regulation, and thus create a more stable business environment.

Resulting risks and opportunities for companies

The important question to address is what risks and opportunities for companies result from the activities of incrementalists. The overall answer is that due to incrementalists' nature described above and their passive role in moving corporate sustainability further, companies have time to develop appropriate strategies to respond to incrementalists' actions.

It remains to be seen to what extent this will change in the future. There are no signs that the importance of sustainability will decline. Some global social and environmental problems are even likely to become increasingly important. Pioneering incrementalists are stepping ahead and are developing innovative instruments to cope with this development. For example, one of our interviewees from the financial markets is dealing with the question of how to integrate qualitative risks into corporate reporting.

> Environmental and qualitative issues are in BASEL II, but only in a very diluted way. In 2015–2017, there will also be a BASEL III. We want to get qualitative risk issues integrated in it. That is systemic change. To succeed, we need to start working now. (Financial Institution)

We asked incrementalists about their perceptions of companies' reactions to incrementalists' actions. The result (see Figure 4.22) shows that incrementalists do not feel that companies ignore their actions. In contrast, the quantitative data illustrate that companies engage in dialogue from time to time, change business processes, defensively change strategy to mitigate risks as well as proactively change strategy to exploit opportunities.

Furthermore, the data show that changes in business processes appear to be significantly less often reported by financial institutions than by customers and suppliers. We attribute this to a more immediate relationship between suppliers and customers (e.g. via material and information flows: product specifications, timing). Financial institutions have a broader focus on environmental and social issues and are more removed from the actual value chain.

It is essential for successful companies to focus on their value drivers. Figure 4.23 shows incrementalists' perceptions of the extent, to which value drivers of companies targeted are affected. Incrementalists consider themselves as having the strongest effect on brand and reputation. This is somewhat counterintuitive, as it suggests that an indirect influence on intangibles is stronger than a (more obvious and direct) lever through

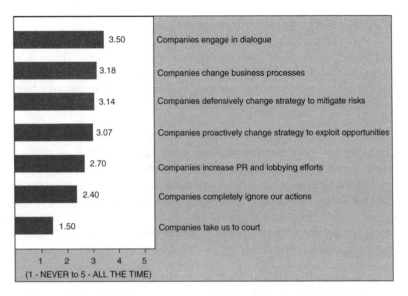

Figure 4.22 Frequency of corporate reactions to stakeholder action (incrementalists)

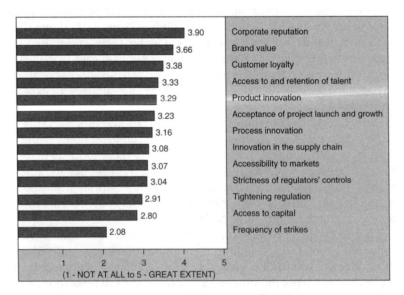

Figure 4.23 Extent to which stakeholder actions affect corporate value drivers (incrementalists)

transactions (i.e. access to capital, customer loyalty, innovation, etc.). We conclude the following:

- From a financial institutions' point of view, influence on access to capital is probably minor, as overall project financing is readily available.
- Actions of suppliers and customers have little direct effects, as they do not trigger significant changes in the targeted companies (i.e. innovation, employee satisfaction).
- The adoption of new social and environmental standards and the use of labeling and certification schemes are perceived to have an effect on brand value and reputation rather than on business models and processes.

Furthermore, the statistical analysis of the quantitative data within the incrementalist cluster shows that financial institutions consider their effect on all value drivers (except access to capital and access to and retention of talent) smaller than customers and suppliers. In line with the findings presented above, this plausibly underpins our finding that:

- Social and environmental issues become more material if you focus on concrete issues or processes. To demonstrate an effect on the corporate value chain seems to be easier than to demonstrate the effect on the company as a whole.
- Influence (and most likely the "felt" responsibility) moves along the value chain. In this respect, financial institutions are one or two stages removed.

Actors within the incrementalist cluster who promote the concept of corporate sustainability are a niche. Nevertheless, we found out that this niche is significant. As one of our interviewees stated:

It does not have to be a majority of the market. All it has to be is a significant minority to be relevant. You cannot afford to rule out significant minorities in the market.

It is difficult to predict where the sustainability activities of incrementalists will be heading in the next years. From our current findings, we would advise companies to observe the developments carefully. Identifying weak signals from the stakeholder environment and interpreting them in terms of their future impact on the business model could be an appropriate precautionary activity for companies.

4.1.4   Media: their strategy and background in corporate sustainability

Simon Tywuschik

In contrast to Chapter 11, which presents and discusses our empirical evidence collected for this study, this section provides more background on the media's mission and background, typology, approach to sustainability and strategy.

Framework and typology

Media operate in various contexts, as depicted in Figure 4.24. The different contexts are determined by certain elements:

- The normative context includes the societal context, prevailing ethical standards, journalistic guidelines and the legal and historical basics.
- The structural context refers to the conditions under which journalistic work is produced, such as economical, political, organizational or technological pressure.
- The functional context refers to the journalistic content and its effects.
- The CSM context refers to media strategy on corporate sustainability, its focus, analytical level and outreach.

Concerning the normative context, media should inform the public appropriately, completely and objectively about the most relevant and

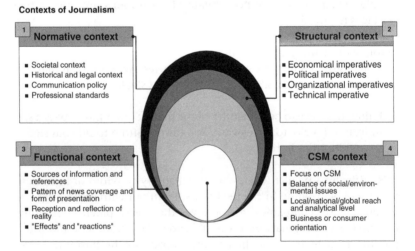

Contexts of Journalism

1 Normative context
- Societal context
- Historical and legal context
- Communication policy
- Professional standards

2 Structural context
- Economical imperatives
- Political imperatives
- Organizational imperatives
- Technical imperative

3 Functional context
- Sources of information and references
- Pattern of news coverage and form of presentation
- Reception and reflection of reality
- "Effects" and "reactions"

4 CSM context
- Focus on CSM
- Balance of social/environmental issues
- Local/national/global reach and analytical level
- Business or consumer orientation

Figure 4.24   Contexts of journalism[1]

pressing issues concerning all societal areas, i.e. it should be neutral and fact-driven. Across Europe, there are several organizations monitoring media behavior and output in order to ensure that media adhere to their institutional mission. Obviously, the normative context of neutrality and objectivity also applies to the topic of corporate sustainability.

Concerning the structural context, media provide relevant facts, backgrounds and opinions for a certain readership or audience. They address a selected area of interest with a certain journalistic style and take into account existing political and economic conditions. In order to remain attractive to the market, they systematically try to attract new consumers, continuously assessing and reassessing the needs and wants of their readers or audiences. This "market research" enables media to select issues, define agendas and communicate content to its audience or readership.

Based on the objective to investigate the importance and the approach of media to corporate sustainability, we will particularly focus on the functional and CSM contexts in the following sections.

Media can be conveniently clustered into print and electronic media:

- We include television, radio and the internet in electronic media. TV and radio can be characterized by factors such as thematic focus, dominant formats or target groups. Internet media are on the one hand an extension of electronic (TV, radio) or print media and, on the other hand, an independent media with a great breadth and depth of information on sustainability.
- Print media consists of newspapers, magazines, journals and books. They can also be characterized by factors such as subjects or frequency of publication.

Sustainability in electronic and print media – A snapshot

Electronic media. Our interviews suggest that corporate sustainability is covered in news programs, as well as in scientific contributions and formats addressing economic and business issues. However, this does not imply that business channels cover corporate sustainability; in fact, it is quite the contrary, most likely because they focus strongly on current market and corporate figures and events. Real-time coverage on business and economics by news channels such as CNN, BBC or Bloomberg provide live information based on a worldwide network of journalists, often at the expense of analytic contents. Given this focus on novelty, it is difficult to capture corporate sustainability properly: an issue assessment in a news format (containing market data and interviews) is rarely sufficient to describe corporate sustainability. Next to methodological barriers (complex and sometimes uncertain issues and marginal relevance), the expectation of the audience to be constantly informed about ongoing changes in the corporate world does not justify the coverage of a strategic issue like sustainability.

In radio, corporate sustainability is covered in a similar fashion to that observed in TV: in more economics-related programs. Coverage does not exhibit a regular fixed pattern. In the period of our investigation, we saw that coverage was frequently triggered by current events, e.g. in Germany as background on the major lay-offs at Deutsche Bank. Local relevance is an important moderating factor: A public radio station broadcasting a discussion about the lay-offs was in fact located in the same federal state as the bank's headquarters. Furthermore, contextual information may increase the attractiveness of the topic. In the case of Deutsche Bank, the fact that it had simultaneously reported record earnings made the story more attractive.

Several internet sites follow a more strategic mission in terms of corporate sustainability. They provide more background information and analysis. They are often "byproducts" of other media (e.g. TV or print media), stakeholders (e.g. NGOs, consumer organizations) and other institutions, such as universities, think tanks, research agencies or consultancies.

One important trend in the internet from a journalistic point of view is the phenomenon of "blogging." Blogging permits individuals to engage in journalistic activities. It is highly decentralized and user-driven. It occurs through weblogs (hence blogging rather than logging) on which individuals post messages, news and articles. At the moment, it is difficult to predict the significance of blogging to companies; however, it can potentially be more harmful and more difficult to manage for corporations than classical media.

Overall, the coverage of corporate sustainability in electronic media depends strongly on the program scheme and analytical level of the particular media. Live television does not use a high analytical level and, hence, is not an appropriate platform for sustainability. Media look for easily accessible topics, which can be transmitted by a few key numbers (this applies to private channels relying on revenue through commercials in particular), primarily because the audiences seem to favor "easy take-aways" around business issues, e.g. packed around the key financials and a CEO interview. Media that include sustainability contents:

- Have program schemes that are more compatible with sustainability
- Have a more analytical journalistic style
- Are attracted by current issues and, most likely, a negative context (accident, fraud, scandal, etc.).

Print media. The coverage of corporate sustainability depends upon the print media's different publication schemes, ranging from one day to several months. At one end of this continuum, there are dailies like the *Wall Street Journal, Financial Times, Les Échos* or *Handelsblatt* and the internet pages. At the other end, there are business journals and magazines, published weekly, monthly or even quarterly. The main difference between these groups is as follows:

- The internet and dailies refer back on the news flow from the last 24 hours at the most.
- Journals, magazines and books can deal with longer time periods.

The ratio between novelty and analytic content is strongly linked to the publication scheme: Whereas internet and dailies focus on novelty, the second group tries to detect patterns and analyze information in a global context. They provide more background (independencies, causal effects). They capture the readers' attention by unfolding a story, instead of merely reporting briefly on the issues and actors. Obviously corporate sustainability fits with the more analytical approach taken by journals, magazines and books. Although some dailies such as the *Financial Times* or *Les Échos* tend to cover corporate sustainability more regularly, the majority of European dailies do not serve this niche and report on a rather generic level.

We conclude that business-oriented media are by far the most important editors of corporate sustainability. They report from a certain contingency perspective, for instance from a certain position (e.g. managerial, accounting), by certain issues (e.g. environment, risk management) or industries (e.g. chemical or insurance). Thus, corporate sustainability is tailored to a certain readership, providing information about a niche, in which the reader, e.g. a manager in a certain industry, is (possibly) inherently interested, e.g. in corporate sustainability in his or her industry. Thus, it combines elements ranging from risk management, issue management and resource efficiency. Outside of the segment of business-related media, corporate sustainability is, as a subject for print media, insignificant, although it is sometimes covered as a political topic.

Our interviewees indicated that corporate sustainability is a niche topic in the majority of print media. The coverage is infrequent, which reflects the rather low strategic importance of and overall modest interest from audiences and readers in corporate sustainability. A few media provide regular information and analysis on corporate sustainability. However, the topic does not represent a permanent point of attraction for media's clientele. Environmental and social issues are covered from time to time, reflecting peaks in public attention.

Ethical Corporation – Business media with a strategic focus on CSM

One title focusing exclusively on corporate sustainability is *Ethical Corporation*, a British monthly. It covers social and environmental issues from a business and an economic perspective. Thus, it could be seen as an example of a business-to-business magazine on corporate sustainability. The magazine features the following characteristics:

- It has a global focus, reporting on corporate sustainability in Europe, the Middle East and Africa, the Asia-Pacific region, North America and Latin America. Often the business perspective is linked to a specific continent, country, region or political/economical organization such as the OECD.
- It covers sustainability from several perspectives such as management strategy and politics (e.g. forthcoming legislation).
- It analyzes issues in a research rather than a journalistic manner, providing the reader with more advanced frameworks and information.
- Every edition features a detailed and systematic analysis of one corporate sustainability report.

Overall, magazines cover a wide range of areas: issues, stakeholders, corporations and their actions. It also provides sector-specific coverage by focusing on issues specific to the automobile, paper or coal industries.

Media's approach: from issue selection to distribution

Why do media increasingly monitor globally active companies and mostly ignore the rest? Why do they focus on issue A rather than issue B? We will provide the answers to these questions by examining the value chain of media, which includes the following steps:

1. To select issues which promise the highest public attention and establish a corresponding agenda.
2. To evaluate the issue factually and subjectively in an editorial process.
3. To distribute the information and evaluate effectiveness.

In the following, we describe this three-step process in more detail:

Issue selection and agenda creation. Issue selection and agenda setting are determined by several critical factors. We have divided these factors into two groups – dependent on whether they are moderated by cultural and national influences or not: The first group consists of factors that are independent from the cultural and national dimension and apply to the issue and its features only. It includes frequency, threshold factor, directness, meaningfulness, expectation, surprise, continuity and variation. In Table 4.1, we describe how the individual factors determine media's agenda setting.

Obviously, the context in which issues occur has a certain impact. For example, negative issues are substantially more often mentioned than positive issues: We also ascertain a certain trade-off between the scale of issues and their lack of local relevance (scope vs. degree of personalization). Media commonly cover an issue of minor social or environmental significance (compared to bigger issues) but of greater relevance to the (local) reader. Further determinants of agenda setting that reflect the context sensitivity of media are included in Table 4.2.

Editorial process. Although media should report objectively on issues (according to their institutional mission and their professional standards), they are overemphasizing outcomes of their assessment to a certain degree to attract greater attention. Public attention is one of the most important success factors for media. However, while tabloids are famous for their "speculative approach," the up-market press such as *The Times* (Consumer title, UK) or *El Mundo* (Consumer title, Spain) sticks closely to the facts. We also detect cultural differences in styles:

We have the UK publication style that is rather offensive. (B2B title, Special Interest, UK)

In Spain, we have a slightly different, more emotional type of journalism. (Consumer title, General Interest, Spain)

Table 4.1 Factors that influence agenda setting (independent from cultural and national context)

Factor	Concrete examples and relationship
Frequency	— The more often the issue occurs, the more probable the issue will become news.
Threshold factor	— There is a certain threshold value, usually defined over relevance and novelty, which an issue or information must meet in order to be recognized by the media.
Directness	— The more direct and straightforward a certain issue is, the higher is the probability of coverage.
Meaningfulness	— The bigger the issue dimension and the more immediate the effects (e.g. on people), the more probable a news story will emerge.
Expectation	— The higher the correspondence between expectation and actual occurrence, the higher the probability of publication.
Surprise	— Surprising issues (= they do not meet with general expectation) have a higher chance of media coverage.
Continuity	— If a certain issue is already defined as news, the chances of it being further regarded as news are high.
Variation	— If certain information can help to provide for more balance in a given context, the probability of media mentions increases.

Table 4.2 Factors that influence agenda setting (dependent on national awareness and culture)

Factor	Concrete examples and relationships
Relation to leading corporations	— Issues related to leading corporations (by economic power) have a higher news value than issues related to less-known or smaller companies.
Relation to leading persons	— Prominent and powerful persons (such as top-managers, politicians and other public persons) have a higher news power.
Personalization	— Personal involvement and proximity increases the probability of coverage. Identical issues occurring in the distance trigger less attention.
Negativism	— The more the issue is centered on "negative" national issues, the higher the media attention. Negative issues vary in dependence of the national context.

Finally, we ascertain that individuals rather than teams are responsible for reporting on corporate sustainability. This points to a significant degree of "managerial" discretion for those individuals.

Distribution. After issues are evaluated and agendas set, media distribute or broadcast their works to the end-user. Thus, certain issues (often-local social or environmental problems that affect a limited amount of people) become public information, which triggers a public monitoring and assessment process for this issue. Two distinct effects can be distinguished here:

- A distribution effect: As the public gains access to new information, public awareness on certain issues rises.
- An amplification (editorial) effect: Since media evaluates and selects information, it affects the public's opinion-making process.

Both effects *can* have significant implications for corporations in the area of corporate sustainability.

Public perception and media influence

How do corporate sustainability management, media and public perception interact? Figure 4.25 depicts corporations (and their stakeholders) and media as the key determinants of public perception and action.

Corporations and stakeholders interact continuously on social and environmental issues. Media screen for interesting issues and distribute information to the public. The public has little direct access to corporate behavior and its social and environmental effects. The outreach of

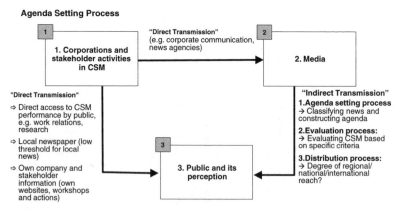

Figure 4.25 Agenda setting and public influence

employees, local newspapers and local stakeholder activities is limited. In addition, corporate reporting can only provide a superficial snapshot on corporate behavior through mini case studies. Hence, direct transmission is weak, and the public relies on indirect transmission, i.e. media distributing information they consider relevant to their target audience. Obviously, this role is significant, since coverage of negative news (accidents, scandals) shapes perception in a different way than coverage of positive news (best practices, innovation). We ascertain two dilemmas:

- Corporate sustainability management is a niche, and thus fails to draw attention from most media.
- Negative news tends to be more spectacular than positive news. Therefore, it is only plausible that media focus on corporate accidents, failures and scandals. It penalizes bad performance and rarely rewards good performance (best practices, pioneering efforts, etc.) with selecting and redistributing corresponding information.

Conclusion

The complexity (plethora of issues, complex global issues) and marginality (many issues are uncertain, only locally relevant, or of little importance because of the high social and environmental standards in Europe, for example) of corporate sustainability make it difficult for media to give this topic more than marginal attention. Obviously, it is most relevant to media focusing on business and economic information.

It remains to be seen how social and environmental issues will develop and how societies will react. Media play a crucial role in shaping public perception. They operate in very competitive markets and therefore cannot be blamed for a system-immanent focus on bad rather than good news. This approach is one important reason for companies to minimize the downside potential (i.e. protecting their reputation and minimizing risks) rather than building upside potential.

We have observed media that have contracted sustainability experts to report on certain issues and corporate sustainability management. This decision to outsource is clearly not a sign for mainstreaming. However, it could suggest that media are reacting to the complex challenge corporate sustainability poses. We have also observed a gradual increase in the coverage of corporate sustainability in the business press.

Media do not have their own agenda, particularly in terms of a current niche topic such as corporate sustainability management. However, *if* the issues (e.g. climate change, water) become more visible (more tangible effects, corresponding activities by NGOs), the media will be one of the first to "jump onto the bandwagon."

4.2   Stakeholders' approach to corporate sustainability: detecting differences and common patterns

Oliver Salzmann

In this section, we will compare the four clusters – challengers (NGOs, consumer organizations), bystanders (governments, communities/ cities, unions), incrementalists (corporate customers/suppliers and financial institutions) and media. We employ quantitative techniques to detect similarities and differences between them and benchmark the results with qualitative data from our interviews.

We identified the main patterns in the quantitative data through factor analysis to reduce the complexity, and compare those factors through analysis of variances (ANOVA) across the four clusters. We will focus on the most interesting results rather than all of the results, i.e. on factors about which stakeholders/clusters exhibit a clear preference or ignorance. We particularly looked out for counterintuitive results as they potentially point to new insights.

We will provide several figures to give a bird's eye perspective on how stakeholders (in total) see corporate sustainability and their role in influencing it. The resulting view is somewhat fuzzy, as it averages out meaningful differences and commonalities between the individual clusters. This is precisely why we report on those nuances in detail in this section.

Criteria for assessing corporate behavior – resulting satisfaction levels

Overall, we see that stakeholders consider corporate regulatory compliance as the most important criteria when assessing corporate performance, followed by accountability and transparency. We also ascertain the clearly minor importance of corporate donations and sponsoring. The remaining mean scores are very similar (see Figure 4.26).

We detected several significant differences in terms of how respondents from the clusters perceive the importance of criteria when assessing corporate social and environmental performance:

- Challengers consider social and environmental issues (both in developing and developed countries), as well as clear target setting by companies, more important than incrementalists, bystanders and the media. This underpins results from our interviews suggesting that NGOs and consumer organizations strongly focus on specific problems associated with primary and secondary corporate activities.

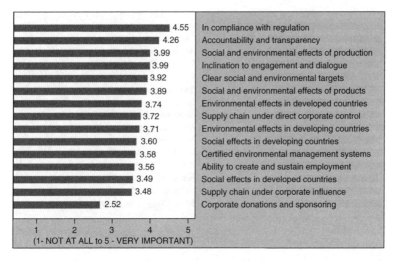

4.55	In compliance with regulation
4.26	Accountability and transparency
3.99	Social and environmental effects of production
3.99	Inclination to engagement and dialogue
3.92	Clear social and environmental targets
3.89	Social and environmental effects of products
3.74	Environmental effects in developed countries
3.72	Supply chain under direct corporate control
3.71	Environmental effects in developing countries
3.60	Social effects in developing countries
3.58	Certified environmental management systems
3.56	Ability to create and sustain employment
3.49	Social effects in developed countries
3.48	Supply chain under corporate influence
2.52	Corporate donations and sponsoring

1   2   3   4   5
(1- NOT AT ALL to 5 - VERY IMPORTANT)

Figure 4.26 Importance of criteria for assessing corporate social and environmental performance (total sample)

- Differences in the importance of engagement and employment can also be linked to certain clusters. Clearly, in line with our interviews, unions, governments and communities are most strongly concerned about engagement and employment, which reflect their concern about regional competitiveness, job security and – in light of their limited bargaining power – companies' willingness to engage.
- Finally, we also ascertain differences in terms of the importance of corporate philanthropy (donations, etc.). It is greater among respondents from the media and bystanders. This most likely reflects a certain level of ignorance (in the media in particular) and bystanders' chronic lack of financial resources.

As one would expect from a European study, stakeholders are relatively satisfied with corporate behavior that is compliant with existing regulation (see Figure 4.27). The remaining items have roughly the same mean scores. We also see that satisfaction levels are not overwhelmingly high. With the exception of regulatory compliance, all are clustered around the mid-point of our scale. Thus, we conclude that:

1. Most stakeholders (NGOs and consumer organizations being the exceptions) are largely indifferent to corporate sustainability.
2. Overall stakeholders are "fairly" satisfied (at least not clearly dissatisfied) with current levels of corporate social and environmental

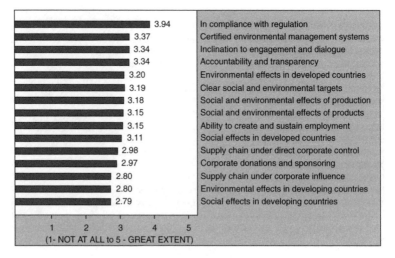

Value	Description
3.94	In compliance with regulation
3.37	Certified environmental management systems
3.34	Inclination to engagement and dialogue
3.34	Accountability and transparency
3.20	Environmental effects in developed countries
3.19	Clear social and environmental targets
3.18	Social and environmental effects of production
3.15	Social and environmental effects of products
3.15	Ability to create and sustain employment
3.11	Social effects in developed countries
2.98	Supply chain under direct corporate control
2.97	Corporate donations and sponsoring
2.80	Supply chain under corporate influence
2.80	Environmental effects in developing countries
2.79	Social effects in developing countries

1   2   3   4   5
(1- NOT AT ALL to 5 - GREAT EXTENT)

Figure 4.27   Satisfaction with corporate social and environmental performance
(total sample)

performance, which one could interpret as an indicator of little future pressure. The corporate sector's recent progress in its ability to deal with issues and stakeholders along with Europe's struggle for competitiveness and employment will also contribute to less pressure in the future.

Satisfaction levels with corporate social and environmental performance deviate across the four clusters. Overall, challengers are less satisfied than incrementalists and bystanders, which reflect the significant demands for corporate sustainability management raised by our interviewees from NGOs.

It was interesting to find *no* difference in terms of respondents' satisfaction with corporate regulatory compliance, companies' willingness to engage and their accountability. This clearly suggests that stakeholders across the board acknowledge widespread compliance with social and environmental regulation in Europe. It also reflects a significant development in the corporate sector toward more openness and transparency since the beginning of the 1990s.

Effectiveness of actions to influence companies

Our data on the effectiveness of actions (see Figure 4.28) reveal – not surprisingly – an overall preference for regulation and legislation, followed

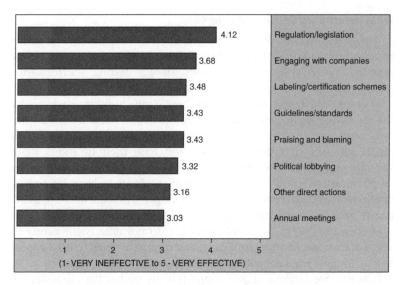

Figure 4.28 Perceived effectiveness of actions in influencing companies' social and environmental performance – regardless of whether used by the individual stakeholder or not (total sample)

by engagement and quasi-regulatory actions (labeling, certification schemes and guidelines/standards). Praising and blaming, actions at annual meetings as well as other direct actions score lower, as NGOs, consumer organizations and the media are underrepresented in the total sample.

Respondents from the clusters perceive the effectiveness of actions to influence companies differently – independent of whether they use that particular action or not. Quasi-regulatory actions (labeling and certification schemes, standards, etc.) combined with engagement are seen as most effective by respondents from challengers and incrementalists. It is obvious that bystanders doubt the effectiveness of those actions more strongly, as they prefer to have "real" regulation. Media appear to be less familiar and therefore more skeptical because they are by their very nature observers and one or two stages removed, i.e. there is virtually no engagement with the corporate sector.

Furthermore, it is very plausible that challengers and bystanders see the effectiveness of classical advocacy (praising and blaming in the public arena, boycotts, etc.) as significantly greater than incrementalists. It is self-evident that companies do not want to be targets of such actions, whereas NGOs, unions as well as local and national governments opportunistically take this approach.

What determines decision-making?

As Figure 4.29 shows, overall decisions to take certain actions to influence (rather than others) are made largely based on experience and (supposedly) more systematic processes (target setting, performance measurement).

As one would expect, our data also show significant differences across the four clusters, in particular between challengers and media on the one hand and incrementalists on the other hand. Challengers and media use less systematic processes and base their decisions more strongly on intuition, because: (1) they have to act quickly (no time for "sophistication"); and (2) decision-making tools are lacking due to lack of resources and systemic factors – there simply is no equivalent of a corporate investment appraisal (e.g. calculating net present value).

Overall, the criteria for decision-making do not differ significantly in terms of their importance. Both issues and corporate characteristics appear to play roughly the same role in influencing stakeholders' decisions.

However, we ascertain a more opportunistic (rather than issue-based) approach to making decisions (for or against certain actions to influence companies) among incrementalists. Obviously, they achieve *incremental* innovations through actions determined by the characteristics of the

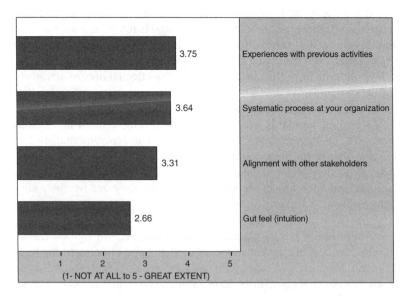

Figure 4.29   Extent to which processes/tools determine actions to influence companies (total sample)

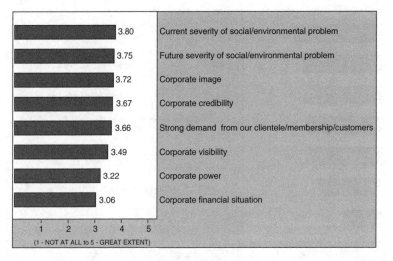

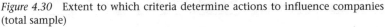

Figure 4.30   Extent to which criteria determine actions to influence companies (total sample)

corporate counterpart (bargaining power, image, credibility as well as technical specifications and processes). Nevertheless, at first sight the result is somewhat counterintuitive, since challengers and bystanders also tend to act opportunistically (given their limited bargaining power). In contrast, challengers and bystanders base their decisions more strongly on issue significance than incrementalists do. This is plausible since both clusters raise demands for corporate sustainability management on the basis of existing social and environmental problems. This applies to NGOs in particular, since issues are at the heart of their mission. This does not – as our interviewees pointed out – exclude an opportunistic approach, e.g. NGOs selecting highly visible companies as campaign targets and the more credible ones as potential partners.

Corporate reactions to stakeholders' actions

Overall, our respondents acknowledge companies' willingness to engage and change their processes and strategies (see Figure 4.31). Considering this figure alongside Figure 4.27 (which shows an "unexcited" or indifferent level of satisfaction with regard to corporate social and environmental performance), we conclude that most stakeholders are not overly ambitious about corporate sustainability, since they are more concerned about corporate and regional competitiveness. They are also met with a significant willingness of companies to engage, which clearly reflects

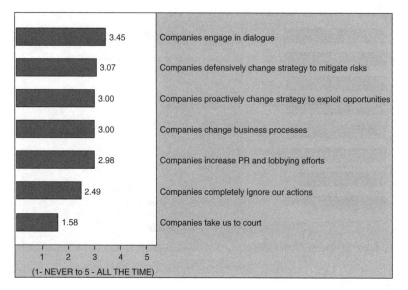

Figure 4.31   Frequency of corporate reactions to stakeholders' action (total sample)

more openness by the corporate sector to engage in stakeholder dialogues, establish stakeholder platforms (e.g. "Tell Shell"), etc.

The four clusters exhibit two significant differences in terms of how
they perceive corporate reactions to their actions:

1. As one would expect, conflict and opposition (PR, lobbying, litigation) with companies is more frequently reported by media and challengers, less frequently by bystanders and especially incrementalists.
2. Incrementalists report no reactions by companies more frequently
   than media and especially challengers and bystanders. This reflects
   both a lack of initiative and activity in the corporate sector, as well as –
   in terms of corporate suppliers – a lack of bargaining power:
   Marketing and sales refrain from telling their customers how they
   should manage social and environmental issues.

Finally, the four clusters report similar frequencies of companies engaging and changing processes and strategies. Incrementalists and media
report more engagement and changes from the corporate sector, challengers and bystanders less; however, the differences are minor and not
statistically significant. In other words, the four clusters are equally
(in)effective at engaging and changing companies. We conclude the

following:

- Companies exhibit a *universal* openness to engagement and stakeholder dialogue. They have come a long way from the beginning of the 1990s.
- The fact that not one of the four clusters is significantly more successful than any other cluster illustrates the strong bargaining power of companies (relative to all clusters) and the modest pressure overall, i.e. of all clusters, in terms of corporate sustainability.

Opportunities and risks for companies

Our sample clearly underlines that corporate sustainability management is primarily related to reputation and brand value (see Figure 4.32). The low mean values of access-to-capital and frequency of strikes are plausible, since both items are largely influenced by one stakeholder group respectively (namely unions and financial institutions).

We also detected several significant differences in terms of how the clusters perceived their effect on certain determinants of corporate success.

Incrementalists and media perceive their effect overall, and on innovation in particular, as greater than bystanders and challengers. The significant difference between incrementalists and challengers is particularly striking, as it underpins substantial skepticism in the NGO

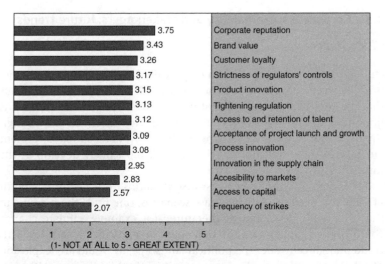

Figure 4.32 Extent to which stakeholder actions affect corporate value drivers (total sample)

community (also in line with our interviews) and its dependence on media (and eventually other transactional stakeholders) to take up a certain social or environmental issue. The relatively high (self-perceived) effect of incrementalists should not be overestimated (especially if one puts it into the context of our data on corporate reactions discussed above), as it can be largely attributed to self-representation and a social desirability bias.

It is not surprising that respondents from the media view their effect on brand value and reputation as being greater than the effects of the other clusters. This reflects the media's significance at "taking up" NGO campaigns, using their investigative resources and disseminating relevant and "juicy" information to the public.

Finally, our data point to a greater self-perceived effect on companies' license to operate (controls of regulators, tightening regulation) through bystanders than through incrementalists and opportunists in particular. This plausibly reflects the role of national, regional and local governments in determining social and environmental legislation and its enforcement. It also underlines the short-term focus and absence of an agenda in media institutions: Although they consider their overall effect on companies (especially on brand value and reputation) significant, they do not make any conscious connection to potential effects on regulation.

4.3 Corporate sustainability and stakeholders: future trends

Ulrich Steger

Our current research revealed an empirically based snapshot of interactions between companies and their stakeholders. However, it is obvious that the current situation will not be static over the years to come. It is important to know where we are and – in this case – to cut through the hype. But in today's changing world, we would also like to present our take on how stakeholder relations will most likely develop in the future.

It is easy to draw up some worst-case scenarios from a corporate point of view (no need to write best-case scenarios, one finds them amass in the sustainable development literature): for example, climate change could happen rapidly and the USA could be particularly hard hit. This could dramatically alter the political landscape, as would any explosion of oil prices, e.g. through more turmoil in the Middle East. Although things would certainly be set in motion, there would be no transition to a more sustainable business model. Instead, there would be substantial turnaround efforts with many frictions and a focus on short-term survival.

It is plausible to think in cycles, which we have seen on both a general and an industry level. There were two decades of massive government regulation, both in social and environmental affairs in the 1970s and 1980s. The collapse of the Soviet Union and other centrally planned economies (e.g. in South America) reversed the trend. The backlash was unfettered "globalization," which in public perception often means: "Let global capital markets work" and "Let's do it the American way." The policy outcome of the Asian (and Russian) financial crisis (to improve governance and transparency) and the rising of an "anti-globalization" movement are the – predictable – countertrends. However, their impact is obviously limited to a rise in awareness. After some break – mostly caused by the burst of the dot.com bubble rather than by the anti-globalization campaigns – foreign direct investments, especially in Southeast Asia, are at an all-time high again, M&As are reaching dot.com-boom levels and hedge funds as well as private equity companies are awash with cash.

Nevertheless, we see a certain "ratchet-effect" – also reflected in our data: the social dimension of sustainable development has moved to the forefront. The job-shift to emerging economies (especially China) continues to be a front-page issue, especially in Continental Europe. So the public scrutiny will not go away.

So what indicates the beginning of a new cycle? We see several major trends that we will discuss in the following:

In praise of incremental change

There is a strong tendency (visible in both of our recent studies) to incremental change that is associated with predictable outcomes and little risk. This is clearly counterintuitive if one – at first glance – looks at the rhetoric of companies, consultants and many academics in the CSR/CSM domain:

- Companies want to create an image of being bold decision-makers and fast movers. Consultants similarly propagate to this end.
- The CSR/CSM community wants to see sustainability as a major driver of new business models and innovation.

However, it is important not to underestimate the effect of long-term incremental change. To take one striking example: Remember the "Banana Republic?" The origin of this expression goes back to the actions of United Fruit, which used to "run" the Central American countries as an "appendix" of their own business, using the "big stick" occasionally – calling in the Marines – when a government stood in the way of their business (this dismissive sketch is of course a simplification, but you will find it in many dictionaries). Today the company is called Chiquita and praised by its former adversaries for its social and environmental performance.

> [...] the company has acknowledged a "debt of gratitude" to the Rainforest Alliance – the New York-based pressure group that developed the banana standards – for demonstrating that these groups could collaborate as well as confront. Chiquita "found a partner they could work with, which wouldn't leave a bad taste in their mouth, and then they learned to leverage their success in the environmental front and move ahead elsewhere in the company," says Daniel Katz, chairman of the Alliance, the world's largest certifier of environmental practices on farms and forests.[2]

Of course, this transition was bumpy rather than smooth (e.g. it included a time in Chapter 11 of the Bankruptcy Law). But Chiquita is a typical example of what has happened in the relationships between MNCs and their host countries in the developing world.

The first code of conduct for multinational companies, the Code of Standards of Advertising Practice, was created by the International Chamber of Commerce in 1937. It intended to restrict competition between companies to prevent damages to the environment or society in locations where the companies operated. Compare the social and environmental impact of foreign investment in developing countries before that time and today and one will see a huge difference, not only in the resource extracting industry. Today, there is unchallenged empirical evidence that an overwhelming majority of foreign direct investments in emerging economies are operated on global standards, which are pretty close to the domestic standards of the (mostly western) multinationals and significantly above the average local standard. Along the way, companies have learned to manage cleaner investments at lower costs and combine low local wages with high productivity. This is the root cause of today's job shift.

Will companies learn to globalize, take opportunities or factor cost differentials and nevertheless preserve jobs at home? Well, why not? Of course, this depends also on macroeconomic conditions in Europe, Japan and the USA. A decade of economic stagnation – as major EU economies and Japan have experienced – has never been accompanied by a booming job market in history. The argument for foreign invest-ment driven by the demand in the emergent economies, apply to the home region as well: as the example of the Spanish fashion maker and distributor "Zara" illustrates, it makes sense to stay close to the cus-tomer. Zara still manufactures nearly all of its clothes in Europe: their fast reaction to volatile fashion trends compensates for a relative cost disadvantage over China, due to higher wages in Europe. Obviously it also helps that the wages in an automated sewing line only account for about 20 per cent of the manufacturing costs.

New effective forms of NGO actions

Our data indicate that companies have learned to "manage" NGOs and they no longer generate PR disasters like Shell with Brent Spar or Nike with child labor. Interestingly, these examples are still quoted – a decade later – and permanently quoted in the academic literature, as there are no recent examples that are similar in significance.

What can we expect in the future? We will continue to see all kinds of opportunity-driven forms of conflict and cooperation, resulting in a new tangled complexity. Furthermore, new types of NGOs with new approaches will emerge, as the following two examples in the (especially fast) food industry illustrate:

Food Watch is – so far – a German NGO, claiming some 30,000 members. It was founded in 2003 by Thilo Bode, who ran Greenpeace Germany during the Brent Spar time and later Greenpeace International. Food Watch is an NGO that combines detective work in the food supply chain with direct marketing, direct actions and skillful PR. It is trying to mobi-lize consumers around those food issues that affect them directly (i.e. in terms of their health and quality of life). Clearly food-related issues are very opportune topics, but do take a unique position in terms of getting consumers' attention. Think about allergies associated with textiles, safety issues around household equipment and you will find other areas (or just look at the USA and what consumers sue companies for). We see many, so far untapped opportunities to mobilize segments of consumers against companies.

Beyond McDonald's (which Thilo Bode thinks is an enemy you should not miss), Food Watch is targeting the (often-unknown) companies in the supply chain. It covers issues it considers posing risks to consumers: hazardous waste in chicken food, genetically modified organisms (GMOs) in milk cow feed, cancerous chemicals in sandwiches, etc.

Information is distributed via direct mail, the internet and through PR activities, and made attractive by direct actions.

Food Watch then turns to regulators and the household names in the branded consumer goods business, skillfully exploiting their propensity for reputation, urging them to stop the risk for their customers or voters. Every scandal in the food business is a feast for Food Watch. During the "rotten food scandal" (meat beyond its expiry date was simply relabeled) in Germany, from October to mid-December 2005, Food Watch got its message across in more than 90 TV shows and about 1,000 articles (print or online).

Among the early successes of the "food savers" (as they call themselves): McDonald's had to stop an expensive marketing campaign about the "healthiness" of their products and – to add insult to injury – pay Food Watch €10,000. Furthermore, certain practices of the animal feeding industry are now under scrutiny and more transparency in the product declarations are under way as regulators get more vigilant. Due to NGO activities (not only Food Watch), GMOs remain a hopeless business case despite some regulatory progress.

Slow Food is very different from Food Watch. Whereas the latter is run by battle-hardened campaigners with management and PR-skills, Slow Food is more of a grassroots movement of concerned gourmets. Founded in Tuscany in 1989, it is growing slowly (of course), but steadily. Today it claims around 83,000 members organized in local chapters in several European countries, the USA and Japan. The heraldic animal is a snail and the slogan reads: "Only slow you can enjoy." The organization was founded as a response to the opening of the first McDonald's in Rome across from the famous "Spanish Steps." The organization opposes the mass-production and homogenization of food. They established the "Ark of Taste" and an Academy to preserve the knowledge of tasty, healthy and locally based cooking throughout the world. In this context, "slow" means good taste, local production, no artificial processing, healthy. To reduce demand for mass-produced food, they create and support a series of niche markets for original local products. Engaging star chefs, they create peer pressure or create kids' cooking clubs to demonstrate the alternatives. They sponsor local markets for wine, meat, vegetables, cheese, etc. And, whenever possible, they bad-mouth mass-produced food and its "bulldozer effect" on diversity. The biggest obstacle for more far-reaching success is the wealthy gourmet image of the organization, although the founders maintain that – "in the half hour, you wait for the pizza delivery in your home, you can cook a cheaper, and tastier meal."

"Food Watch" and "Slow Food" have very different strategies and actions, and they both differ from traditional consumer and environmental organizations, which gives an indication about the dynamic developments in the NGO community. You should expect a lot of creativity and engagement, particularly if you are a corporate planner or communications manager.

New generation – new values

During the dot.com boom the unscrupulous, tough-dealing investment banker was idolized. In the aftermath, things looked different: infamous practices were discovered, which cost the involved investment banks billions in settlement fees, not to mention the damaged reputations. Ethics were suddenly fashionable – the number of ethics officers in the US skyrocketed overnight, propelled by sentencing guidelines, which gave corporate violators a lesser sentence when they have an ethics program in place. Codes of conducts were everywhere, advocating integrity, honesty, openness for every corner of the company.

Where is this leading us? Economists believe that people behave according to the incentives or disincentives they are given (a skeptical vision of humankind, but surely a realistic one with respect to large organizations). Therefore, they remain skeptical as long as a major incentive to "cut corners" remains in place, such as the strong short-term financial pressure created by a "consensus" of financial analysts, stock options, etc.

Will this framework last? What will happen when those people who are now 10–20 years younger than the current CEO generation (early 30s to mid-40s) make their mark? Currently we can only guess, but there is some indication that there will be a different set of values. In their book, *What's Important to Us – a New Leader Generation Defines the Corporate Values for Tomorrow,*[3] young German executives define six values, including sustainability. Their bottom line is: earning money is not a goal in itself, but a means for other purposes. What counts is the conduct of business, how the profit is achieved. Obviously, some industries will be more susceptible to such a philosophy than will others: A recent WBCSD study found that younger financial analysts disregard sustainability as much as their older peers.

Alongside these new management values, a revival of government intervention could lead to more momentum toward corporate sustainability. The early predictions of the irrelevance of national government have not proved well-founded. The rising security concerns and the "War on Terror" have brought back governmental power with significant implications for industry: the financial services industry is now subject to tight regulation and control over money laundering and other dubious financial practices. This would have been unthinkable before "September 11." Furthermore, business itself is now sometimes asking for a more "level playing field," an issue that is dealt with in international treaties and in the "Doha Round" of the World Trade Organization (WTO).

What if the performance of capitalism is heading for another disappointment? As the memory of the counterproductive effects of massive government intervention fades – is a more active government strategy for job protection completely unthinkable? After all, the majority of voters in Europe have no "natural affection" for the market economy. This is why there was no new Maggie Thatcher (N.B. no other European country came as close to bankruptcy as the UK in the late 1970s) in Europe or any other success of the "raw meat version" of capitalism. People accept capitalism because of its higher performance than other economic systems. But what if the expectations are disappointed? Here lies the real risk for business: In the exaggerated expectation of CSM/CSR lies the seed for disappointment and with that a potential for a backlash.

What is clearly needed is a better understanding and a clarification of who is best doing what and when. This issue can be observed in many aspects. Many social and environmental issues have to do with the "common good" or "collective good" and that means it cannot be offered solely through markets, which are based on individual demand and individual willingness-to-pay. That does not mean that business and consumers do not also have their own responsibility, but someone has to "bring it together" and that can only be the government.

For example, poverty on a regional level can be addressed through various measures: more jobs, education, upgraded housing, environmental improvements, etc. Business can bring competencies including vocational training, and invest under economic criteria, but a lot of agencies and not-for-profit organizations need to be brought in too. Someone has to create a platform – or, in today's speak, a public–private partnership – to ensure that the tasks are allocated, efforts coordinated and the goals efficiently achieved.

It is already difficult enough to bring several players with different interests and competencies together on a regional level. The task is orders of magnitude more complex when one looks at the emerging "mega-issues" of climate change, water scarcity or poverty. In an interconnected, interdependent world, the nature of problems has developed such that they go beyond a specific industry or consumption activity.

Hence, progress can only be achieved if multiple players work together. This is always simple in principle: Goals have to be set, responsibilities and resources allocated and progress measured. But in reality, it is an immense challenge due to different interests and cultures, strong competition and egos, etc.

Alongside decentralization and standardized processes to manage the complexity in today's world, transparency is needed to answer the simple question: Who is doing what and when? As a kind of meta result of our research, we can conclude that this transparency is missing today. Thus, sustainable development runs the risk of being continuously ignored.

There was an important job to be done and everybody was asked to do it.
Everybody was sure somebody would do it.
Anybody could have done it, but nobody did it.
Somebody got angry about that, because it was everybody's job.
Everybody thought anybody could do it but nobody realized that nobody would do it.
At the end everybody was blaming somebody and nobody did what anybody could have done.

Notes

1 Based on S. Weischenberg, "Das neue Mediensystem. Ökonomische und publizistische Aspekte der aktuellen Entwicklung." *Politik und Zeitgeschichte*, 26 (90) (1990), 29–43.
2 "The Banana Giant that Found its Gentle Side." *The Financial Times*, London, 1 December 2002.
3 S. Unger, K. Hattendorf and S. Korndörffer (eds), *Was uns wichtig ist* (Weinheim: Wiley, 2005).

5
What is it with Stakeholder Pressure?

Ulrich Steger

Little pressure on companies

To put it in a nutshell, companies can relax. Despite the rhetoric in academia and by the public, the pressure on companies to shift into a higher gear for CSM/CSR simply does not exist. We cannot detect any massive discontent with corporate social and environmental performance; there is no evident opposition to the current basic (financially driven) business model. Those who are asking for more (the challengers) are also those who are least important to companies, and companies have learned to manage them. There is no sustainability juggernaut in sight that can match the pressure of the financial markets – this can be subject to debate, if it makes the lives of managers easier. And as long as sustainable development remains a largely intellectual endeavor, it will not stir up masses through reality TV. (For those readers who are now upset: Please don't shoot the messenger. We have summarized what the empirical evidence has uncovered, not how the world could be a better place.)

However, as every businessperson knows, a look at the bottom line is no substitute for a more detailed analysis of the balance sheet and P&L statements. As always, the interesting facts are in the fine print. Here we see several dilemmas and challenges

- Transparency and accountability are two keywords, which describe general social trends. Today capital markets demand much more transparency from companies than they used to a decade ago. Management is immediately held accountable for the results. For the media, transparency and accountability determine how they view the world. CSR/CSM clearly profited from the resulting dynamic, as the elaborate reporting guidelines and activities indicate (just read the GRI Guidelines). However, to dampen the potentially exaggerated optimism: reporting and the transparency that comes with it does not mean that corporate social and environmental performance has increased in parallel.

- The dominant benchmark for stakeholders is compliance with existing rules and regulations. These are considered high in Europe. However, the rise of regulatory standards lost its momentum in the environmental area a decade ago. In fact, social standards have eroded in most EU countries in the last years. If compliance is a benchmark – where should social and environmental progress come from in the future? The powerful stakeholders – financial institutions, customers – expect marginal improvement through technical progress and better management. We called them incrementalists because they call for operational risk management, not for radical innovation, and most certainly not for spending more on the cost side.
- The bystanders, who could change the benchmarks through regulation, standards or collective agreements (in the case of the unions), are much too concerned about regional competitiveness and job creation as their main priority. Therefore, they will not dare to be too "pushy" about sustainability. Sure, they are a bit more demanding (on average) than incrementalists, especially if they see an opportunity to jump on the bandwagon of public opinion (e.g. in the case of an environmentalist scandal or plant closure).
- And those who are pushing for progress? The challengers – in their own view – often lack the resources and political leverage to push companies. In addition, companies have learned to manage them – to a degree that NGOs feel overwhelmed by the requests for stakeholder dialogue, cooperation, invitations to speeches, conferences, etc. It is not accidental that the real PR disasters in the CSR/CSM area happened a decade ago.

There are several interesting "footnotes" in this context:

1. Those who are least demanding for CSR/CSM performance are those who are best equipped to assess the performance through tools and processes: Coming from a business environment, incrementalists could just apply the usual decision-making standard if they wanted. The challengers turn to past experience and gut feelings – as they need to act quickly to jump on an opportunity with no detailed analysis possible (few challengers are as structured and organized as companies).

2. Most stakeholders tend to think that the value driver for CSM/CSR that they can influence, i.e. the lever they can apply to make companies

move, is more important than the typical value drivers of other stake-holders. Furthermore, they consider their influence on "their" value driver stronger than the influence of other stakeholders, i.e. the media has the greatest self-perceived effect on reputation, bystanders on the license to operate.

3. We detect a certain alignment of interests across different stake-holders, which points to the potential for alliances and coalitions in the future, e.g. shareholder activism and rallies through unions and NGOs, joint praising and blaming by NGOs, governments and the media.

4. The boundaries between the (traditional) regulators and non-regulatory bodies have become blurred through quasi-regulation. As our research shows, quasi-regulatory functions are today occupied by various stakeholders such as financial institutions (e.g. SEC guidelines), NGOs and consumer organizations (e.g. labeling schemes) and unions (e.g. collective agreements).

Reputation as a key lever

Stakeholders influence companies by targeting corporate reputation. Some corporations persistently demonstrate that you can live splendidly with a bad reputation in certain quarters. Just take Exxon Mobil Corp., which has been labeled by NGOs as the "Darth Vader" of the energy business: It even draws its sense of identity, mission, self-confidence (some say: arrogance) and demonstrated competence from NGO attacks. For many other companies, especially in Europe, reputation matters, as it is part of the (informal) license to operate and part of the quality assurance for their products.

Reputation matters differently and to different audiences. In the sustainability area, this explains why you read the same names repeatedly. The sustainability rating agencies focus on the big global companies, especially those that are publicly listed, as they make their living with advice to investors. The challengers use the ratings also for their assessment and actions. Engaging against a well-known, mighty company is often effective, as it ensures a "David–Goliath" situation, in which a small campaigner takes on a profit-driven corporate giant with destructive power. Similarly, NGOs tend to cooperate with big (hence more resourceful) multinationals rather than small and medium-sized enterprises, since they believe they can have greater impact – also in terms of media coverage.

Media also play their role in amplifying and redistributing messages based on corporate reputation. They choose a household name that ensures the interest of a wider audience and report bad news (rather than good news), since this is what people supposedly want to see, read or hear. A juicy scandal or even drama – we know this to be true since Shakespeare – is always more enticing than a plain success story. In conclusion, we see a clear pattern, characterized by a focus on the few names (ah, it's Nestlé again…) and the punishment of laggards (in many instances also criticism of "stumbled" leaders) rather than rewards for pioneers.

The level playing field

Were there any surprises in our research? We expected that unions and some consumer organizations would be struggling to find a new – and important – role for themselves in light of global competition and price-sensitive consumers respectively. However, to some degree, it was surprising how the issue of a "level playing field" was "popping up" under different headings and from different stakeholders, plus from the managers themselves.

In the 1980s and early 1990s, there was a long debate about the industrial and employment impact of environmental protection. Legislation was accelerating and inducing structural change. There were significant concerns about tight regulation driving industry into "pollution havens."[1] The outcome of the debate – in essence – was: In individual cases, especially in energy-intensive commodity businesses, relocation might have been the "last straw" for companies that were struggling anyhow. Overall, the effects of environmental legislation were minor – simply because the environmental investments and costs were marginal – even in most cases of back fitting. In general, life cycle costs are lowest if reinvestment cycles are synchronized with stricter pollution standards, as "clean integrated technology" is able to combine pollution prevention with cost-effective manufacturing. In conclusion, the burden of environmental costs cannot be a serious problem for a "level playing field," because the effects of legislation are already absorbed. There might be cases in which clean production by foreign direct investments is associated with a competitive disadvantage against local, "dirty" producers, when they compete in the same market. For example, a foreign producer of washing powder shut down his factory in China, as he could not compete against the low-cost domestic producers. However, the contribution of environmental aspects to this "un-level" playing field was – again – marginal. Differences in capital costs and the inability to increase the raw material yield to a level similar to Europe were much more important.

The social dimension – which basically means the differences in wages and social security contribution – is different from the environmental one. Wage differentials have been a driver of trade and industrial development since the beginning of the industrial revolution (in 1860, Germany was a low-wage competitor to the United Kingdom). What has drastically changed through globalization is that the old formula "low wages–low productivity, high wages–high productivity" is no longer working. The transfer of knowledge and technology as well as the organizational and logistical competencies of global companies make a high productivity process possible in every corner of the world – regardless of the wage level. Hence, high productivity–high wage locations compete against high productivity–low wage locations (especially China, but also other Southeast Asian countries, India and last but not least Eastern Europe). This is the reason for the massive deindustrialization, which can be currently observed in Europe (and which already started in the US 20 years earlier driven by exports from Japan and the "Four Tigers."[2]

There is an easy, even tempting but also counterproductive, answer to this problem of creeping deindustrialization: protectionism. US unions, especially, embark on such a strategy to protect themselves from (Chinese) "slave labor." Protectionism would slow down the structural change for a while, but would widen the competitive gap even more. To go through this change is painful, but easier now than later. Our research indicates that the impact of globalization on jobs in Europe has now fully reached the executive suites – as a problem, with no obvious solution yet. To demand a "level playing field" is either a politically correct circumscription for protectionism, or reflects perplexity or fundamental ignorance of economic drivers for trade and foreign direct investment: They are driven by differentials of natural resource endowments, capital or labor availability. A "level playing field" might be the managerial expression for the neoclassical static equilibrium of perfect markets. However, in this theoretical equilibrium, global trade would be largely obsolete, since prices are the same everywhere. It will definitely be worthwhile to see how the opinion of managers will develop here. One can argue about "facts" and economic theory. In the end, it is the perception of the decision-makers that will drive actions (or as Keynes impolitely wrote: "Practical men are the intellectual slaves of a defunct economist a century ago...").

If we see the "level playing field" as one end of the spectrum, then the fragmentation of demands and the diversity of standards for sustainability represent the other end. Suppliers in particular complained about the many different requests their customers impose on them (and they can do little, as one noted: "The power is moving up the supply chain, not down"). ISO 14000 does not say anything about performance. Performance-driven standards, such as SA 8000, were seen – by many companies – as beyond reach, reflecting the wishful thinking of NGOs, not what the global company can commit to. This reflects a certain dilemma: standards without acceptance by the NGO and regulatory community are not credible and are unlikely to have a significant positive impact on corporate reputation. Standards without acceptance from the business community are practically irrelevant (such as SA 8000).

What does this mean for companies?

For companies, sustainability seems to be like driving a car: You can expect to arrive safely and on time, when your car is well maintained and especially if the brakes are working. Nevertheless, sometimes cars crash in accidents, are stuck in traffic jams or are even stopped by snow-storms. Sustainability is obviously not a risk to the core business model of companies, if issues are managed professionally and the company is generally a well-organized, responsible organization. Even then, some-thing unforeseen and (typically) unpleasant may happen. As Murphy's law states: If something can go wrong, it will go wrong – at least occa-sionally. And it will mostly likely happen at a time, when you do not expect it and definitely do not need the additional trouble.

The risks are due to: (1) a "tangled landscape" that is difficult to survey; (2) challengers' actions against companies; and (3) the increased opportunism of all players. The trenches that separated companies and stakeholders are gone. Today NGOs cooperate with companies in one area and fight them in another area at the same time. For example:

- Since March 2000, Lafarge has a comprehensive cooperation agree-ment (a so-called conservation partnership) with WWF International on several issues, such as CO_2 emissions, the use of alternative fuels and quarry rehabilitation. However, this partnership did not keep WWF Scotland from campaigning against a superquarry on Harris in the Western Isles.
- Industry associations support environmentalists in pushing through legislation they want (e.g. the auto industry and the environmental-ists against the oil industry in the EU Auto Oil Programme).
- Politicians in local communities normally do not want to confront companies – but when the opportunity is there, they will lead the anti-corporate demonstration. This is especially true if companies appear to "hurt" the community through massive layoffs or even plant closures. Furthermore, unforeseen local players enter the stage – suddenly the local church organizes a boycott, when "unethical" behavior is perceived.

There will be more coalition building and alliances. Since NGOs' resources and their personal capacity are very limited, teaming up with their peers gives them power for "heavy lifting." All anti-globalization demonstrations, with up to hundreds of thousands of demonstrators, were the result of that kind of loose, event-driven alliance. All it needs today is a laptop and a mobile phone. If such an alliance has locked itself onto a certain issue, companies can get stuck. Just observe the powerful grassroots movement fighting genetically modified food products in Europe: Despite some legal and regulatory progress, GMOs are a dead business case in Europe.

In conclusion, despite overall low pressure on sustainability today, expect everything – and do not assume that it will not hit you.[3]

One nagging question remains from our research: Managers get excited, but also frustrated about NGOs. They are excited because a good battle with an NGO or any other adverse stakeholder is good for the blood pressure and an interesting experience. They are frustrated about the fact that they make so little progress on the political level (see section 3.3). This is surprising, as the business lobbyists in Brussels or any other European capital outnumber the NGOs by a factor of 10, if not more, in terms of resources and personnel. Even if one takes into account that business lobbyists have a somewhat broader agenda, the result is nevertheless surprising: It is the perception of managers that there is at best a stalemate.

In our interpretation, there are a couple of reasons for this situation:

1. Given the time pressure on executives in global companies, few corporate decision-makers get personally involved in political debates. The professionals who might be knowledgeable, articulate experts and skilful networkers do it all. However, this cannot overcome the lack of credibility, the "they would say that, wouldn't they?" syndrome, which hits all communication managers or lobbyists.

2. Industry associations work on a consensus principle, the least common denominator. Innovative ideas are rare and associations tend to protect the status quo, and thus the laggards. As those laggards have something to lose from a proposed legislation, for example, they are more active in preventing that. The others usually stand by, because they are concerned that the next time they could be laggards and then be without the protection of the industry association (that is why even proactive companies in CSM/CSR rarely break ranks). This "rear-guard" strategy has

little credibility: All the bleak predictions of industry associations in political controversies, e.g. over environmental standards, never materialized. This handicap is difficult to overcome for the sustainability officers in companies. Often they find themselves "between a rock and a hard place": internally they have to motivate and push for progress in CSM/CSR against the reluctance of most of their colleagues. Externally they have to defend the company against the exaggerated demands of NGOs and fight for credibility, which is often damaged by the insensitive actions of industry associations.

Notes

1 For a brief overview of the debate and its results see, U. Steger, *The Strategic Dimension of Environmental Management* (Basingstoke: Palgrave Macmillan, 1998), p. 71.
2 Just compare the following two references to ascertain striking similarities with the current European debate: S.S. Cohen and J. Zysman, *Manufacturing Matters* (New York: Basic Books, 1987) and R. Lawrence, *Can America Compete?* (Washington: The Brookings Institutions, 1984).
3 For a diagnostic tool and strategy recommendations on such a broader business environment, see U. Steger, *Corporate Diplomacy* (London: Wiley, 2003).

Part II
Stakeholder Reports

In the following chapters, we present a detailed analysis of the individual stakeholder groups, i.e. financial institutions, cities and communities, governments, NGOs, consumer organizations, media, corporate customers, corporate suppliers and unions. More specifically, we will elaborate on the stakeholders' background, their approach to corporate sustainability, their actions and effectiveness. The findings are primarily based on the qualitative and quantitative evidence collected through interviews and self-completion questionnaires.

6
Financial Institutions: Corporate Sustainability as a Significant Niche?

Alexander Nick

This chapter presents empirical evidence collected from financial market institutions through 31 self-completion questionnaires and 37 semi-structured interviews (lasting on average 90 minutes). The following participated in the study: Allianz (Germany), ASSET4 (Switzerland), Basler Versicherungen (Switzerland), BNP Paribas (France), CERES (USA), Deutsches Aktieninstitut (Germany), Dit (Germany), Dresdner Bank (Germany), Goldman Sachs (UK), Innovest (Spain), Irish Business Employers Confederation (Ireland), Irish Life & Permanent plc (Ireland), Irish Stock Exchange (Ireland), KfW Development Bank (Germany), KfW IPEX Bank (Germany), Munich Re (Germany), Oekom-Research (Germany), PricewaterhouseCoopers (Switzerland), Rabobank (Netherlands), SAM (Switzerland), Sarasin (Switzerland), SEB Invest (Sweden), Swiss Re (Switzerland), UNEP FI (Switzerland), VantagePoint (Switzerland).

The chapter is structured as follows: in section 6.1 we provide general background information on the study and the stakeholder. In section 6.2 we describe the stakeholder's approach to corporate sustainability (mission, incentives and motives, processes and tools, criteria and expectations). Section 6.3 features our key findings on current stakeholder strategies, their actions and effectiveness as well as success factors and obstacles. In section 6.4 we elaborate on future trends, and in section 6.5 we conclude by highlighting the key findings and implications.

6.1 Stakeholder background

Research scope

The financial industry is by no means homogeneous. We conducted interviews with institutions involved in banking, insurance and reinsurance.

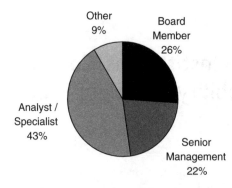

Figure 6.1   Functions of interviewees (financial institutions)

We also spoke to research and information providers, market providers and sustainability experts.

As this chapter takes an outside-in approach and tries to assess corporate performance in the field of sustainability, we considered financial institutions as stakeholders of corporations. Therefore, we did not assess the sustainability performance of the institutions interviewed. We also selected our target group in a similar way, and mainly interviewed those entities dealing with companies as clients and suppliers.

As Figure 6.1 indicates, we carried out 26 per cent of our interviews with board members, including CEOs, general managers and vice presidents on a corporate level. Of the rest, 22 per cent of our interviewees held a position in senior management, e.g. director or head of unit. The biggest group (43 per cent) consisted of people in an analyst or specialist role. Most interviewees in this group were experts from big financial institutions dealing with sustainability on a daily basis in different functions (analysts, project managers). Nine per cent of our interviews held an executive managing function in a specialized organization (e.g. sustainability think tank, consultancy).

Trends in the financial market

Over the last decade, the financial market has undergone tremendous change and developments, including:

- The emerging market crises in Russia and Asia in the late 1990s.
- The burst of the dot.com bubble in late 2000 and through 2001.
- The stream of bad corporate governance and accounting fraud-related scandals post-Enron.

- The introduction of corporate governance codes in financial market regulation (e.g. stock markets, information disclosure) all over the world to promote transparency in company accounting and accountability (e.g. Sarbanes–Oxley Act).
- The fact that shareholder activism has also become a reality in Europe.
- The rising issue of pensions due to an aging workforce and overall population.

Datamonitor recently examined the global asset management and custody bank sector and identified the following three main developments:[1]

1. Rising interest rates and inflation have fostered a trend toward shorter-duration bond investments.
2. The growing attraction of mutual funds should act as a growth engine for the asset management industry.
3. Companies have taken steps to ensure that client concerns raised in the wake of Sarbanes–Oxley are addressed in order to regain their trust.

In recent years, we have observed that investors have increasingly delegated the management of their investment portfolios to institutional asset managers. Looking at the insurance sector, consisting of the markets for life insurance and pensions, accident and health insurance, and property and casualty insurance, one might observe that the introduction of the euro has considerably improved capital investment opportunities for European insurers. The move toward regulatory harmonization in Europe and the single European financial market offers opportunities and a range of investment options.[2] The global reinsurance sector remained largely untroubled, in spite of the high number of natural catastrophes in 2004. However, the latest natural disasters, especially hurricanes Katrina, Rita and Wilma in 2005, will reduce the scope to lower prices for underwriting premiums.[3] Looking forward, the reinsurance sector has been forecast to continue posting high growth rates.[4]

Sustainability issues in the financial market

Before presenting the results of our empirical study, it is helpful to differentiate two aspects of sustainability in the financial market.

- **Sustainable investments.** In this study, we use the term "socially responsible investment" (SRI) for any form of ethical, social or ecological investment. A common definition does not yet exist.

Nevertheless, the common basis for SRI is that besides the traditional investment criteria of *liquidity, rate of return* and *risk, sustainability* criteria are also taken into account. The method and the stringency with which they are applied vary greatly from case to case.

- **Integrating sustainability issues into the business model.** Companies take on the challenge of integrating into the business model business risks and opportunities resulting from social and environmental issues (e.g. climate change, water scarcity, disease, poverty). This might result in changes in lending policies, insurance policies, underwriting criteria or logistics and purchasing guidelines.

The scope of issues discussed is broad. Nevertheless, to indicate the type of issues, we propose to refer to the definition of the Enhanced Analytics Initiative.[5] It defines environmental, social and governance issues as being one or more of the following:

- The focus of public concern (e.g. genetically modified organisms).
- Qualitative and not readily quantifiable in monetary terms (e.g. intellectual capital).
- Reflective of externalities not well captured by market mechanisms (e.g. environmental pollution).
- (Often) the focus of a tightening policy and regulatory framework (e.g. greenhouse gas emissions).
- Present throughout the company's supply chain (e.g. labor issues at supplier factories).

We left it to our interviewees to address the issues that are relevant for their own actions and did not limit the scope of their answers. As a result, we encourage you to be aware of a potential bias while reading this chapter. Sustainability in the financial market is still a niche issue. We chose our interview partners according to two main criteria: the interviewee had (1) to be familiar with the concept of corporate sustainability; and (2) to deal with companies daily. We challenged our interview partner to mirror the whole view of his or her institution and asked about the relevance of his or her job to the corporate strategy.

Evolving debate. If over time you compare the whole debate of sustainable development with specific emphasis on corporate sustainability, it is important to recognize that the issue is still in its infancy. The debate started on an international level in the early 1990s and it is therefore still a young discussion. Some of our interviewees stated that one must be aware of overambitious expectations:

> You cannot accelerate learning processes. Sustainability is a societal innovation and not a technical one and, therefore, it needs time to develop. (Financial institution N)

6.2 Approach to corporate sustainability

Mission

The financial market is primarily concerned about the economic performance of its activities. It follows an economic logic. Competition is perceived to be high. Some financial institutions have niche business models based on sustainability. However, even they do not claim that they want to improve the social and environmental performance of companies. Instead, their goal is to provide information and create transparency:

> We are trying to identify companies that seize opportunities and manage risks deriving from economic, environmental and societal developments better than their peers do. (Financial institution U)
> Our mission is to be able to measure what companies are doing in terms of management systems and how this leads to specific results. (Financial institution O)

We did not find only companies that have specialized – nearly all the big players in the financial market deal with the issue of sustainability. This results in the mainstream institutions setting up departments to deal with sustainability even though they do not have a specific mission:

> We do not have a special mission, we do not want to convert people, we are not at the top of the movement. Yet, we noticed a trend on the market and that is why we are engaged in sustainability. (Financial institution V)

Incentives and motives

It is not the declared goal of financial market institutions to improve the social and environmental performance of companies. The answers we received varied from "we can only see disincentives" to "we do not have any incentives" to a variety of motives for becoming engaged in this issue. The main argument against a sustainability assessment, which always requires a long-term perspective, is the short-term logic of the markets:

> As a public company, you have the obligation to disclose to investors everything that they would consider to be material to their investment decision. An investor will not invest in a company for thirty years. They do not care, for instance, if a company is putting sludge into the ground that is going to be robbed in thirty years time. If the investors knew, it would be in thirty years from now and nobody else would know it until thirty years from now, they wouldn't give a sugar. That is the reality of the market. They only care about the risk that is going to crystallize tomorrow. (Financial institution E)

Nevertheless, we observed a rising awareness within the mainstream financial community that takes on issues of sustainability. We identified several key motives, which can be generally divided into the categories "value protection" and "value enhancing."

We noted that the majority of our interviewees related their incentives to the business case argument. Most obvious seems to be the business case for sustainability in the reinsurance industry in relation to climate change:

> We are directly hit by the effects of climate change. Our business models allow us theoretically to adjust our premiums but you should not forget the competition between re-insurers if you adjust the premiums each year. Consequently, we want to show the effects of climate change and start a discussion on how to overcome this risk, for instance through supporting the development of new technologies. (Financial institution L)

Another incentive is the growth of SRI funds:

> Our product, sustainable investment, is the main argument. We cannot prove that companies integrating CSR have a better performance in the long run. The only proof is about 150 studies related to this question: Most of the studies show that there might be a positive link between sustainability performance and share price. (Financial institution R)
>
> Ethical investment funds are probably the biggest growth area in the Western economy. Investors are becoming more sophisticated and educated in social and environmental issues. This is happening very rapidly and increasingly. (Financial institution D)

It does not have to be a majority of the market. All it has to be is a significant minority to be relevant. You cannot afford to rule out significant minorities in the market. If the political environment of a region is increasingly moving toward a green society, then you will see investors following this trend. I don't think an investor will look for ethical funds but I think the ethical fund will come to him, advertising through the agencies. (Financial institution D)

Table 6.1 Financial institutions' motives for addressing sustainability

	Key motive	*Aim*	*Concrete examples*
Value protection	Pressure from outside	Value protection	— Corporate scandals — Lobby pressure from NGOs — Bad experiences with the public in the past — Exposed industries — Engagement is perceived as a social insurance, e.g. to satisfy the local community
	Observer	Keeping up to date	— Analyzing the trend for SRI on the market — Conducting research
	Business case	Mitigating business risks	— Relevant credit risks, including material, social and environmental issues — Qualitatively better risks — Risks of climate change — Price of fossil fuels — Better and lower risk for our business
Value enhancing	Business case	Exploiting business opportunities	— Conviction that better sustainability performance leads to better shareholder value for investors — Product sustainable investment — Customers are taking part in same initiatives
	Business model	Generating value through addressing sustainability	— SRI departments — Ethical investment funds — Specialized rating agencies and information providers
	Individual conviction	Doing the "right thing"	— Leading by example — Acting as a change agent

Assessing corporate performance

Looking at the whole financial market, the vast majority of corporate assessments rely on only the economic dimension. As we stated earlier in the chapter, sustainability is a niche issue. We found that financial institutions assess sustainability performance in two cases:

1. It is the core business of the institution, e.g. SRI investors, CSR rating agencies.
2. Social and environmental issues are perceived as a risk for the company.

The case for the first group is clear. Their business model depends upon a comprehensive and credible assessment. We found that these assessments are undertaken very systematically and that they are increasingly transparent. This seems to be quite an important finding if one looks back a few years, because criticism about corporate sustainability assessment used to be a major barrier to sustainable investing.

It seems that the case for the second group is still in its infancy. The interviewees definitely see the need to integrate social and environmental criteria in their assessments. This is mostly related to the changing business environment. They observe developments like the rapidly growing global population, which relies on resource-intensive lifestyles, and the future valuation of natural resources or risks from newly emerging social and ecological issues. The challenge nearly all the interviewees in this group are facing is the development of appropriate innovative processes, tools and criteria that can grasp the mentioned risks and quantify them. For reputational risks related to environmental and social issues at clients, the case seems to be clearer and assessments are more mature.

Processes, tools and criteria. For those institutions that have a well-defined assessment process – case 1 above – the main sources of information are the following:

- Screening and analysis of annual reports and sustainability reports.
- Acquiring information by contacting companies (e.g. through the use of questionnaires).
- Working with a database (containing, e.g. media and press clippings).
- Cooperation with NGOs (e.g. to check the information provided by companies).
- Working in cooperation with external researchers.

In general, there is a choice between active and passive SRI approaches.[6] Active approaches focus on engagement between shareholders and management, e.g. through exercising shareholder rights at annual meetings or through dialogue with management. Passive approaches can be further divided into negative and positive screening. Negative screening is based on the exclusion of companies with certain business activities. Positive screening comes closest to the conventional, benchmark-oriented investment approach and mostly works with a best-in-class approach.

Most of the companies we interviewed have defined an institutionalized screening process based on positive screening. Our interviewees reported that their systems are quite stable and well developed over time. The screening process is based on a set of criteria. There are general and industry-specific criteria. They are in the social, economic and ecological fields. Some institutions also include a governance dimension. The criteria are based on sustainability trends. Identifying these sustainability trends is perceived as most difficult and crucial. Because most of the criteria are qualitative, there is a need to identify indicators that allow the criteria to be measured.

For the second case, which refers to the business model dimension, a systematic screening process used throughout the financial market is still wishful thinking. Most of the interviewees striving to integrate sustainability noted that they are not that far yet:

> Currently, our process for sensitive business risks is not binding. It is up to the judgment of our colleagues to decide whether a case is sensitive or not. Then, a task force will be set up to examine the case. The task force and the respective colleague then give a recommendation. (Financial institution K)

In some cases, for example, lending, we observed systematic approaches. The focus lies on environmental risks and much less on embracing the social dimension. We conclude that the significance of environmental issues is greater and more obvious and, therefore, there is a need to conduct environmental due diligence. An example that also integrates the social dimension is the Equator Principles in the banking industry.

Example: Equator Principles. The Equator Principles are an industry-wide approach for financial institutions for determining, assessing and managing environmental and social risk in project financing. They represent a common framework for the project finance industry based on an external benchmark, namely the World Bank and International Finance Corporation (IFC) sector-specific pollution abatement guidelines and IFC safeguard policies. Projects are categorized according to high, medium and low environmental and social risk. Financial institutions require their customers to demonstrate in their environmental and social reviews, and in their management plans, the extent to which they have met the applicable criteria. In the loan documentation for high- and medium-risk projects, financial institutions include covenants for borrowers to comply with their environmental and social management plans. If these plans are not followed, and if deficiencies are not corrected, financial institutions can declare the project loan to be in default.

We observed that the Equator Principles are limited in scope, since they focus on project financing internationally. As the businesses of lending, project co-financing and export financing are all equally relevant for sustainability risk assessment, this raises the question of why the banking industry does not also address these activities so that it does not finance projects with unsustainable long-term outcomes. The Equator Principles definitely signify an important first step, but the question of their credibility and strategic corporate intent still needs to be proven. Financial institutions are under scrutiny from NGOs such as Banktrack, the Berne Declaration and Urgewald. We have also learned that a growing number of banks have recently come up with specific sector policies, e.g. for forest protection, or they no longer lend money on dams that do not comply with the recommendations of the World Commission on Dams.

We ascertained that assessment criteria are best developed in purchasing and real estate. For instance, some financial institutions in Switzerland follow the MINERGIE standard – a quality label granted to buildings that meet ambitious criteria with regard to user comfort and energy efficiency at a minimal additional cost. The heat consumption of certified buildings is some 60 per cent lower than required by current Swiss regulations.

Our quantitative data show that regulatory compliance is the most important criterion (see Figure 6.2). This was also reflected in the interviews, especially with those interviewees who do not conduct any assessments and who believe that the burden for companies should not be increased. They claimed that it is sufficient for a company to act according to laws established by governments. The second most important

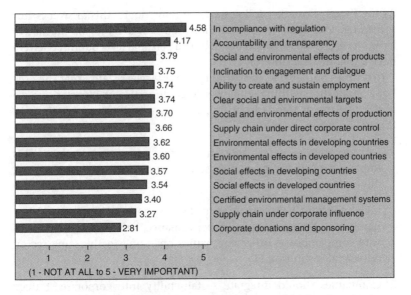

4.58	In compliance with regulation	
4.17	Accountability and transparency	
3.79	Social and environmental effects of products	
3.75	Inclination to engagement and dialogue	
3.74	Ability to create and sustain employment	
3.74	Clear social and environmental targets	
3.70	Social and environmental effects of production	
3.66	Supply chain under direct corporate control	
3.62	Environmental effects in developing countries	
3.60	Environmental effects in developed countries	
3.57	Social effects in developing countries	
3.54	Social effects in developed countries	
3.40	Certified environmental management systems	
3.27	Supply chain under corporate influence	
2.81	Corporate donations and sponsoring	

(1 - NOT AT ALL to 5 - VERY IMPORTANT)

Figure 6.2 Importance of criteria for assessing corporate social and environmental performance (total sample)

factor is perceived to be accountability and transparency. Throughout this chapter, we will show activities from financial market institutions that are based on this criterion. Corporate donations and sponsoring was perceived as the least important criterion. This finding is quite revealing as we observe many multinational companies that engage in corporate giving as a form of corporate sustainability management. In terms of our finding, we can conclude that these efforts are at least not successful when dealing with the financial market.

Expectations

We asked our interviewees to what extent their expectations in the social and environmental arena are currently met by companies. The overriding answer we received was that the financial market does not have any expectations. We also received this answer from those institutions that are involved in sustainability and which conduct sustainability assessments:

> We do not have any expectations; we do have criteria. (Financial institution R)

> We do not draw our own conclusions. The assessment is made public and clients can make their own choice. (Financial institution O)

As the financial market follows an economic logic, this answer is not surprising. Our interviewees did not argue on a moral or normative level. Nevertheless, we found out that on a personal level our interviewees have a well-defined opinion.

In a time comparison, nearly all our interviewees stated that they see huge progression within companies. Regarding current expectations, we found two major trends from interviewees who have expectations in this field:

1. Our interviewees expect more transparency from corporations. This implies a need for more robust and more focused non-financial disclosure:

   It is important for companies to disclose both good news and bad news about their sustainability performance, and to make this disclosure comparable to other companies operating in the same sector. (Financial institution FF)

2. Companies should integrate sustainability into corporate strategy and mainstream business.

6.3   Current stakeholder strategies

Actions and their effectiveness

Our hypothesis that sustainability is a minor issue for the financial market as a whole was confirmed with a closer look at the current actions to influence companies' social and environmental performance. Business in the capital markets does not include a sustainability dimension. In fact, the opposite is true – social and environmental requirements are perceived as a disincentive for companies, e.g. for going public:

   We see a need to be careful not to put extra responsibility on listed companies as opposed to private companies. As the compliance burden becomes too heavy compared to their competitors in the private sector then it will stop companies from going public. It will be another disadvantage for companies to go public. Already you see enormous compliance burdens placed on listed companies that are not on private companies, and it is increasingly difficult to persuade companies nowadays to go onto the public market. Our approach will be to hold back any other requirements unless the legal system will catch private companies in the same way. But if the investment community goes in that direction, it is fine. The social and environmental agenda is mainly driven by law. (Financial institution D)

Yet there are signs that reveal that the majority of financial institutions are taking this issue seriously and investigating how to approach it.

Disclosure and transparency. One major expectation financial market actors have of companies is for them to be increasingly transparent. Consequently, we observed that most activities carried out by the financial market aim to increase the transparency and disclosure policy of companies. The focus lies on the disclosure of material non-financial information. In the post-Enron era, the regulatory framework is taking on this challenge. We can observe government regulations heading in this direction. In the context of the corporate governance debate, most of the discussions about transparency have typically focused on financial transparency. They include the Sarbanes–Oxley Act of 2002 created in the United States to protect investors by improving the accuracy and reliability of corporate disclosures. The Operational Financial Review (OFR) in the United Kingdom includes the requirement to disclose material non-financial information. In Germany, changes in the Commercial Code have led to the inclusion of a passage on non-financial disclosure (§ 289 HGB). Currently, these developments do not have an immense impact on the way corporate accounting is done. Our interviewees revealed that any potential progression also depends on the actions of other stakeholder groups:

> Those are only first steps, but they are taken. It now depends if other actors like NGOs use this opportunity, refer to the regulatory changes and demand more appropriate reporting from companies. (Financial institution AA)

We identified the following strategies and activities being undertaken by financial institutions, which can be clustered into three groups and will be described in more detail:

- Awareness building, dialogue and research.
- Development of economic instruments and products.
- Coalition building.

Awareness building, dialogue and research. The majority of our interviewees stated that awareness building is currently one of the most effective activities. Companies are engaged in dialogue with internal and external stakeholders. For instance, campaigns to sensitize asset management departments have been successful. The same applies to cooperation with clients. After a company is rated, it is common for the rated company to invite the analysts back to explain their results. A third example can be given with regard to the interested public. Our interviewees revealed that more and more public conferences on sustainability and the financial market are taking place. An indication that these events are perceived as a business need is that management board members of leading financial institutions are participating as keynote speakers. To illustrate this, in Germany in spring 2005 a conference on SRI took place with the participation of three board members from blue-chip companies. According to research on this issue, we ascertained that the number of studies on the link between sustainability and the financial market undertaken by sustainability actors as well as by mainstream institutions is rising.

Development of economic instruments and products. Since they are part of the economic system, for the vast majority of our interviewees it seemed appropriate and best to work out solutions that are compatible with the current system. Therefore, they are investigating the possibility of integrating sustainability issues into their business practice, e.g. in lending policies, insurance policies and underwriting premiums. They are thinking about the possibility of introducing deductibles. Currently, our interview partners admitted that they are still in the investigation phase and most of the instruments are not yet in place. Already quite successful is the concept of micro-credits, which is regarded as a useful tool in developing countries for helping to start small businesses or projects that can make big improvements in local capacity.

We should not forget the whole field of SRI, which serves to reward companies making efforts and progress in sustainability. One of the best-known financial instruments is the Dow Jones Sustainability Index.

Example: Sustainability Indices. In 1999 the Dow Jones Sustainability Index (DJSI) was launched, followed by the FTSE4Good Index series two years later. Today, there are more than a dozen sustainability indices worldwide. These financial indices serve as equity benchmarks to track the financial performance of sustainability leaders on a global scale:

> The evidence that there are indices like DJSGI or FTSE4Good should demonstrate the fact that they are growing in importance. The FTSE people would not have invented such an index unless they thought there was a significant demand. (Financial institution E)

There is an increasing demand for these indices by the investment community. They don't do the index for the public. The public does not matter. The financial community wanted that index to differentiate their products. It is just another way of branding. (Financial institution D)

Coalition building. Many of our interviewees pointed out that actors dealing with sustainability in the financial market are becoming more visible through coalition building (see Table 6.2).

Our quantitative data suggest that engagement with companies has become the key strategy of financial market institutions (see Figure 6.3).

Determinants of effectiveness

Success factors. The determinants of effectiveness can be clustered into the following three categories: (1) involvement-related factors; (2) instrumental factors; and (3) contextual factors (see Table 6.3).

Table 6.2 Overview of selected coalition-building activities in the financial market

Initiative	Description
UNEP Finance Initiative (UNEP FI)	UNEP FI is a global partnership between UNEP and the financial sector. Over 200 institutions, including banks, insurers and fund managers, work with UNEP to understand the impacts of environmental and social considerations on financial performance.
Carbon Disclosure Project (CDP)	The Carbon Disclosure Project represents the world's largest collaboration of institutional investors on the business implications of climate change. More than 150 institutional investors with assets of more than $21 trillion collectively signed a single global request for disclosure of information on Greenhouse Gas Emissions. More than 350 of the 500 largest corporations in the world currently report their emissions through the CDP website.
Enhanced Analytics Initiative[7] (EAI)	The EAI is a group of institutional investors and fund managers who have decided to allocate individually a minimum of 5 per cent of their respective brokerage commission budget to sell-side researchers who are effective at analyzing material extra-financial issues and intangibles. The initiative is designed to give brokers a commercial incentive to produce innovative and differentiated research that captures the value of intangibles or corporate performance on extra-financial issues and intangibles.

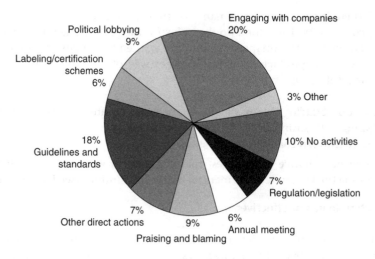

Figure 6.3   Financial institutions' portfolio of actions

We ascertained that individuals involved in corporate sustainability management tend to have different motives and evaluations. Nevertheless, we found out that success is not easy to present and to pinpoint:

You need to work a long time for little success. (Financial institution K)

Our activities receive good feedback from the public, for example from media and NGOs, but only minor interest from companies. (Financial institution Q)

We are very successful if you consider the complexity of the issue. (Financial institution C)

Obstacles. We identified three major obstacles that currently prevent sustainability from gaining in importance in the financial market.

1. Short-term thinking and current financial reporting model: Probably the most obvious argument is the short-term functioning of the capital market:

We experience a trend toward shorter reporting periods. It is very difficult for us to integrate sustainability issues, which are mostly long-term factors (Financial institution L).

Table 6.3 Determinants of effectiveness

Determinant	Further remarks/quotes
Involvement-related factors	
Management attention	— Board-level commitment
	— Internal campaigns for asset managers
Public awareness	— Demand from customers
	— Scrutiny from media and NGOs
Mainstream involvement	— Signs from mainstream institutions, e.g. Goldman & Sachs energy report
Instrumental factors	
Integration into core business	— Appropriate business instruments
	— Development of targets and incentives
	— Integration into existing management systems (e.g. balanced scorecard)
Adequate reporting instruments	— Corporate reporting needs to grasp the intangibles
	— Reporting model for service-based industries needs to be developed
Contextual factors	
Political leadership	— Progress depends on regulatory environment
	— Setting incentives through regulation
Environmental and social disasters	— Increasing damage shows urgency to act
	— Calculation of risks needs to be adapted

What is the value of additional information? The crucial problem is that in the short term other information will be more relevant. (Financial institution AA)

It is a disincentive to care for the long term. Because you would have to look proactively for that information, and if you found it, you would have to disclose it. Companies would be creating a disclosure obligation for themselves. (Financial institution E)

In addition to this dominant factor, the current financial reporting model seems to be falling behind the times. It has been developed over the last 150 years and is mainly suitable for mass-production in industrial companies.

2. Competition and lack of demand from customers: Some interviewees on the sell side in the insurance industry stated that it is currently not possible to address additional questions when selling a policy. The customer would just turn to a competitor.

3. Organizational structure and standing of sustainability managers: Processes and incentive systems do not seem to support the goals of sustainability. Our interviewees stated that as long as sustainability is not seriously addressed by the board, financial institutions will not be a strong driver. In some institutions, we observed a trend that sustainability is becoming part of strategic planning and is therefore strengthening its position:

> One of the major problems is that people in sustainability are often alone. That is changing, as sustainability is becoming part of the governance debate. (Financial institution I)

We also noted that unintended consequences could hinder the spread of sustainability instead of moving it in the planned direction:

> We currently observe a boomerang effect due to the social and environmental reporting duty of pension funds: Those providers that stated clearly that they do not integrate sustainability issues into their products have increased their sales. (Financial institution V)

Influencing corporate behavior. Respondents to our questionnaire perceived media as the stakeholder that is best able to influence corporate behavior, followed by financial institutions (Figure 6.4). We can clearly state that this general ability is obvious, but at least for the financial sector the influence is currently not put into practice in terms of sustainability.

Resulting risks and opportunities

Resulting risks. We challenged our interview partners and asked them if they could discover risks and opportunities for companies resulting from their current activities. The overall response was that a company would face almost no financial risks if it did not follow the sustainability requirements of financial institutions. This finding applies to SRI as well as to the business model dimension:

> The idea is that you can influence the share price through your investments. This is quite illusionary for SRI because this is only a

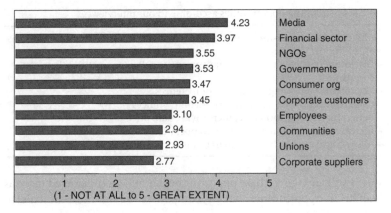

Figure 6.4 Extent to which stakeholders are able to influence corporate behavior (financial institutions)

minimal aspect. This does not have any consequences for the share price. Only in case of "ethical businesses:" Then, changes in rating might influence the share price. (Financial institution R)

Our business model does not allow us to impose additional assessments on our clients. If you want to sell something, it is difficult to address additional criteria. Currently, our clients could just go to a competitor. (Financial institution C)

Despite the fact that we could not find any financial risks for companies, our interviewees painted another picture with regard to reputational risks within the financial market:

Risks might be peanuts with regard to financial factors, but material with regard to the reputation. (Financial institution DD)

The dynamics here are quite interesting. The financial market will not take on an active or even activist role and blame companies for their poor sustainability performance. Yet, especially in exposed industries, the financial market is under scrutiny from the public and from NGOs. Therefore, there is a need to set up appropriate instruments to deal with these challenges (e.g. Equator Principles). These reputational risks mostly occur within the financial market; the changes in business practices emerge in both financial market institutions and corporate stakeholders.

Resulting opportunities. It was much easier for our interviewees to give us examples of resulting opportunities than of resulting risks. As the

Table 6.4 Resulting opportunities according to our interviewees

---

— Ability to take better-informed decisions (when dealing with sustainability as an additional criteria)
— Disclosure of solved problems: transparency enables competition between companies
— Competitive advantages, gain in competences
— Companies could be listed in sustainability indices
— Better financial performance, increase in share price
— Increase in reputation and license to operate
— Allow companies to improve management systems

---

issue is still emerging, these opportunities should be considered more as theoretical opportunities which companies would find difficult to exploit (see Table 6.4).

Recommendations for companies

We asked our interviewees if they could come up with concrete recommendations that would enable companies to better satisfy their demands. Although we have already ascertained that the financial market has few expectations in terms of the sustainability performance of companies, we received some answers that are worthy of note. In general, our interviewees proposed speaking the language of investors more, investigating further, showing the individual business cases and quantifying.

Further concrete recommendations include:

1. Lobbying for good regulation:

   Companies should spend more effort on lobbying for good regulation. They don't do at the moment, but they should – out of purely selfish reasons. For big companies, the rationale is very simple: Companies in the spotlight are conforming to higher and higher standards. But the twenty smaller companies they compete with don't. None of the single companies is a problem for the big company, but the sum is a big problem. Look at the corporate governance debate. Big companies want other companies to suffer the same pain. (Financial institution D)

2. Going beyond a PR-based approach to corporate sustainability:

   All activities that only focus on reputational issues but do not make sense for the business in the long run should be decreased.

Communication is important but it will become critical if the company only relies on communication. (Financial institution L)

3. Developing a culture of innovation:

Companies must be persuaded for themselves; it is not sufficient if pressure comes from outside. You need to develop a culture of innovation. Adopt processes. The top management is responsible for this process. Additionally, pressure from outside must be there. The question is if companies are doing more than urgent measures. (Financial institution L)

4. Working in partnership with externals:

The problem often lies in communicating internally. A solution could be to ask externals to give a status quo assessment. In this way, critical points can be communicated in a credible way. (Financial institution C)

6.4 Future trends

We observed several indications from our interviews that corporate sustainability will become more important in the future. There are signs that this will happen from the corporate environment as well as from inside the corporate sector.

Addressing future-oriented sustainability risks. Observing the business environment, we find many unknown variables that companies will have to deal with. Our interviewees pointed out that their colleagues dealing with corporate strategy are well aware of the business need to address the challenges of the future today. As globalization increases, the interdependencies concerning major issues such as climate change, fossil fuels and changing lifestyles are becoming more complex. Risks are becoming more systemic. Managers have to deal with more uncertainty in decision-making processes. As a result, we can observe that corporate strategy departments are developing new tools to deal with the future, e.g. corporate foresight or scenario processes. Our interviewees pointed out that financial institutions will internalize these risks in their business model, which will have definite consequences for companies:

First, we want to adapt internal processes, and then we intend to ask our clients about their procedures and guidelines. In the future, we plan to integrate sustainability criteria. We hope that in five years a systematic identification of future-oriented sustainability risks will be implemented at least in parts of our business. (Financial institution K)

New generation of managers. Some of our interviewees observed that the perception of corporate sustainability within the financial market is changing with a new generation of managers. The key drivers to foster this development are: (1) the management culture ("tone of the top"); and (2) proactive individual behavior. The new management generation was described to us to as being more open and familiar with sustainability and therefore might address this issue more intensely. On the contrary, there is empirical evidence that this anticipated generational change is not happening. A recent survey by the World Business Council for Sustainable Development Young Managers Team concluded that young analysts appear unconvinced of the potential substance of sustainability issues.[8]

Merger of the sustainability and corporate governance debates. Many of our interview partners mentioned that the sustainability and corporate governance debates seem to be merging. While there does not seem to be a direct correlation, we needed to investigate further to get to the underlying reasons for these statements. Our interviewees stated that both debates are about values and good management. A recent study from Systain assessed this question in more detail.[9] They concluded that there is no direct correlation between sustainability and corporate governance. None of the examined corporate governance codes had a reference to sustainability-related issues. Nevertheless, the study found out that there are indirect links, e.g. in the context of risks and disclosure of company information. A possible explanation for this argument might be as follows: On the one hand, we observed that management attention toward sustainability is often lacking. On the other hand, corporate governance is a board issue and, therefore, a priority for management. If both issues are combined, sustainability will become part of the corporate governance debate and, therefore, a material issue.

Integration of qualitative risks into corporate reporting. As we stated earlier, the current corporate reporting model is falling behind the times. Our interviewees anticipate that in 10 to 15 years reporting practice will change. The resources of twenty-first-century business clearly lie in intangible competences and capabilities. To find competitive companies, there seems to be an inevitable need to develop appropriate measures to capture the intangibles:

> Environmental and qualitative issues are in BASEL II, but only in a very diluted way. In 2015–2017, there will also be a BASEL III. We want to get qualitative risk issues integrated in it. That is systemic change. To succeed, we need to start working now. (Financial institution I)

Transformation of share ownership and leading role of institutional investors. We ascertained that activities in the future will be driven by institutional investors and pension funds more than by the retail market. It is also quite interesting that we are currently undergoing a change in the nature of client interest and beneficial owners of pension funds and mutual funds. Today, the beneficial owners are the huge majority of working people who have their pensions invested in the shares of the world's largest companies. If one looks across Europe, the biggest shareholding bodies are, for instance, the mineworkers' pension scheme in Britain, the workers' pension fund in Denmark or the civil service fund in the Netherlands. The underlying ratio about the main interest of shareholders is on retirement and other long-term financial needs. Some of our interviewees stated that this might be a lever for sustainability-related issues.

We believe that this assumption must be questioned. The mechanics of asset management and fund manager selection are based on short-term results within a yearly, or even shorter, time frame. Therefore, what is in the interest of the pension fund beneficiaries is not necessarily in the interest of the trustees, as they have to show yearly positive developments on the basis of principles, and certainly not in the interest of fund managers who are often only hired for a year and have tight performance targets to meet.

Increasing short-term dynamic. While a majority of our interviewees pinpointed the mentioned developments that could lead to the increased relevance of sustainability in the financial market, we also got some answers that the current dynamic to short-term thinking will increase:

> I don't think you can change it. That is a basic problem with the market. And it is becoming a more acute problem as we are following the US market. Now you have the hedge funds, the momentum investors, the sectoral investors. They do not care any more about the single company. On a portfolio analysis they only look at the amount of money they will make. (Financial institution O)

If one considers that our interview sample was mainly affiliated with sustainability, one might conclude that the quoted minority answer could have been the majority answer in another interview sample.

Outlook. To sum up with a general outlook, there are good indicators that the importance of corporate sustainability issues will increase. Optimists pointed out that in ten years' time sustainability units will no longer be necessary. By that time, sustainability would be integrated into mainstream business. The integration approach seems to be quite promising as it should deliver value for the corporation and is undertaken out of enlightened self-interest. Nevertheless, our interviewees remain realistic and vote for a strong political framework to support the goals of sustainable development:

> Asset management will not change the world. It cannot be the main driver. You first need to set up the right political framework, for instance through tax incentives or subsidies. It does not make economic sense if we only invest because this is something good for humanity. We would bite the hand that feeds us. We need to earn money with asset management. (Financial institution L)

6.5 Conclusion

Key findings

After having discussed: (1) the stakeholder background of financial institutions; (2) the approach to corporate sustainability of financial market actors; (3) current financial market strategies on sustainability; and (4) future trends, we come back to answer our research questions.

With our first research question, we asked about the relevance of corporate sustainability to the financial market as a key corporate stakeholder. Evidently, financial markets exert a tremendous influence on companies nowadays. The potential impact on the sustainability performance of companies has been widely discussed in the last decade.[10] Our study found that the financial market as a stakeholder of companies is not a strong driver for corporate sustainability. Missions and incentives to address sustainability are not obvious. Otherwise, the financial market would have incorporated social and environmental factors. This implies that the economic logic and business advantages of sustainability are not evident and the business case must be detected and built. We reached the same conclusion in our previous study on the business case for sustainability.[11]

Our second research question (success factors and obstacles when assessing and influencing companies' social and environmental performance) assumed that financial market institutions would assess and influence the sustainability performance of companies. We can now conclude that overall this is not the case. Assessments are only done by some actors and those undertaken do not apply for mainstream analyses. Nevertheless, the determinants of effectiveness that we identified reflect drivers to build the case better.

Our third research question asked about the implications for companies resulting from financial market demands and activities related to sustainability. For people involved in sustainability the answer might be discouraging. Our study reaches the conclusion that companies will not be punished through the financial market if they do not address sustainability in their business activities. We could observe that currently there are only a few significant associated risks. Although we detected opportunities, it must be mentioned that most of those listed still need to prove their empirical applicability:

As long as financial market institutions are opportunists and not strategists, the financial market will not be a strong driver for corporate sustainability. (Financial institution D)

Even so, the niche we examined is an evolving niche and a significant one. Companies cannot deny that the issue is on the table and evolving. The evidence brought up in this study imply that companies should deal with sustainability on a strategic level out of enlightened self-interest.

Further investigations

The empirical evidence we observed in our study clearly shows that the financial market could play a crucial role in fostering sustainability. The debate on sustainable development which started on an international level in the 1990s is ongoing and far from over. Current societal problems as well as the long-term challenges humankind is facing definitely need further investigation from all parts of society. We would like to sum up this chapter with two findings that might provoke further debate on sustainability in the financial market.

Overcoming short-term thinking. Our study clearly indicated that "quick money" still overrules potential risks in the medium- or long-term range. This approach is risky, as the practice on contaminated sites in collateralized corporate lending and real estate business demonstrates: A lender prefers to walk away instead of underwriting an unknown essential risk. This also indicates the importance of more work being carried out on the economic significance of sustainability risks. The rise of shareholder activism can also contribute to overcoming short-term thinking. Some companies already value the importance of having a strong base of SRI shareholders as a means of stabilizing sudden market reactions due to technical developments or the coming up of rumors. The result is reduced volatility.

Integrating sustainability criteria in the bottom line. For further investigations into this issue, we propose examining in more detail how sustainability criteria can be applied to the "traditional" criteria (liquidity, rate of return, risk). There is good evidence to suggest that a better understanding of these dynamics will change the landscape of the debate. Most importantly, sustainability should not be treated as an additional criterion because in this case it will be a struggle to build a financial case. The image of the triple bottom line might be misleading because only one bottom line exists and, therefore, the question should be how sustainability issues can be quantified and integrated into the existing economic criteria. To some extent, we observe that brand value and reputation risk are already doing so.

Notes

1 Datamonitor, *Global Asset Management & Custody Banks Sector*, Industry Profile (May 2005).
2 Datamonitor, *Insurance in Europe*, Industry Profile (November 2004).
3 Reuters News, *More Disasters Mean No Price Cuts, Swiss Re Says* (24 October 2005).
4 Datamonitor, *Global Reinsurance*, Industry Profile (May 2005).
5 http://www.enhancedanalytics.com.
6 See H. Garz, C. Volk and M. Gilles, *From Economics to Sustainomics: SRI – Investment Style with a Future* (WestLB Panmure, May 2002).
7 http://www.enhancedanalytics.com.
8 Young Managers Team 2004, *Perspectives. Generation Lost: Young Financial Analysts and Environmental, Social and Governance Issues* (Geneva: WBCSD and UNEP FI, 2005).
9 Systain Consulting GmbH, *Sustainability in Company Management: The Interface between Sustainability (CSR) and Corporate Governance* (Hamburg, 2004).
10 See, for instance, S. Schmidheiny, *Financing Change: The Financial Community, Eco-efficiency, and Sustainable Development* (Cambridge, MA: MIT Press, 1998).
11 U. Steger, *The Business of Sustainability* (Basingstoke: Palgrave Macmillan, 2004).

7
Cities and Communities: Local Players in Corporate Sustainability

Oliver Salzmann and Jens Prinzhorn

This chapter presents empirical evidence collected from cities and communities through 32 self-completion questionnaires and 16 semi-structured interviews (lasting on average 60 minutes) with mayors, city managers, local and regional authorities, and similar agents. The participating communities, cities and regions were: Basel (Switzerland), Bern (Switzerland), Catalunya (Spain), Erfurt (Germany), Innsbruck (Austria), Leipzig (Germany), London (UK), Metz (France), Oslo (Norway), Quierschied (Germany), Solna (Sweden), Starnberg (Germany) and Stockholm (Sweden).

In section 7.1 we provide general background information about cities and communities (without a specific focus on corporate sustainability). In section 7.2, we describe their approach to sustainability, including their mission, incentives and motives, processes and tools, criteria and expectations. Section 7.3 contains our key findings on communities' and cities' current strategies, on their actions to influence companies and their effectiveness in doing so. It also looks at success factors and obstacles. In section 7.4, we elaborate on future trends, and in section 7.5 we conclude by highlighting the key findings and implications.

7.1 Stakeholder background

Since the mid-1980s, major economic, political and social changes have occurred in Europe as a result of European integration and globalization. These changes have put considerable pressure on both national and regional governments as well as on communities and cities, which have to cope with the new levels of complexity generated by:

- The growth of knowledge-based and service-oriented business activities
- The de-industrialization of major cities, along with the rise of high-tech science parks
- Increasingly multicultural societies
- The challenge of sustaining and increasing employment levels, as companies downsize, outsource and relocate to deal with global competition
- Rising levels of social inequality.

As a result, the boundaries between national, regional and local governance have become blurred, leading to multi-level governance. Today the most important issues of competitiveness and employment are often negotiated between (supra-) national, regional and local authorities. Thus some argue that the importance of communities relative to national governments has actually increased. Very often, this has gone hand in hand with an increase in conflict: Whereas companies consider communities as "insensitive to the ever increasing competitiveness of the global economy," communities view companies as no longer interested in their well-being.

7.2   Approach to corporate sustainability

Mission

Cities and communities are primarily concerned about economic development, regional competitiveness and social issues such as the integration of immigrants. Depending on local biophysical and economic conditions, interviewees also mentioned environmental issues such as noise and air emissions associated with traffic, or site contamination. Large cities generally feel greater environmental pressure (e.g. waste, shortage of water) due to their great population density. The City of London, for example, is taking climate change seriously and has introduced a series of initiatives, such as the newly formed Climate Change Agency, to safeguard against future water shortages in the summer, potential flooding and health risks due to higher temperatures.

Given the high environmental standards across Europe and substantial improvements in corporate environmental performance over the last two decades, it is not surprising that overall the environmental issues are clearly dominated by the social challenge of sustaining and generating employment. Although most large cities have local Agenda 21 processes in place, sustainability in general, and with a corporate focus in particular, is clearly of minor importance.

Cities and communities also reflect country-specific characteristics in their missions. For example, in Sweden, they generate revenues for social welfare, i.e. they have to balance regional competitiveness (requiring lower duties and taxes) with the stability of social systems (requiring higher duties and taxes).

Incentives and motives

The key drivers of cities and communities are clearly globalization and regional competitiveness. Automation and productivity improvements have persistently decreased the need for labor. In this situation, communities and cities are – together with national and regional governments – "stuck in the middle." To retain the stability of social systems, they are forced to compromise between: (1) companies' demand for deregulation and low labor costs; and (2) citizens' (voters') desire for secure, well-paid jobs.

We identified several significant characteristics of cities and communities that act as factors moderating the importance of corporate sustainability. They include size and land use, location, and community income and the role of industry in generating it.

- Size and land use determine population density (the higher the density, the more severe the local environmental constraints), the availability of managerial and technical resources as well as responsibility (larger cities have more resources and responsibility).
- Location obviously affects the significance of local environmental issues. For example, proximity to environmentally sensitive areas that may generate community income through tourism is likely to be a factor, as is a situation below sea level, which may increase sensitivity to climate change and flooding.
- The greater a community's or city's need for income and the more significant the role industry plays in generating this income, the higher the inclination to compromise. We also note that areas with higher per capita income tend to be more sensitive to local environmental issues.

Processes and tools

Assessing corporate performance. We found very few initiatives aimed at assessing corporate performance at the micro, i.e. company, level. Some larger cities have conducted cost–benefit analyses and introduced environmental monitoring (of air pollution in particular) with corresponding sustainability or "quality of life" indicators (including economic growth, energy consumption and waste). The leaders calculate the ratio of CO_2 emissions to gross value added and build industry-specific scenarios.

For their assessment, smaller communities, in particular, rely on personal contacts with companies and information provided by third parties (e.g. chambers of commerce). In many cases, responsibility for enforcing environmental regulations (e.g. controls by regulators) has been allocated to regional authorities.

> We do not control and enforce environmental regulations; this is done by a regional authority. The bundling of resources to this authority was necessary, since communities do not have the resources to deal with such issues. (City F)

We ascertain that apart from tracking local contaminated sites, company- or site-specific assessment in small communities and cities hardly ever takes place.

Our quantitative data (see Figure 7.1) point to a wider and more balanced portfolio of assessment means, most likely because the data are biased toward larger cities. Nevertheless, the dominant role of own investigations (e.g. testing environmental quality, monitoring of corporate activities and their effects) is largely in line with the findings from our interviews, if one takes into account that these investigations occur at the macro rather than the micro level.

Determining actions to influence companies. When it comes to making decisions about appropriate action to take in order to influence companies, past experience with previous activities and (more or less systematic) political decision-making processes play a strong role (see Figure 7.2).

Furthermore, alignment with other stakeholders, such as other cities and local pressure groups, is significant:

> A lot of good initiatives already exist, so one just has to pick a suitable one and adapt it. (City B)

Criteria

Assessing corporate performance. The assessment of corporate performance is clearly oriented toward compliance with social and especially environmental regulations (see Figure 7.3).

> We do not apply any criteria [beyond compliance] because our challenge is to promote the region of [City B] to companies. There is strong competition between communities across Europe. We only win

those "battles" if we do not ask for more than what the regulators wants. (City B)

In addition, several other criteria are mentioned, such as local and regional conditions and effects, guidelines and certification schemes

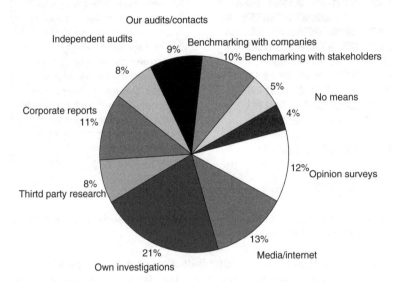

Figure 7.1 Means of assessing corporate social and environmental performance (cities and communities)

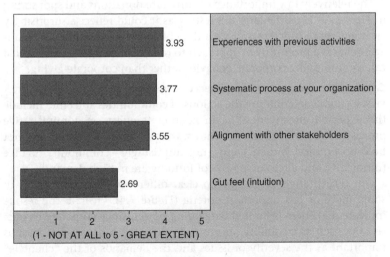

Figure 7.2 Extent to which processes/tools determine actions to influence companies (cities and communities)

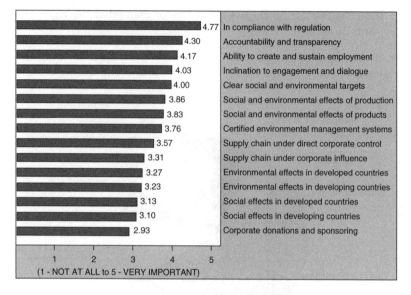

Figure 7.3   Importance of criteria for assessing corporate social and environmental performance (cities and communities)

(e.g. ISO 14000, EMAS), and other indicators of corporate goodwill (the winning of local awards, reputation). This is clearly in line with the quantitative data collected: Respondents emphasize the importance of (1) regulatory compliance; and (2) accountability and transparency.

The relatively low importance of corporate donations and sponsoring in Figure 7.3 is particularly interesting as it could reflect a surprisingly clear and more concrete understanding of corporate sustainability management (as a profit-driven approach to resolve or mitigate issues) and a call for improving corporate behavior rather than corporate giving.

Criteria determining actions to influence companies. According to our interviews, criteria determining the actions of communities and cities include the expected effectiveness of an action, its effect on administrative processes ("[it] should not slow down the provision of permits and not hold up a project launch") and – not surprisingly – community finance (innovative and alternative ways of funding are in high demand).

Our quantitative data show no clear difference that could point to some more or less important criteria (Figure 7.4). Overall, the results indicate that there is limited bargaining power, since corporate characteristics such as credibility, image and power are considered at least as important as the severity of issues and the demands of the "clientele" (i.e. residents, voters, etc.).

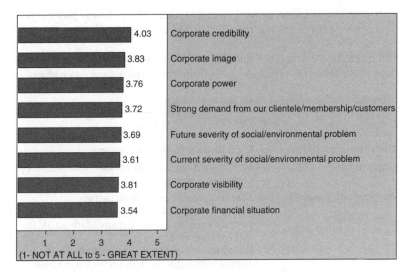

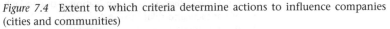

Figure 7.4 Extent to which criteria determine actions to influence companies (cities and communities)

Expectations

Overall, our interviewees' responses reflect the willingness of communities and cities to compromise in their relationships with companies. Expectations of cities and communities can be categorized as shown in Table 7.1.

Companies are also perceived as being impatient about slow, democratic decision-making processes.

> If the community was kept in the loop from the beginning, permits could be as quickly provided as in the US. (City B)

We also detected significant variation in terms of participating communities' and cities' satisfaction with corporate performance, which clearly reflects the strong local characteristics of corporate–community relations. Most interviewees are satisfied with the general corporate compliance with social and environmental standards, although they also report:

- SMEs lagging in performance, which is attributed to a lack of (technical or managerial) resources
- Largely reactive corporate attitudes ("wait-and-see position"), which is often reflected in a lack of corporate transparency.

If companies come up with creative ideas, the political process will not adopt them all, but they will adopt some of them. (City E)

Our quantitative data (see Figure 7.5) are in line with the findings from our interviews. Whereas respondents indicate the highest level of satisfaction

Table 7.1   Expectations of cities and communities

Category	Concrete examples/expectations
Philanthropic activities	— Local projects (sponsoring, giving)
Employment	— More respect for work–life balance, disabled people — Employee training
Dialogue and goodwill	— Take community as a serious partner — Be both a local and global player — Increase capacity building (particularly in SMEs) and commitment — Introduce and certify management systems — Timely communication: to prevent significant bottlenecks (lack of communication is due to lack of contacts and relationships) — Read relevant policy documents of the community to know political climate and agenda — Take consumer interests into account

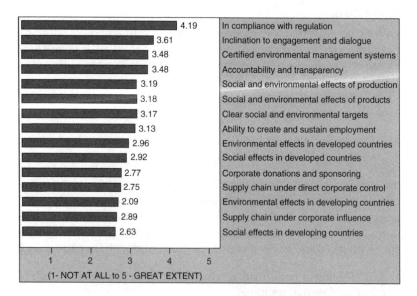

Figure 7.5   Satisfaction with corporate social and environmental performance (cities and communities)

with corporate regulatory compliance, they are significantly less satisfied with companies' environmental and social effects in developing countries and their supply chain management. These low satisfaction levels most likely reflect communities' and cities' concern about an "unlevel playing field," i.e. low social and environmental standards in developing countries undermining regional competitiveness in Europe.

Current stakeholder strategies

Actions and their effectiveness

The portfolio of actions cities and communities use to influence companies includes five broad categories, as shown in Table 7.2.

Our interviewees also pointed to significant differences between the portfolios of actions of small communities and large cities: The latter can have the competence to introduce significant local policy measures:

> Overall, our [local] policy is more proactive than national policies; this is because our local environmental issues are more severe than in any other parts of the country. (City D)

Table 7.2   Actions of communities and cities

Category	*Concrete actions/measures*
1. Regulation	— Ordinances
	— Policy targets, e.g. by 2008, 50 per cent of the cars in Oslo should be low emission vehicles
2. Incentive systems	— Awards
3. Participation	— Task forces
	— Face-to-face discussions, e.g. between city manager/mayor and companies
	— Multi-stakeholder dialogue involving NGOs, unions, industry associations, etc.
	— Involve umbrella organization of national communities and cities to have a broader platform for interaction with companies
4. Communication and coaching	— Speeches, articles, media coverage to inform about community issues and to coach companies (SMEs in particular)
5. Cooperation	— Public–private partnerships
	— Contracting arrangement (city as custtomer), e.g. assessment of construction projects takes environmental and social effects into account (contracting in particular concerned with energy efficiency)

Since social and environmental standards are largely complied with and tightening them further would compromise regional competitiveness, communities and cities have increasingly focused on engaging with companies. New policy measures are clearly geared toward increasing the attractiveness of a community or city (e.g. through city marketing featuring account management of key corporations). However, interviewees also noted that existing environmental standards are not being compromised – at most, when negotiating with companies, a transitional period for compliance is granted. Figure 7.6 suggests that engagement (including participation, and cooperation in general and public–private partnerships in particular) has actually become a key strategy of communities and cities.

Given the high social and environmental standards in Europe and tough global competition, one may question how meaningful it is to use regulation to influence companies. In any case, our data clearly show that regulation is still viewed as the most *effective* action to influence companies (see Figure 7.7).

As our interviewes also mentioned, local and national legislation/-regulation in global industries is only one of many standards companies must comply with. A life-sciences multinational headquartered in Switzerland, for example, has to meet standards set by the US Food and Drug Administration (FDA).

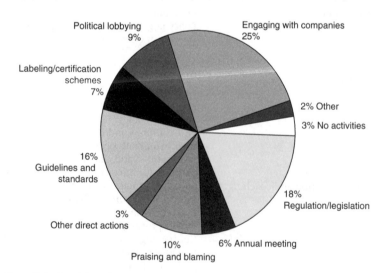

Figure 7.6 Portfolio of actions to influence companies' social and environmental performance (cities and communities)

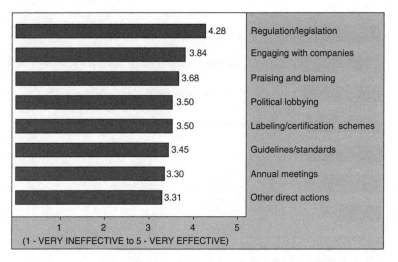

4.28	Regulation/legislation
3.84	Engaging with companies
3.68	Praising and blaming
3.50	Political lobbying
3.50	Labeling/certification schemes
3.45	Guidelines/standards
3.30	Annual meetings
3.31	Other direct actions

1 2 3 4 5
(1 - VERY INEFFECTIVE to 5 - VERY EFFECTIVE)

Figure 7.7 Perceived effectiveness of actions in influencing companies' social and environmental performance – regardless of whether used by the individual stakeholder or not (cities and communities)

So how do communities and cities view companies' reactions to their actions? Our data suggest that companies actually engage in dialogue, even if they – according to our interviewees – do not necessarily regard the city or community as a "serious partner." Companies are seen to change strategies and business processes but also to increase PR and lobbying efforts (see Figure 7.8).

Overall, the actions of communities and cities have a limited effect on companies:

> Companies get a lot [of concessions from communities and cities] these days. (City A)

Nevertheless, interviewees suggested that leading companies benefit from an improved license to operate, i.e. accelerated provision of permits/contracts (e.g. if ISO 14000 certified), fewer and quicker controls, i.e. in general a more stable and favorable operating environment.

> The risk of being fined is low, but there is significant risk of losing contracts in the future in our community. (City A)

> There are no risks. We have a cooperative approach. We look for discussion. (City B)

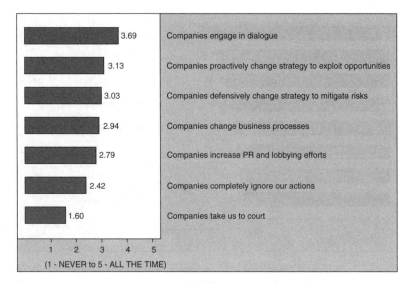

Figure 7.8 Frequency of corporate reactions to stakeholder action (cities and communities)

Responses to our questionnaire (see Figure 7.9) put this claim somewhat into perspective: Whereas it could be expected for communities and cities to have a relatively strong lever on companies through regulators' controls, it is surprising that they perceive themselves as having an even greater effect on corporate reputation. It is also surprising that tightening regulation and, in particular, acceptance of project launch and growth have lower scores. We suggest that these two levers are hardly used, as they would compromise regional competitiveness. The remaining discretion for communities and cities to influence companies appears to be limited to: (1) regulatory enforcement (i.e. how strictly companies are controlled); and (2) the mobilization of the public (to influence corporate reputation).

Respondents to our questionnaire perceived the media as the stakeholder that is best able to influence corporate behavior, followed by the financial sector and (corporate) customers (see Figure 7.10).

In light of the evidence presented above, this self-assessment of communities/cities appears somewhat overoptimistic. However, it could also hint at multi-level governance through which – as suggested earlier in this chapter – communities' potential to determine competitiveness has actually increased.

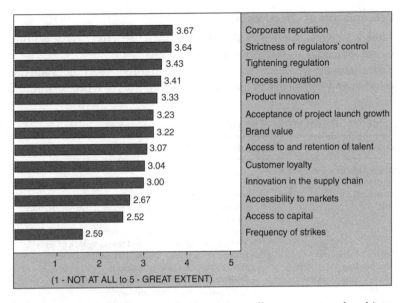

Figure 7.9 Extent to which stakeholder actions affect corporate value drivers (cities and communities)

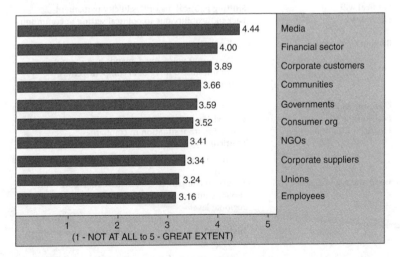

Figure 7.10 Extent to which stakeholders are able to influence corporate behavior (cities and communities)

Determinants of effectiveness

Table 7.3 details the factors that determine the effectiveness of actions by communities and cities to influence companies.

Furthermore, we detected divergent views on corporate attitudes and the mindset and knowledge of managers, which appears to reflect significant

Table 7.3 Determinants of effectiveness

Determinant	*Further remarks/quotes*
Moderating/situational factors	
Trust and commitment	— Trust (due to a stable political situation), close personal contacts (with unions, management, etc.)
	— Commitment at the top (city council, administration and companies)
	— Awareness and willingness to work together
	— Violation of agreements, and resulting lack of trust
Financial situation and funding	— Innovative funding (leasing and renting rather than buying), additional funding
Market opportunities	— Positive effect on brand value
Public	— Local public awareness and buy-in
Allocation of responsibilities	— Unclear allocation of responsibilities
	— Lack of local control: Allocation of responsibilities between regional and local authorities (e.g. *Landratsamt* in Germany); responsibilities largely given up by local authorities because they lack knowledge and resources
Community-/city-related factors	
Political will	— Shifting political majorities in city parliament
Flexibility	— Lack of flexibility due to political setting in community, or national or regional legislation
Bargaining power	— Lack of bargaining power:
	We cannot voice any demands in order not to compromise our regional competitiveness. (City H)
Company-related factors	
Positioning	— Clear vision of corporate sustainability
Financial situation	— Severe financial situation in companies (particularly SMEs):
	We cannot fine them without destabilizing them. (City C)
Local and regional ties	— Industrial companies less sensitive than SMEs and service companies, since they are less active on a regional level
	— Certain local and regional bonds (due to relatively high level of regional competitiveness; historically developed):
	Companies will not just simply leave or blackmail us. (City A)

local and company- or industry-specific variation in (1) corporate behavior; (2) local ties between communities/cities and companies; and (3) different expectations on both sides.

> Usually companies are very willing. (City A)
>
> In general, we find industrial companies more difficult. (City G)

7.4 Future trends

Given (1) their limited bargaining power and financial capacities, (2) widespread corporate social and environmental compliance in Europe, and (3) the imperative of regional competitiveness, it is not surprising that communities and cities have a tendency to pursue participatory rather than regulatory actions (e.g. taskforces), negotiated agreements and engagement. A tightening of social and environmental standards seems unlikely:

> The balance of power is changing in favor of companies due to globalization: Creating and sustaining employment is per se not a goal for companies. (City A)
>
> It is impossible to introduce new social regulation; the most obvious option is a participatory approach. (City A)

We expect – in larger communities and cities in particular – a more systematic approach to corporate sustainability, which will feature:

- More public–private partnerships (in the Nordic countries in particular), also including funding and running pilot projects.
- Foundations to promote corporate sustainability.
- More incentives (e.g. award schemes).
- Clearer strategic positioning to provide greater certainty for corporate long-range planning.

However, corporate sustainability is unlikely to take a more prominent role in the short to medium term.

7.5 Conclusion

In most cases, communities and cities can exert very little influence on companies today. Obvious exceptions are industries that rely on local communities (e.g. power generation, mining). These communities and cities have considerable bargaining power.

We draw the following key conclusions:

- The missions of cities and communities in term of corporate sustainability reflect their weakening bargaining position and the widespread corporate compliance with social and environmental regulation in Europe.
- There are few systematic approaches to corporate sustainability. Assessment of corporate social and environmental performance is largely limited to the micro level. Technical and managerial capacity are lacking.
- Satisfaction levels with corporate regulatory compliance are rather high. Concern about an unlevel playing field – compared to developing countries – is significant.
- Although it may be desirable – from the point of view of communities and cities – to keep current regulations or even tighten them, it is increasingly difficult to justify under the current circumstances (globalization and the need for regional competitiveness).

Currently cities and communities appear to lack the drive, capacity and leverage for more distinct actions to drive corporate sustainability. In addition, in light of their financial constraints, they are likely to increasingly search for engagement and partnerships with companies. This is unlikely to change in the near and medium-term future.

Overall, cities and communities are currently more concerned about social issues than environmental ones: employment, social inequality, immigration and the like. Compared to the environmental domain, this is clearly the greater challenge: It is easier to find win–win situations between companies and communities/cities on environmental issues: First, environmental win–wins can be achieved through technological innovation, which is less expensive than (employment-related) social change. Second, corporate environmental responsibility (e.g. for cleaning up a contaminated site) is intuitively stronger than social responsibility (e.g. providing employment).

8
Governments: The Challenge of Addressing Corporate Sustainability at the Macro Level

Fabian Baptist

This chapter presents empirical evidence collected from national and regional governments, international institutions and experts in this field gathered from 31 self-completion questionnaires and 47 semi-structured interviews (lasting on average 60 minutes). The following participated in the study: Directorate General for Employment, Social Affairs and Equal Opportunities (European Commission), Directorate General for Enterprise (European Commission), Directorate General Trade (European Commission), Ministry for Foreign Affairs (Sweden), Ministry for Sustainable Development (Sweden), SIDA Swedish International Development Cooperation Agency (Sweden), Ministry of Economics and Labour (Austria), Ministry of Economics and Labour (Germany), Ministry for the Environment, Nature Conservation and Nuclear Safety (Germany), Ministry for Economic Cooperation and Development (Germany), Ministry of Health and Social Security (Germany), Ministry of Consumer Protection, Food and Agriculture (Germany), Hessian Ministry of Economics, Transportation, Urban and Regional Development (Germany), Ministerio de Trabajo y Asuntos Sociales (Spain), Ministerio de Industria, Turismo y Comercio (Spain), Ministerio de Medio Ambiente (Spain), Ministerio de Economia y Hacienda (Spain), Ministerio de Sanidad y Consumo (Spain), Ministry of Environment and Traffic Baden-Württemberg (Germany), Department for Environment, Food and Rural Affairs (UK), Department for International Development (UK), Department of Trade and Industry (UK), Institute for Organizational Communication (Germany and Belgium), The Danish Labour Market Authority (Denmark), Passages Magazine (France), Ministry of Economic Affairs (The Netherlands), UN Global Compact.

The chapter is structured as follows: In section 8.1 we provide a general background on governments. In section 8.2 we describe government approaches to corporate sustainability (mission, incentives, motives, processes, tools and criteria). Key findings on current stakeholder strategies, their actions and effectiveness as well as future trends are given in section 8.3. Section 8.4 highlights corporate risks and opportunities and includes some recommendations, before section 8.5 concludes the chapter.

8.1   Stakeholder background

Governments have the power to determine how corporations and individuals achieve their goals by defining laws and regulations. Governments have exercised their regulatory powers to a greater or lesser extent over the last few decades.

During the 1960s, the policy of western countries was characterized by a strong state and a command-and-control approach. The state, with its centrist approach, provided goods and services such as energy and communications systems. Hence, it was believed that societal problems could be solved by developing detailed programs and policies and imposing them on corporations. Institutions were expected to behave in a manner specified according to regulations. A wide variety of areas, such as safety at work and equal opportunities for women and minorities, began to be regulated. Increasingly corporations had to deal with a far wider range of market and non-market issues. They perceived that the potential for corporations to play a voluntary role in society was restricted by compulsory statutes. However, it turned out that the policies often did not reach their intended goals and outcomes. The specific monitoring of the broad range of regulations turned out to be far more difficult than expected. Governments have continually failed to regulate corporate behavior at a reasonable cost because of practical and economic limitations.[1]

From the 1980s, there was a strong move toward the privatization of some public industries. Public transport, postal services, telecommunications and utilities increasingly became the domain of private corporations. Particularly in the UK, the phenomenon of privatization meant extensive deregulation, which paved the way for private businesses to be allowed to enter former state-dominated markets.[2]

Increasingly since the 1990s, governments' power and the intensity of regulation have tended to decline because of the internationalization of trade. Globalization facilitates the relocation of companies to low-cost regions, with low taxation and limited environmental and social statutes. As soon as corporations act beyond the scope of countries, they are no longer directly accountable to them. Globalization challenges the regulatory authority of national governments, since multinational corporations (MNCs) can exploit the environmental regulations of individual nation-states. To avoid the "race to the bottom," governments have increasingly set up systems for transnational negotiation (e.g. the EU). In this context, an increasing level of regulation at the transnational level can be observed. Simultaneously organizations of civil society (e.g. NGOs and trade unions) have also established (civil) rules and codes for business conduct. This makes it clear that national governments are no longer the only authority determining the "rules of the game."[3]

8.2   Approach to corporate sustainability

Mission

In 2000 the governments of the EU member states agreed on an ambitious goal: To turn the EU into "the most competitive and dynamic knowledge- based economy in the world, capable of sustainable economic growth with more and better jobs and greater social cohesion" (strategic goal for 2010 set for Europe at the Lisbon European Council in March 2000). In 2002, at the World Summit on Sustainable Development in Johannesburg, governments committed themselves to the Millennium Development Goals. As corporate sustainability (CS) is considered to be business's contribution to achieving sustainable development, governments publicly place it high on the policy agenda. In this context, governments proclaim that they want to take the lead in the sustainability arena. In particular, this means that governments try to stimulate corporate sustainability in a "soft manner" based on a voluntary, engaging and cooperating system.

> We try to promote corporate sustainability by setting the right framework, raising awareness, improving CS knowledge and bringing greater transparency. (Government G)

Local, regional and national governments intend to define a framework including minimum standards for business performance and enabling or providing incentives for companies to engage in social and environmental projects. New research work should be funded identifying the "business case" for corporate sustainability. Governments are trying to provide businesses with ideas and concepts on how to implement corporate sustainability and to empower corporations to address CS issues proactively. Governments believe that many firms, especially smaller and medium-sized companies, regard corporate sustainability solely as a PR campaign. One of the priorities for governments is to show that:

> Corporate sustainability is more than "funding a kindergarten." (Government A)

Furthermore, public authorities themselves want to lead by example, examining their practices to understand their economic, social and environmental impacts. Governments also want to act as a meeting point, bringing together heterogeneous actors and finding solutions to specific problems, as well as being a facilitator by encouraging the development and dissemination of best corporate sustainability practices.

> Governments do not have enough money to provide all the services citizens are expecting. Therefore, we have to mobilize companies to meet their responsibilities and to be more active in corporate sustainability. (Government B)

However, the primary focus of governments is on programs linked to the main goals of the "new" Lisbon Strategy – employment and growth – outlined in 2005. Former Dutch prime minister Wim Kok and a team of experts had concluded in November 2004 that only minor progress had been made after almost half the time had elapsed for Europe to become the most competitive economy in the world. Economic growth is considered a prerequisite for achieving social and environmental goals, and the lack of it affects sustainable development negatively.[4] In March 2005, therefore, the European Commission relaunched the Lisbon Strategy, since its original goals seemed to be almost out of reach. Lower levels of economic growth are forcing the European Commission to react by reviewing the objectives and prioritizing them. The Commission proposes to focus strongly on economic growth and employment in order to increase pensions, salaries and the standard of living.[5]

> All corporate sustainability proposals have to be scrutinized in terms of effects on growth and employment. (Government R)

In this context, it is hardly surprising that many of the associated programs are characterized by low budgets and staff levels. In some countries there are only between two and five people working on corporate sustainability. Thus, many government programs are not specifically designed to facilitate or promote companies' global CS activities. Considering the staff levels, governments' self-defined mission to be promoters seems to be difficult to fulfill. It is becoming clear that for the time being governments do not intend to intervene too strongly in the corporate sustainability arena and market.

Incentives and motives

Governments' main driver for fostering corporate sustainability is obvious. Corporate sustainability, as the business contribution to sustainable development, helps to increase social welfare. Governments, as elected institutions, therefore have the mandate to increase the welfare standards of their citizens.

> We see companies as the main contributor to reach our goals and increase welfare. Therefore, of course we want to push corporate sustainability very intensively and try to help it become mainstream. (Government C)

Further, ministries consider corporate sustainability as an appropriate instrument to compensate for market and policy failure.[6] Market mechanisms are not effective in all fields and many imperfections, known as negative externalities, come into play.

> We see corporate sustainability as one of various approaches to internalize existing negative externalities. Public policy promoting CS is considered as the right response. (Government D)

Policy failure is a result of the inability of governments to resolve the catalogue of economic, social and environmental problems a society faces.[7] In addition, national governments have the challenge of finding the ideal regulatory instruments for "borderless corporations." They therefore see the voluntary part of corporate sustainability as an appropriate tool to promote, since it could compensate for policy failures and replace government regulation.

> We do not want to burden global companies with an extensive amount of national regulation. Therefore, corporate social responsibility with its voluntary and self-regulating characteristics is the right instrument in the era of globalization. (Government C)

Governments expect corporations to come up with their own proposals for corporate sustainability if they wish to avoid legal regulations. Additionally, governments strongly believe in the long-term business case for corporate sustainability.

> Corporate sustainability can maximize companies' long-term returns by minimizing their negative impacts. Through responsible actions, corporations can become more competitive. Nevertheless, we are aware that CS will only become mainstream if there is the appropriate economic growth. (Government C)

An existing demand for corporate sustainability is essential for the business case and for promoting corporate sustainability. Only when this is a given, can corporate sustainability and sustainable products help increase companies' competitiveness. Governments observe increasing customer concern regarding the social and environmental impacts of products they buy. However, these customer groups are still a niche that governments intend to promote using, for example, campaigns.

Assessing corporate environmental and social performance

Processes and tools. Before explaining the tools in detail, two levels of corporate environmental and social performance assessment need to be distinguished: the micro level, which involves the direct assessment of single companies; and the macro level, in which all companies are assessed together (indirect assessment) using aggregated figures.

Governments are always in direct contact with multinational corporations. Nevertheless, the corporate environmental and social performance assessment on a micro level rarely takes place in ministries. Of course, governments try to monitor and control to make sure legal expectations and requirements are being fulfilled, but efforts beyond compliance are rarely scrutinized on the micro level. Only a few ministries assess the corporate sustainability reports of various multinationals in order to be able to publish a success ranking. The instrument of publishing rankings is regarded as very effective in changing corporate performance. Occasionally, different societal groups such as NGOs inform governments about potential social or environmental corporate misdeeds or risks. When this happens, governments try to act as an intermediary and also try to find out more about the named company. Other institutions such as NGOs or rating agencies assess corporations on a micro level, whereas governments do not have the resources to assess single companies – they are more focused on the overall outcomes.

> We do not have any criteria for assessing single companies. But via the sustainability indicators we do know in which direction we have to push the sustainability process. (Government H)

Governments use sustainability indicators for macro-level assessments with which they are partly able to assess the corporate performance of all companies together. These sustainability indicators are calculated regularly and systematically. Regional and local governments mainly conduct research on a macro level selectively, sporadically and unsystematically.

Our quantitative data show that, to obtain the information for the sustainability indicators, governments conduct their own research and also use third-party research by calling for bids. Direct government research is mainly carried out via media/internet screenings and surveys. Both research types aim primarily at generating and disseminating information regarding corporate sustainability.

Figure 8.1 illustrates a wide and balanced portfolio of assessment means, which is in line with the qualitative results (interviews). The assessment tools predominantly apply to the macro level, as opposed to the micro level.

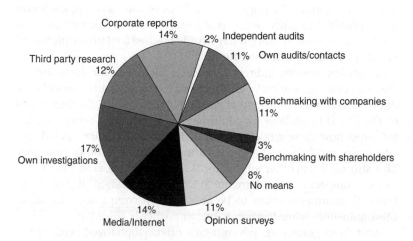

Figure 8.1 Means of assessing corporate social and environmental performance (governments)

Criteria. The criteria for direct assessment of single companies on a micro level are clearly based on the existing social and environmental regulation in the country concerned (see Figure 8.2). Predominantly governments on the national and regional level monitor and control compliance with existing legal standards in areas such as environmental protection, health and safety and employment rights. Companies that comply with regulations get the formal license to operate in the corresponding market.

In terms of indirect assessment (macro level), the criteria of the sustainability fields with their indicators offer an orientation for companies. Several of the following most mentioned sustainability fields are linked to the social and environmental effects of corporate production (see Table 8.1).

Table 8.1 Sustainability fields linked to social and environmental effects

Environmental effects	Social effects
— Energy productivity	— Education
— Climate protection	— Equal opportunities
— Renewable energies	— Safety at work
	— Economic growth and employment

All interviewed ministries listed almost the same sustainability fields. Nevertheless, each country has its own specific focus, reflecting its various problems and differing understandings of the nature of corporate sustainability. Currently Germany, for example, is less focused on environmental protection, since it has already reached a relatively high level in this area (e.g. climate protection).

In addition, positive indirect assessment takes place for all companies that are committed to make an effort and to comply with codes of conduct. For example, at the annual meeting of the National Contact Points of the OECD Guidelines for Multinational Enterprises, companies are informed how these guidelines can be implemented, how related specific issues can be solved and what the situation is in other countries. This also applies to other international codes and standards, e.g. the UN Global Compact or the International Labor Organization (ILO) conventions. Governments claim to be able to help companies implement these guidelines while the nature of compliance is voluntary.

Apart from guidelines, governments often emphasized certification schemes (e.g. EMAS, ISO 14000) as positive instruments for supporting corporate environmental and social performance assessment. These schemes

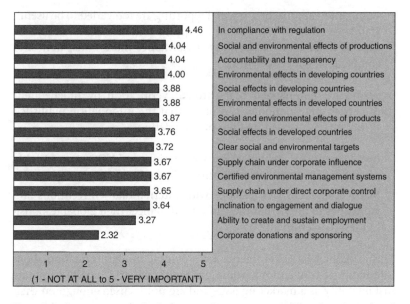

4.46	In compliance with regulation
4.04	Social and environmental effects of productions
4.04	Accountability and transparency
4.00	Environmental effects in developing countries
3.88	Social effects in developing countries
3.88	Environmental effects in developed countries
3.87	Social and environmental effects of products
3.76	Social effects in developed countries
3.72	Clear social and environmental targets
3.67	Supply chain under corporate influence
3.67	Certified environmental management systems
3.65	Supply chain under direct corporate control
3.64	Inclination to engagement and dialogue
3.27	Ability to create and sustain employment
2.32	Corporate donations and sponsoring

1   2   3   4   5
(1 - NOT AT ALL to 5 - VERY IMPORTANT)

Figure 8.2 Importance of criteria for assessing corporate social and environmental performance (governments)

and codes of conduct clearly illustrate the efforts of a particular company to mitigate the social and environmental side effects of their products and production methods.

The quantitative data (see Figure 8.2) highlight other important criteria, such as accountability and transparency, when assessing companies. The stream of bad corporate governance and accounting-related scandals such as Enron has obviously spurred governments to be increasingly focused on accountability and transparency, which is essential to make assessment possible. Furthermore, the data show that governments consider the ability to create and sustain employment and corporate donations and sponsoring somewhat apart from the other criteria listed. This shows that governments perceive the ability to create and sustain employment more as a prerequisite for corporate sustainability than a part of it, and reflects a call for genuine corporate sustainability activities rather than corporate giving.

Outcome of the assessment. Many multinationals try to increase transparency and accountability by issuing social responsibility reports.

While environmental, health and safety reports are included, reports often do not tackle issues such as human rights and child labor.

Companies' approaches to social reporting are too varied to be useful. Standards such as The Global Reporting Initiative (GRI) should be used to make the sustainability performance more transparent and comparable. (Government L)

Governments emphasized that through verification by independent third parties, multinationals can prove that the information published in corporate reports is more than public relations.

Involvement of stakeholders, e.g. trade unions and NGOs, considerably improves the quality of verification. (Government E)

Many companies lack practice with international conventions and guidelines to prove that they do intend to meet their global responsibilities. (Government G)

This explains why governments are providing more information about international conventions. Some multinationals still handle corporate sustainability as a marketing issue and are not focused enough on their real impacts on society.

A better integration of corporate sustainability policy, involving management, enables CS to become far more than a "PR issue." (Government F)

Several times the future challenge of "demographic change" was mentioned. Governments emphasized that multinational companies underestimate and are far too passive with regard to this problem. Corporations will face problems recruiting employees and should therefore be more focused on training and on the work–life balance in order to recruit talents.

Only a few corporations have recognized the problem of demographic change. For the future, we have to put more effort into raising awareness of demographic change. Both governments and corporations have to cooperate in order to be able to solve and to counter. (Government NN)

Governments' relatively low satisfaction with both social effects in developing countries and corporate donations and sponsoring is of particular interest (see Figure 8.3). Apparently, governments think that multinationals should explore the implications of their activities more

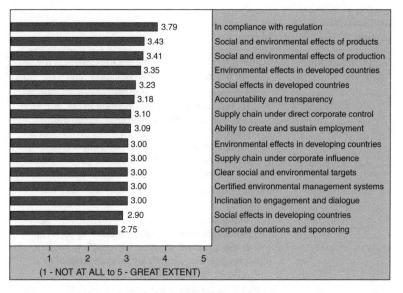

Value	Category
3.79	In compliance with regulation
3.43	Social and environmental effects of products
3.41	Social and environmental effects of production
3.35	Environmental effects in developed countries
3.23	Social effects in developed countries
3.18	Accountability and transparency
3.10	Supply chain under direct corporate control
3.09	Ability to create and sustain employment
3.00	Environmental effects in developing countries
3.00	Supply chain under corporate influence
3.00	Clear social and environmental targets
3.00	Certified environmental management systems
3.00	Inclination to engagement and dialogue
2.90	Social effects in developing countries
2.75	Corporate donations and sponsoring

(1 - NOT AT ALL to 5 - GREAT EXTENT)

Figure 8.3 Satisfaction with corporate social and environmental performance (governments)

deeply. This expectation of greater corporate responsibility in the supply chain most likely also reflects European governments' desire for a more level playing field between developed and developing countries, which could, for example, be achieved if companies move beyond regulatory compliance in countries with low social and environmental standards. The low satisfaction level with corporate donations and sponsoring reflects a call for corporate sustainability activities that are linked to own corporate efforts.

8.3   Current and future stakeholder strategies

Actions and their effectiveness

Portfolio of actions. The portfolio of government actions aimed at stimulating or facilitating corporate sustainability is extensive and varied. The actions can be categorized into three main groups:

1. Modifying existing regulation
2. Enabling corporate sustainability (raising awareness and promoting initiatives)
3. Standardizing corporate sustainability

Table 8.2 Actions of governments

Category	Actions
Modifying existing regulation	— Shifting from bureaucratic detail regulation toward voluntary agreement, "soft regulation" and frameworks
	The environmental regulation in our country is far too excessive. There's nobody in our ministry who has an overview. Through deregulation, companies have more freedom in their activities and more space for innovation. In addition, we have more capacities and can be more focused on environmental laggards. (Government KK)
	— Harmonizing the various codes/regulatory frameworks
	Our goal is it to have "better regulation." Better regulation means analyzing existing social and environmental regulation on appropriateness for economic growth and competitiveness (Government MM).
	— Ratifying international agreements
	— Shifting away from exclusive toward participative decisions
Enabling CS	— Providing information on labor conditions
	— Promoting best CS practice
	— Public tendering for goods and services linked to companies meeting CS standards
	— Giving fiscal incentives for CS reporting, certification schemes (EMAS, ISO 14000)
	— Facilitating cooperation between stakeholders through workshops
	— Giving awards to particularly progressive companies
	— Providing information about international standards (ILO, UN Global Compact, OECD guidelines, GRI)
	— Fostering the triple bottom line
	— Fostering socially responsible investment (SRI)
	— Fostering fair trade
	— Fostering socially responsible consumption
	— Educating and raising awareness regarding eco- and social labels
	— Giving incentives to strive for gender quality
	— Giving incentives for employing older people and people with disabilities
	— Increasing demand for CS products through campaigning
	— Providing consumer information on products

Continued

Table 8.2   Continued

Category	Actions
Standardizing CS	— Harmonizing eco-labels — Negotiating international guidelines for reporting — Negotiating internationally accepted CS standards — Negotiating standards in social labeling

The large number of actions in the enabling CS category shows that governments put much effort into actions that are based on a voluntary system. Governments often emphasized that they did not wish to put too much pressure on companies in order to ensure regional competitiveness. This is also reflected in our quantitative data (see Figure 8.4). Governments want to engage with multinational corporations to promote and facilitate corporate sustainability (18 per cent). Further, they are working on guidelines and standards (14 per cent) and existing regulations (24 per cent) in order to: (1) provide an enabling framework; and (2) make corporate sustainability more transparent and easier to compare. Consumer protection ministries often use praising and blaming to inform consumers about e.g. healthy and fair-trade products.

Effectiveness of government actions. Governments have continually pointed out that regulation is the most effective instrument for changing companies' behavior (also reflected in our quantitative data – see Figure 8.5). The compulsory, binding nature of regulation forces companies to behave in a certain way. Not complying with the rules means fines and, in the worst case, the revocation of the license to operate.

Nevertheless, governments hesitate to issue new "hard" regulation for various reasons. Nowadays, society, technology and knowledge changes rapidly and continuously. Furthermore, many environmental problems such as climate change are characterized by their borderless and global aspect. This makes static and national regulation ill-suited to solving problems.

> We need far too much time to issue new regulation. Environmental technologies can change significantly during the time it takes for a proposal to become law, which can lead to fatal results. (Government N)

Due to the static nature of regulation, it has proliferated immensely in the past, particularly in the area of environmental measures. Hence, it is

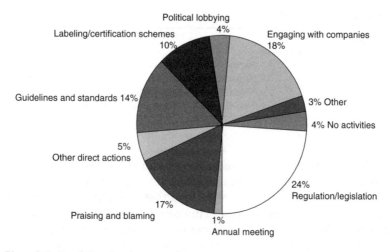

Figure 8.4   Portfolio of actions to influence companies' social and environmental performance (governments)

economically inefficient for governments as well as multinationals because of the high administrative and monitoring costs.

> Corporations have the impression that they are too intensively monitored by different ministries. Therefore the ministries try to coordinate their monitoring efforts to reduce the costs of compliance and of monitoring. (Government KK)

In 2000 US manufacturers spent roughly $1,700 per employee to comply with federal workplace regulations.[8] A regulatory burden limits the international competitiveness of countries in the era of globalization. Multinationals, in particular, have to manage a variety of regulations and the resulting costs. They have to contend with the laws of their own nation, international laws and the laws of the nation in which they will be trading. Therefore, multinationals tend to prefer countries with low standards.

> Whenever we issue new regulation, we always have Adam Smith's invisible hand in mind. Corporations will use the resources that are set free by deregulation in the most effective way. (Government O)

Given the high social and environmental standards in Europe, the described disadvantages of regulation and particularly the imperative of regional and national competitiveness, the phenomenon of deregulation and government efforts to set appropriate frameworks and guidelines do not seem to be surprising. Several ministries confirmed that this process is ongoing. Other governments refused to use the word "deregulation," but called it "better regulation." Better regulation means the simplification of existing laws and the analysis on appropriateness for economic growth.

The quantitative data are in line with the qualitative interviews. Figure 8.5 shows that, apart from regulation, labeling and certification schemes and guidelines and standards are seen as effective instruments in changing corporate behavior. This finding illustrates that quasi-regulatory actions aimed at stimulating voluntary corporate efforts are seen as a more genuine alternative for addressing social and environmental problems than engaging with companies.

Determining actions to influence companies. During many of the interviews with governments, it became clear that the political decision-making processes do not seem to be particularly systematic.

> Corporate sustainability is a very young topic and we are in an early phase. Firstly, we have to learn more about CS and then we are able to develop appropriate processes and tools. (Government NN)

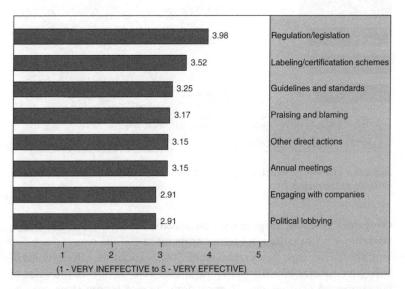

Figure 8.5 Perceived effectiveness of actions in influencing companies' social and environmental performance – regardless of whether used by the individual stakeholder or not (governments)

In addition, the quantitative data (Figure 8.6) show that the decision-making processes are primarily driven by the current and future severity of the problems, followed by the demands of governments' "clientele" (which includes citizens as voters and companies). Corporate characteristics play a less important role, most likely since governments act at the macro level, at which they most often deal with industry associations rather than individual companies. This does not mean that corporate characteristics do not sometimes moderate decisions, as the following quote shows:

If the company is powerful, we expect that the companies solve their problems without our engagement. (Government G)

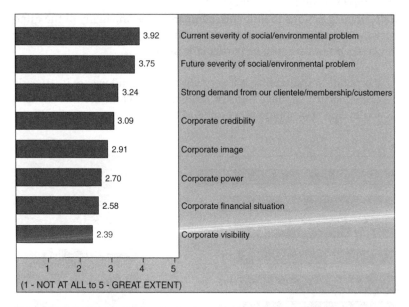

Figure 8.6 Extent to which criteria determine stakeholder actions to influence companies (governments)

Companies' reactions to governmental actions. As Figure 8.7 illustrates, governments primarily react with engagement and dialogue.

However, our interviews raised some doubts about the effectiveness of this: governments confirmed that multinationals do not see the value of governments' engagement. Corporations do not ignore their engagement activities, but are nevertheless reluctant to become actively

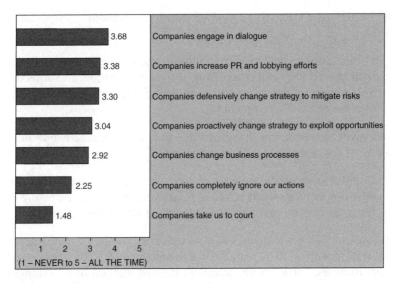

3.68	Companies engage in dialogue
3.38	Companies increase PR and lobbying efforts
3.30	Companies defensively change strategy to mitigate risks
3.04	Companies proactively change strategy to exploit opportunities
2.92	Companies change business processes
2.25	Companies completely ignore our actions
1.48	Companies take us to court

1   2   3   4   5
(1 – NEVER to 5 – ALL THE TIME)

Figure 8.7 Frequency of corporate reactions to stakeholder action (governments)

involved in initiatives. This can be traced back to the fact that corporations are not used to the new role of governments.

> Our strategy of promoting corporate voluntary initiatives has resulted in more corporate independence. Ironically, because of this, multinationals are reluctant to engage in our initiatives. (Government V)

Hence, corporations might believe that governments have not recognized how markets work, since they have not internalized the market logic. The different way of thinking makes cooperation difficult. Further, companies might have recognized that government initiatives are characterized by small budgets and minimum staff levels. Due to the undifferentiated approach of government programs, the value for companies of participating in the workshops is negligible. In some European countries, the number of environmental certified companies has not increased, despite government incentives.

> Corporate sustainability first went through a sharp rise. Although now it is on a plateau and neither decreasing nor increasing. (Government M)

One interviewee stated that cooperation with corporations is problematic. Their experience was that:

> Corporations do not like to communicate about successful partnerships with the public authorities. They also do not approach us directly. This is quite a frustrating experience because we cannot explain this phenomenon. (Government O)

Moreover, governments have realized that companies are not fully aware of the business case for sustainability:

> Companies should be more active in ecological R&D, since demand for environmental products is said to be growing immensely especially in faster developing countries like China and India. (Government H)

Because of this, governments want to influence companies through fiscal R&D incentives to increase their involvement and exploit new-found opportunities. Furthermore, an often observed reaction to government praising and blaming is an increase in PR efforts. Ministries for consumer protection in particular experienced the following:

> As soon as we inform consumers about products in a positive way, the corresponding corporations try to exploit this opportunity by intensifying their PR efforts. The same applies when we alert consumers. Corporations try to protect themselves through PR efforts. (Government N)

Future strategies

In the short term, a tightening of social and environmental standards is extremely unlikely. However, petty and existing regulations may well be reduced. Governments do not want to negatively affect companies' competitiveness. Governments will want to make further use of the volunteer system and will be continually interested in raising awareness and promoting corporate sustainability activities.

> We are aware of the fact that raising awareness for corporate sustainability will take a long time. The processes have to be continued. (Government D)

Some ministries predict that they may oblige companies to issue sustainability reports, which must meet the minimum reporting standards. The GRI might represent a way to do so, not only because many companies have already started using it, but also because it has been sanctioned by the UN. This will inevitably lead to more accountability and transparency of the sustainability performance of companies.

Governments are awaiting internationally legal corporate sustainability standards and a corporate sustainability certification (for example, the forthcoming ISO 26000). The discussion about whether internationally accepted minimum laws should be created and enforced has existed for a long time. International codes of conduct, e.g. the UN Global Compact or OECD guidelines, are often criticized because of their voluntary nature and the lack of compliance monitoring. Interviewees saw legal minimum corporate sustainability standards quite differently. Some ministries expect them, while emphasizing that they have to be introduced on a European level to guarantee a level playing field for all countries. Other ministries believe in and prefer non-legislative intervention due to the imperative of international competitiveness. Nevertheless, a harmonization of the codes of conduct and accountability standards must and will happen in their view.

8.4   Corporate risks and opportunities

The risks and opportunities companies face through government actions when actively or passively involving themselves in corporate sustainability can be divided into internal and external opportunities and risks. Governments provide a lot of (general) information regarding risks and opportunities, as illustrated in the Table 8.3.

The chance to forestall legislation and to ease regulators' controls is of great importance for managers. According to a study conducted by the Economist Intelligence Unit, regulatory risk – arising from new or existing regulations – is one of the greatest threats to business. In the eyes of managers, regulatory risk is a greater source of concern than other risks such as country risk, market and credit risk, IT and people risks, terrorism and natural disasters. Managers are aware that regulation is partly needed. Nevertheless, a majority believe that the problems outweigh the benefits of regulations.[9]

The strength of the opportunities and risks seen through the governments' lens is illustrated in Figure 8.8.

Besides the opportunity to influence regulation and enforcement, Figure 8.8 highlights government influence on corporate innovation and corporate reputation. As described earlier in this chapter, governments strongly believe in the business case for sustainable products, which they try to promote by incentivizing corporate R&D efforts.

192

Table 8.3 Internal and external risks and opportunities

Dimension	Opportunities/risks
Internal	— Gaining insight and knowledge of how to apply CS tools — Cutting costs through eco-efficiency — Anticipating and minimizing internal risks — Improving working environment leading to a more committed and productive workforce — Attracting and retaining a skilled and motivated workforce — Being fined when not complying with existing regulation
External	— Presenting an attractive investment — Promoting active relationships with stakeholders — Establishing and protecting reputation — Government procurement — Increasing the market opportunities while retaining consumer and government trust (especially in foreign countries) — Helping corporations to retain the license to operate — Anticipating stakeholder expectations (e.g. customer demands) — Forestalling stricter legislation

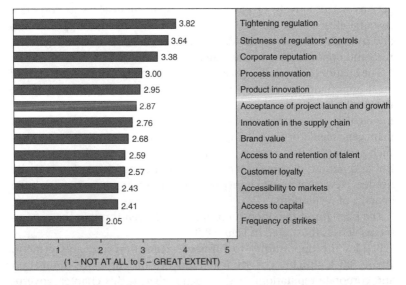

Figure 8.8 Extent to which shareholder actions affect corporate value drivers (governments)

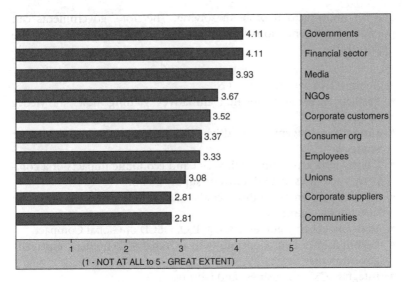

4.11	Governments
4.11	Financial sector
3.93	Media
3.67	NGOs
3.52	Corporate customers
3.37	Consumer org
3.33	Employees
3.08	Unions
2.81	Corporate suppliers
2.81	Communities

(1 - NOT AT ALL to 5 - GREAT EXTENT)

Figure 8.9 Extent to which stakeholders are able to influence corporate behavior (governments)

The relatively high mean value of corporate reputation suggests that governments consider public statements (such as criticizing Deutsche Bank for layoffs after it achieved record profits) and awards reasonably effective. In light of the imperative of national and regional competitiveness, such actions may in fact be seen as the currently most feasible and hence effective approach.

Influence of stakeholder groups. Governments perceive themselves, financial institutions and the media as stakeholders with the greatest power to change corporate behavior (see Figure 8.9). Governments see themselves as having as much influence as financial institutions, which seems to be surprising, since compared to financial institutions governments are "only" contextual and not business stakeholders. This makes it clear that regulation and the provision of guidelines are still regarded as powerful instruments. Nevertheless, the qualitative data showed that governments no longer want to or think it appropriate to remain "commanders" in the markets.

Recommendations for mitigating the risks and exploiting the opportunities

Through workshops and especially through research projects, it has been possible for governments to build up valuable knowledge on CS and on multi-sectoral problem solving. Therefore, governments can provide recommendations for mitigating the risks and exploiting the opportunities:

- Be proactive with regard to CS.
- Participate in governmental initiatives gaining new knowledge about CS.
- Commit management to drive and integrate CS into corporate strategy.
- Consider all environmental, social and economic impacts of a company's activities up and down its supply chain.
- Consider different context, challenges, minds and perceptions in developing countries.
- Integrate existing guidelines, e.g. ILO, OECD or Global Compact.
- Communicate and cooperate with external stakeholders, especially governments.
- Integrate CS into business and culture.
- Use the existing standards for CS communication, e.g. GRI.
- Integrate workforce in CS development and programs.
- Identify the business case with regard to the growing demands for CS of consumers, investors and the workforce.

The recommendations governments have given are very general in nature. The appropriateness and added value for concrete corporate issues seem to be low.

8.5 Conclusions

From the questionnaires and the interviews in particular, it became clear that governments are predominantly struggling with three different corporate sustainability related issues.

- Is corporate sustainability only an instrument to allow companies to minimize risk or is it an instrument for new innovation? With regard to the latter, will corporate sustainability become mainstream in all aspects of business? How can governments promote the mainstreaming of corporate sustainability in a more effective manner?
- The aim of governments is to define a level playing field. High corporate sustainability performers are already lobbying governments in order to have minimum corporate sustainability standards.

In 2004, NIKE proclaimed the wish to have concrete standards enacted. This is an example of high performers calling for standards to avoid unfair competition. (Government E)

Standards lead to increasing costs for competitors and penalties for free riders. What should standards look like? Should these standards be set up on a national, European or international level? Is a voluntary or a compulsory character the right approach for these corporate sustainability standards? How can multinationals as "borderless corporations" be monitored?

- Corporate sustainability is a market-driven concept. Several governments are trying to promote corporate sustainability by increasing the demand for it. Therefore, some have launched various campaigns facilitating consumers' access to information. For example, the issue of harmonizing labels has to be tackled, since the large number of different labels irritates consumers. How can governments increase corporate sustainability demand by raising the awareness of consumers and companies more effectively? How can companies be included in this process?

Notes

1 J. C. Ruhnka and H. Boerstler, "Governmental Incentives for Corporate Self-Regulation," *Journal of Business Ethics*, 17 (1998) 309–26.
2 J. Moon, "Government as a Driver of Corporate Social Responsibility," *ICCSR Research Paper Series*, No. 20 (2004).
3 A Crane and D. Matten, *Business Ethics: A European Perspective* (Oxford: Oxford University Press, 2004), p. 389.
4 See http://europa.eu.int/comm/commission_barroso/president/topics/growth_en.htm.
5 See http://europa.eu.int/growthandjobs/intro_en.htm.
6 Statements are in line with e.g. J. Moon, "Government as a Driver of Corporate Social Responsibility," *ICCSR Research Paper Series*, No. 20 (2004).
7 D. Thorne McAlister, O.C. Ferrell and L. Ferrell, *Business and Society: A Strategic Approach to Corporate Citizenship* (Boston: Houghton Mifflin, 2003), p. 110.
8 See http://www.mercatus.org/article.php/57.html.
9 Economist Intelligence Unit, *Regulatory Risk: Trends and Strategies for the CRO* (London: The Economist Intelligence Unit, 2005).

9
NGOs: Catalysts of Corporate Sustainability

Jens Prinzhorn and Oliver Salzmann

This chapter presents empirical evidence collected from NGOs through 44 self-completion questionnaires and 50 semi-structured interviews (lasting on average 60 minutes) with heads or directors of NGOs. The participating NGOs were: Amnesty International – International Secretariat – United Kingdom; Amnesty International – Business Group – United Kingdom; Amnesty International – United Kingdom; BUND – Germany; Business and Human Rights Resource Center – United Kingdom; Bishopric Trier – Germany; Citizen initiative "Environmental protection" (Bürgerinitiative Umweltschutz) – Germany; Childright – Netherlands; DanChurchAid (Folkekirkens Nødhjælp) – Denmark; Danish Society for Nature Conservation (Danmarks Naturfredningsforening) – Denmark; Danish Association for International Cooperation (Mellemfolkeligt Samvirke) – Denmark; Deutsche Umwelthilfe – Germany; Equipo Nizkor – Spain; Fair Trade Foundation – United Kingdom; Forum for the Future – United Kingdom; Friends of the Earth – United Kingdom; Fundació Natura – Spain; Fundació Un Sol Món – Spain; Fundacion desarrollo sostenible – Spain; Future in our hands (Framtiden i våre hender) – Norway; German Agro Action (Welthungerhilfe) – Germany; Germanwatch – Germany; Gesellschaft fuer technische Zusammenarbeit (GTZ) – Germany; Greenpeace International – Netherlands; Greenpeace – Switzerland; HIVOS – Netherlands; Ibis – Denmark; Lutheran Church – Germany; National Deaf Children Society (NDCS) – United Kingdom; Nature and Youth (Natur of Ungdom) – Norway; Respect Europe – Denmark; Terre des Hommes – Germany; Transparency International – Germany; Umbrella organization of Muslims (Zentralrat der Muslime) – Germany; Umbrella organization of Spanish NGOs in human rights (Federación de Asociaciones de Defensa y Promoción de los

Derechos Humanos) – Spain; URGEWALD – Germany; World Economic Forum – Switzerland; WWF European Policy Office – Belgium; WWF International – Switzerland; and WWF – United Kingdom.

The chapter is structured as follows: in section 9.1 we provide general background on NGOs (without a specific focus on corporate sustainability). In section 9.2 we provide information about their approach to sustainability (mission, incentives and motives, processes and tools, criteria and expectations). Section 9.3 features our key findings on NGOs' current strategies, their actions and effectiveness as well as success factors and obstacles. In section 9.4 we elaborate on future trends, and in section 9.5 we conclude by highlighting the key findings and implications.

9.1 Stakeholder background

The process of globalization began after the end of World War II, and with it came the foundation of intergovernmental organizations (IGOs). With increasing globalization, national autonomy weakened as policy areas that were previously mainly nationally dominated – such as security, trade, environmental protection and social issues – became more interdependent.

In light of this, one might have expected IGOs to grow in importance. However, IGOs can only express themselves as much as their member states permit.[1] As a result, and prompted partly by the economic changes after the break-up of the former Soviet Union, national and transnational non-governmental organizations (NGOs) have come to the fore, "taking over" state autonomy on single issues such as human rights, the environment or development aid.[2]

The NGO community is very complex and diverse, which makes classification and definition difficult.[3] For the purposes of this chapter, we define NGOs in line with the ECOSOC-Resolution 1269 (XLIV), established in 1968, as "any international organization which is not established by inter-governmental agreement." However, it seemed necessary to concentrate on those institutions and public pressure groups that have an interest in and the greatest potential to influence corporate sustainability. This includes large multinational NGOs focusing on conservation and human rights, for example, as well as think tanks, local civic action groups and religious organizations.

In light of the wide and diverse range of NGOs, one might presume that they lack influence. In fact, the opposite is true. Pressure groups and consumer organizations are the key drivers of public perception of corporate attitudes. In the non-business sphere, NGOs are the most important stakeholders after media and national governments, and their importance will continue to grow in the future.[4]

NGOs are not legally bound by the opinions of others, and can thus "operate without all political constraints [...] in several of the more controversial areas such as human rights."[5] Since NGOs tend to focus on a single issue (or a cluster of similar issues), they "can serve as focal points for the mobilization and articulation of interests shared by many people living in different countries."[6]

9.2   Approach to corporate sustainability

Mission

Our interviews revealed clearly formulated mission statements (also available on NGOs' websites). They depend on the individual NGO's focus, e.g. human rights – Amnesty International; conservation – WWF.

We also noticed a traditionally strong NGO strand focusing on classic advocacy through campaigns. However, over the past decade, several other business models have emerged:

- Knowledge dissemination: The Business and Human Rights Resource Centre provides an internet-based library and communication platform for both NGOs and companies.
- Engagement with companies: e.g. WWF's conservation partnerships.[7]
- Solutions provider: e.g. The Forum for the Future as a facilitator and consultancy.

Finally, in light of an increasingly global and financially and politically powerful economy, NGOs put a lot of effort into their networks. Thus, they achieve local presence and global outreach: Pressure groups "in poorer countries have surprisingly extensive resources at their disposal."[8] Therefore, despite the variety of NGO missions, public pressure groups are clearly "a means of ensuring a uniformity of concern throughout the world."[9]

Incentives and motives

Our interviewees indicated that the membership and clientele of NGOs play an important role, as they determine the strategic agenda, governance and funding. Their importance has increased over recent years, as the competition among NGOs for funding intensifies: The clientele demands more activities and more accountability. However, there are exceptions:

> Beneficiaries, for instance in the case of development projects, have restricted possibilities to influence. (NGO A)

The more resourceful NGOs survey their clientele to keep track of satisfaction levels and shifting demands (e.g. whether or not to cooperate with companies). In light of the different business models described above, it is important to note that each NGO essentially has its own clientele. Pressure groups design their programs around the interests of their members and/or contributors. Some prefer a more confrontational approach, others a more cooperative one:

> Our supporters are generally happy with us taking money from companies as long as the policy changes companies make are visible. (NGO B)

In conclusion, approval of or dissatisfaction with contributors is a meaningful means of quality control, particularly for those NGOs that mainly or completely rely on individual contributions. Next to NGOs' immediate clientele, other drivers for NGO activities exist: IGOs and the European Union (EU) call for NGO engagement. The UN Global Compact and High Level Groups established at the EU would not be possible to the same extent without NGO participation:

> I should like non-governmental organizations to occupy an increasingly significant place [...]. From the standpoint of global democratization, we need the participation of international public opinion and of the mobilizing powers of non-governmental organizations.[10]

Processes and tools

Assessing corporate performance. Overall, we detected significant variation in NGOs' means of assessing corporate performance. There is no corporate screening on a daily basis, but there are ad hoc investigations. Furthermore, some NGOs concentrate on issues rather than companies, e.g. Amnesty International focuses on the testimonies of victims. Although NGOs often simply lack the resources to carry out their own comprehensive and local assessments, we detected a trend toward more local involvement (e.g. tapping into the knowledge of local or regional partners). Some issues such as corruption are particularly difficult to assess:

> When trying to assess corruption, in some cases it simply starts with guessing. If there are no internal corporate measures for corruption, how should one – as an NGO – assess this from the outside? (NGO C)

Also, since some issues, particularly environmental ones, have become more accessible to the public, NGOs increasingly generate and make use of scientific knowledge and data. Quantitative data collected through our questionnaire point to four primary means NGOs use to assess corporate performance (see Figure 9.1):

- Media/internet (newspapers, news alerts, etc.): Information provided by the media and internet is inexpensive and abundant. Thus it makes sense for NGOs – small ones with fewer resources in particular – to rely on these sources. However, such information may lack accuracy.
- Third-party research: This source (by rating agencies, local journalists and consultants) tends to be costly and is only affordable to the bigger NGOs, which also combine it with their own investigations, audits and contacts. The result is often a very comprehensive and powerful assessment.

  > Prior to engaging with a company, we carry out a due diligence process. We commission a comprehensive assessment of our potential partner – carried out by a third party. Our potential corporate partner pays for this assessment – as a demonstration of goodwill. (NGO D)

- Corporate reports (see media/internet): Material produced by companies themselves is readily available, but may not paint an unbiased picture.
- Own investigations: These can be very resource-intensive, as they require a local presence ("that means a lot of traveling") and skilled personnel.

Determining actions to influence companies. Our data on factors that determine NGOs' actions to influence companies (see Figure 9.2) largely depend on size and resources. Whereas large multinational NGOs such as WWF, Friends of the Earth and Greenpeace have more systematic processes in place (e.g. multidisciplinary coordination committees involving managers from different divisions such as fundraising, campaigning, corporate relations – often with top management involvement),

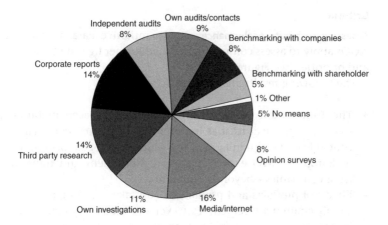

Figure 9.1 Means of assessing corporate social and environmental performance (NGOs)

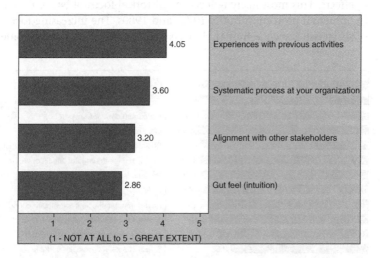

Figure 9.2 Extent to which processes/tools determine actions to influence companies (NGOs)

it is plausible that, overall, NGOs determine their actions largely on the basis of past experience.

We also found out that alignment with stakeholders (other NGOs in particular) is growing in importance because coalitions facilitate the bundling of resources and bargaining power.

Criteria

Assessing corporate performance. Our quantitative data on the criteria NGOs apply to assess companies has shed further light on their agendas and priorities (see Figure 9.3).

The following results are particularly revealing:

- The formulation of clear targets as well as accountability and transparency are at least as important as regulatory compliance. We conclude that – also in light of the widespread regulatory compliance in Europe – NGO expect stronger commitment and transparency from companies – beyond compliance.
- Effects of products and production still take a leading position over supply chain management. However, our interviews suggest that the importance of supply chain management, i.e. upstream activities in developing countries, has increased substantially over recent years.
- Social effects are still considered less important than environmental effects. This most likely reflects the historical focus of NGOs on environmental protection in the 1970s and 1980s. The increasing focus on social issues such as human rights is a comparatively new development.

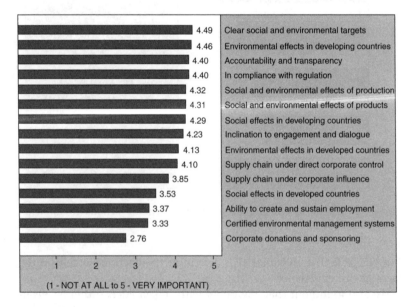

	Value	Criterion
	4.49	Clear social and environmental targets
	4.46	Environmental effects in developing countries
	4.40	Accountability and transparency
	4.40	In compliance with regulation
	4.32	Social and environmental effects of production
	4.31	Social and environmental effects of products
	4.29	Social effects in developing countries
	4.23	Inclination to engagement and dialogue
	4.13	Environmental effects in developed countries
	4.10	Supply chain under direct corporate control
	3.85	Supply chain under corporate influence
	3.53	Social effects in developed countries
	3.37	Ability to create and sustain employment
	3.33	Certified environmental management systems
	2.76	Corporate donations and sponsoring

(1 - NOT AT ALL to 5 - VERY IMPORTANT)

Figure 9.3   Importance of criteria for assessing corporate social and environmental performance (NGOs)

- Overall, NGOs' attention appears to be shifting toward developing countries: A comparison of the importance of social and environmental effects reveals that problems in developing countries are considered more important than those in developed countries.
- The low level of corporate donations and sponsoring (in line with our interview data) suggests that NGOs prefer socially and environmentally responsible business models over philanthropic activities.

Determining actions to influence performance. Our interviews point to several significant criteria that determine decisions to take a certain action rather than another. They include:

- Corporate characteristics such as a company's visibility (e.g. brand recognition), reputation and actual performance:

  When looking for a corporate partner, we are interested in corporate leadership, in the "willing sinners," preferably in a high-impact sector. (NGO E)

  The most visible companies are, of course, the most attractive ones. (NGO F)

- The issue: its severity, existing scientific evidence, its complexity ("Is it easy to communicate?")
- Actions of other NGOs ("Where is a gap for us?")
- Parameters related to the organization: resources and expertise, contacts and networks and probable impact.

Our quantitative data highlight the importance of the current and future severity of social and environmental problems rather than corporate characteristics such as corporate credibility and corporate image (see Figure 9.4). This reflects issue-driven missions and actions of NGOs: However, as our interviews suggest, it does not exclude a certain opportunistic approach, i.e. taking visibility and credibility of companies into consideration when deciding to campaign or engage.

Expectations

We note that, with the exception of regulatory compliance, NGOs are most satisfied with those aspects of corporate performance that are less important to them: certified management systems, corporate donations and sponsoring, as well as social/environmental effects in developed countries (as a comparison of Figure 9.3 and Figure 9.5 reveals).

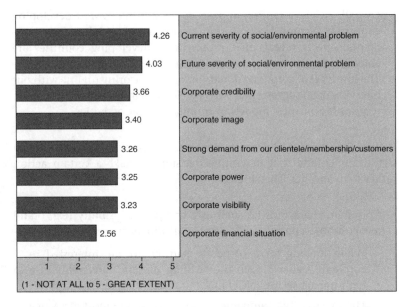

Figure 9.4 Extent to which criteria determine stakeholder actions to influence companies (NGOs)

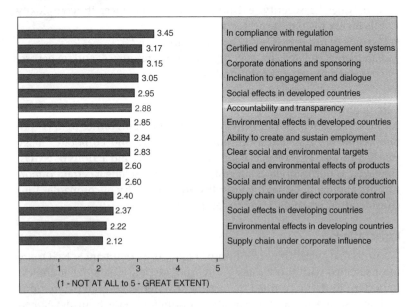

Figure 9.5 Satisfaction with corporate social and environmental performance (NGOs)

The quantitative data are also in line with expectations voiced by our interviewees who stated a need for:

- Greater transparency (e.g. readiness for external audits).
- Accountability ("all management levels should be accountable").
- More consistency in environmental and social performance across all operations, i.e. moving beyond compliance in developing countries:

  We do not expect companies to resolve issues that should be managed by governments. However, a number of projects are not thought through; hence, they are not sustainable. (NGO G)

Current stakeholder strategies

Actions and their effectiveness

The actions and roles of NGOs are as diverse as the NGO community itself. Our interviews revealed the following activities aimed to influence companies:

- Participation and political lobbying: some NGOs have historically focused on governments (e.g. human rights issues), because they (not companies) can be legally bound by the human rights charter.
- Classical advocacy through reports, press releases, rallies, online libraries, face-to-face meetings, shareholder activism, etc.
- Monitoring corporate performance ("watchdog" function).
- Cooperation and partnerships (engaging with companies): partnerships with the corporate sector remain a controversial strategy in the NGO community. Most interviewees noted that such engagement could be very effective, as it has a potential upside for companies (innovation, credibility). They also acknowledged that companies rarely engage, i.e. "rarely take the carrot" without complementary pressure – "without the stick." Several NGOs also reported that they are overwhelmed by companies' requests for cooperation and partnerships.

As our quantitative data – in line with the interviews – shows (see Figure 9.6), NGOs concentrate on four major activities to influence companies: engaging with companies; quasi-regulation (guidelines and standards as well as labeling and certification schemes); regulation and legislation (and political lobbying); and praising and blaming.

Figure 9.7 somewhat mirrors the previous chart: Companies' engagement in dialogue stands out, which is also in line with our interviews:

In the early days, we could not get to the factory gates; today they serve us tea and cookies. (NGO H)

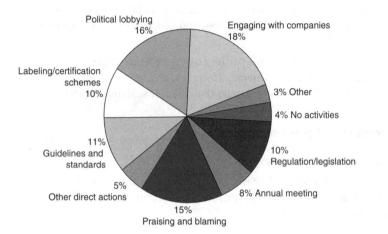

Figure 9.6   Portfolio of actions to influence companies' social and environmental performance (NGOs)

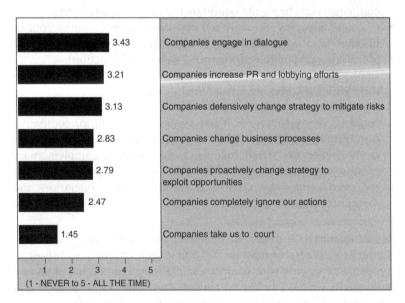

Figure 9.7   Frequency of corporate reactions to stakeholder action (NGOs)

Overall, we detect significant frustration from the NGO community because they feel they are "being managed" by the corporate sector. Interviewees pointed to the limited reactions of companies beyond incremental changes to business processes and increased sophistication in dealing with NGO campaigns. A twofold confrontational and cooperative ("carrot and stick") approach is often criticized by campaigning NGOs. This is largely because – as an interviewee from a cooperative, "convening" NGO pointed out – the "convener" is able to claim the success of a partnership with the company that would have been difficult (if not impossible) to establish without the pressure generated by the "campaigner."

Both the interviews and the questionnaires (see Figure 9.8) point to three primary areas that NGOs believe they can affect. They include:

- Corporate reputation (plus brand value) through partnerships and campaigns.
- Innovation of products and processes, as a result of both campaigning and engagement (e.g. Greenpeace's Greenfreeze, Brent Spar campaign, WWF's Forest Stewardship Council).
- The corporate license to operate (regulation and its enforcement), which is also affected through political lobbying – increasingly at the EU level:

    The alignment between regulators and NGOs was a key for REACH's success (NGO I).[11]

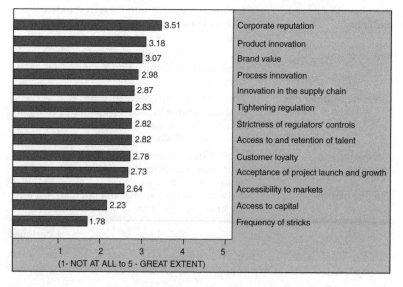

Figure 9.8 Extent to which stakeholder actions affect corporate value drivers (NGOs)

Determinants of effectiveness

We identified various factors determining the effectiveness of actions
carried out to influence corporate social or environmental performance
(see Table 9.1).

Table 9.1   Determinants of effectiveness

Determinant	Further remarks
Moderating/situational factors	
Support from third parties	— Public — Political community — Other NGOs — Media — Multi-stakeholder alliance.
Close personal contacts at top level	The closer the contact, the greater the trust. Some interviewees were also critical of the fact that – whereas contacts with corporate CSR staff are good— there is little connection to mainstream business staff.
Complexity	Great variation in cultural and economic conditions across countries and in environmental and social issues.
NGO-related factors	
NGO brand value and credibility	Greater brand recognition and trust in NGO increases upside for corporate partners and downside for corporate opponents.
Resources: time and money	Corporate performance becomes more complex, competition among NGOs more intensive.
Governance structures	Strong bottom-up governance affects decision-making processes (slow, difficult to find common denominator, impossible to ensure organizational alignment).
Knowledge and awareness	Lack of knowledge and understanding of economic necessities (e.g. religious organizations in particular).
Existing networks	Networks on the national and international level facilitate local presence and global outreach.

Continued

Table 9.1 *Continued*

Determinant	Further remarks
Company-related factors	
Corporate ownership	Some forms of ownership (in particular family businesses) are seen as more proactive and receptive.
Company size and visibility	The larger the company, the greater its bargaining power. On the other hand, greater visibility makes companies more vulnerable.
Corporate attitude and PR	Some companies have a "softer" attitude than others (e.g. Shell and BP compared to Exxon Mobil). "Overall corporate PR machines are very effective; hence, public perception is often ahead of reality."
Corporate involvement	More proactive companies contribute more resources; engage more distinctly through funding, technical support and political lobbying.
Corporate presence in political arena	At EU level, corporate presence is largely limited to lobbyists. There are no decision-makers.
Top management awareness and commitment	Higher levels of awareness and greater involvement at the top facilitate innovation (e.g. changes in business processes and business models).

9.4 Future trends

Our interviews point to two major future strategies, namely political lobbying/consultation for more regulation and legislation and engagement with companies. This finding is also in line with the quantitative data shown in Figure 9.9.

Respondents perceive regulation/legislation as the most effective action, followed by engagement and praising and blaming in the public arena. Overall, we ascertain an ongoing "division of labor" between NGOs, which results in a complementary "carrot and stick" approach of "conveners" and "campaigners." The traditional campaigning activities are continuing their decline:

> The times of the big demonstrations are gone. (NGO J)

Finally, accountability will most likely increase in terms of importance, in particular for convening NGOs, as cooperation with the corporate sector is associated with greater reputation risk.

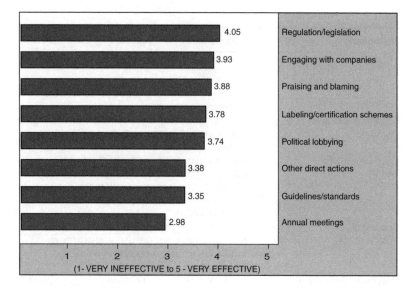

Figure 9.9 Perceived effectiveness of actions in influencing companies' social and environmental performance – regardless of whether used by the individual stakeholder or not (NGOs)

9.5 Conclusion

From both elements of this survey, the questionnaire and the interviews, we detected a broad variety of perceptions and attitudes that appear to be contingent upon underlying issues, culture and the political, social and economic framework.

In his survey on managers' perceptions of stakeholders, Steger noted the growing importance of NGOs as stakeholders in the future.[12] This chapter sheds further light on their roles and actions. As Figure 9.10 surprisingly shows, NGOs ranked themselves low on their effectiveness at influencing companies.

Taking into account qualitative evidence from our interviews, this is not overly surprising, as several respondents complained about companies' increasing proficiency in managing NGOs and their campaigns. The corporate sector has developed this ability over the last decade. The result also reflects NGOs' reliance on buy-in from companies' primary and transactional stakeholders (governments, communities and customers in particular) and the need for coalition building.

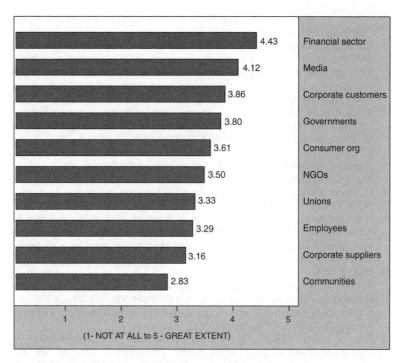

Figure 9.10 Extent to which stakeholders are able to influence corporate behavior (NGOs)

A "carrot and stick" approach has emerged. We ascertained a "division of labor" between NGOs concentrating on special competencies, in particular: (1) regulation and legislation; and (2) engagement with companies. This finding is also in line with – compared to other stakeholders – clear mission statements and a need for more NGO accountability. NGOs remain a significant catalyst of opinions of social groups. Naturally, they present a diverse picture. We expect attempts to strengthen influence on regulation/legislation – ideally through coalitions, including those with other stakeholder groups – and foster innovation through partnerships, particularly in developing countries to achieve a level playing field.

Notes

1 R. Thakur, "Human Rights: Amnesty International and the United Nations," in P.F. Diehl (ed.), *The Politics of Global Governance: International Organizations in an Interdependent World* (Boulder, CO: Lynne Rienner Publishers, 1997), p. 261.

2   I. Take, *NGOs im Wandel – Von der Graswurzel auf das diplomatische Parkett* (Wiesbaden: Westdeutscher Verlag, 2002), pp. 37–8.

3   According to the International Classification of Nonprofit Organizations (ICNPO), the NGO sector contains organizations in areas such as culture, social services, environment, development aid, education, research, etc. This includes civic and philanthropic initiatives, employee and employer associations, religious communities, etc.

4   As concluded by U. Steger, "A Mental Map of Managers: An Empirical Investigation into Managers' Perceptions of Stakeholder Issues," *Business & the Contemporary World*, 10 (1998), 579–609 (p. 596).

5   P.F. Diehl, *The Politics of Global Governance – International Organizations in an Interdependent World* (Boulder, CO: Lynne Rienner Publishers, 1997), p. 244.

6   Thakur, "Human Rights," p. 261.

7   U. Steger, *Flirting with the Enemy: The WWF/Lafarge Conservation Partnership* (A), IMD Case No. IMD-2–0101, 2003.

8   H.K. Jacobson and E. Brown Weiss, "Strengthening Compliance with Environmental Accords," in P.F. Diehl (ed.), *The Politics of Global Governance: International Organizations in an Interdependent World* (Boulder, CO: Lynne Rienner Publishers, 1997), pp. 305–33.

9   Ibid., p. 328.

10 Boutros Boutros-Ghali as quoted in C. Ritchie, "Coordinate? Cooperate? Harmonise? NGO Policy and Operational Coalitions," in T.G. Weiss and L. Gordenker (eds), *NGOs, the UN, and Global Governance* (Boulder, CO: Lynne Rienner Publishers, 1996), pp. 185–6.

11 The proposed REACH (Registration, Evaluation and Authorization of Chemicals) directive should bring greater consistency in the way new and existing chemicals are regulated throughout the European Union (see http://europa.eu.int/comm/environment/chemicals/reach.htm).

12 Steger, "A Mental Map of Managers."

10
Consumer Organizations: Aligning Corporate Sustainability and Consumer Interest

Aileen Ionescu-Somers

In this chapter we present empirical evidence collected from the managers of consumer organizations (a spread of middle-ranking and senior managers, including the top management of some organizations) on their perception of corporate sustainability performance. We obtained this information through 33 self-completion questionnaires and 15 semi-structured interviews. We interviewed representatives of a combination of national consumer organization representatives, policy organizations and testing organizations. The following consumer organizations participated in our survey: Consumers International (UK), the European Association for the Co-ordination of Consumer Representation in Standardization (ANEC), the European Consumer's Organization (BEUC), the Consumer's Association of Ireland, Consumentenbond (Netherlands), Forbru-gerradet (Danish Consumer Council), Stiftung Warentest (Germany), Verbraucherzentrale Bundesverband (Federation of German Consumer Organisations), Verein für Konsumenten-information (Consumer Association of Austria), Kuluttajat-Konsumenterna r.y. (Finland), Konsumentföreningen Stockholm (the Stockholm Cooperative Society, Sweden).

The chapter is structured as follows: in section 10.1 we provide some general background on consumer organizations. In section 10.2 we provide information about their approach to sustainability (mission, incentives and motives, processes and tools, and criteria). Section 10.3 outlines the expectations and resulting corporate risks and opportunities. Section 10.4 contains our key findings on consumer organizations' current strategies, their actions and effectiveness as well as corporate risks and opportunities. In section 10.5 we elaborate on future trends, and in section 10.6 we conclude by highlighting the key findings and implications.

10.1   Stakeholder background

In recent decades, the world has witnessed an unprecedented increase in consumerism. With the rapid growth of the world economy, significant rises in incomes and a global approach to trade, people are consuming a wider array of products and services than ever before. Consumer organizations in Europe play an important practical role in consumer affairs. They are non-profit organizations, often registered as charities, and are mostly funded by their memberships. Some benefit from governmental contributions, the level of which varies greatly from country to country. Some organizations also benefit from the sale of consumer product-testing magazines, but this is by no means a universal characteristic.

National consumer groups are chiefly supported by organizations based at a regional level and are involved in a variety of areas, from welfare and tenancy to environmental and social issues linked to products. Consumer organizations exist to serve society and therefore act as members of civil society. In their role as consumers, citizens require a contact point where they can present their concerns about the products and services they buy. The consumer organization is an independent entity that represents "the voice of the consumer" and which can compensate for consumers' lack of knowledge by supplying independent information about products and services. Given the interface between consumer organizations and both consumers and companies, we elected to include the consumer organization as one of the prime stakeholders that would be able to give us an informed perspective on the social and environmental performance of companies, as well as the dynamic between companies and the consumers of their products and services.

10.2   Approach to corporate sustainability

Mission

While some consumer organization representatives we spoke to felt that sustainability, particularly corporate social responsibility, is not "in the typical realm" of the work of their organizations, most of those we spoke to had nevertheless a very clear view of the importance of their organization's contribution to sustainable consumer behavior and corporate transparency in this regard. They defined their mission variously as:

- Above all, providing information to consumers in order to allow an informed consumer choice – this included information about corporate sustainability performance.

- Ensuring that companies tell "the whole truth and nothing but the truth" about their products. Consumer organizations tend to want to distinguish the public relations activities of companies from their real efforts to be sustainable. Transparency is their goal. We found it interesting that consumer organizations claimed not to have a traditional activist-type stance of "naming and shaming," but rather one of stating the facts, describing the reality with scientific objectivity and allowing the consumer to make more sustainable choices based on the newly available criteria.
- One more idealistic mission was defined as "creating the responsible consumer." By helping the consumer to be more informed and aware, this helps the consumer to move away from egotistical goals.

Incentives and motives

The activities of consumer organizations are driven by a large "clientele"; one of our interviewees summed up their clientele as "basically the 6 billion people on this planet." While they work through consumer groups mostly on a national level, consumer organizations put time and resources only into activities that interest their consumer audience. Therefore, they only address the need for more information in social and environmental areas if the consumer asks for it. Most people we interviewed reiterated that their interest in sustainability management at companies is fueled by consumer interest:

> We see ourselves as a countervailing force for business and we are empowered by consumers to do so. (Consumer organization K)

The national consumer groups are very diverse in terms of interest and demand, structure, resources and experience. Their objectives with regard to social and environmental issues in developed countries are mainly anchored to sustainable consumption. Conversely, in developing countries the issues are access to consumption and introducing basic consumer protection legislation (regarding food safety, for example). However, it was clear that in terms of their overall mission and purpose, interviewees had very similar views.

Processes and tools

Our survey indicates the means by which consumer organizations assess companies (see Figure 10.1). We observe that consumer organizations make use of various means at their disposal, but principally their own

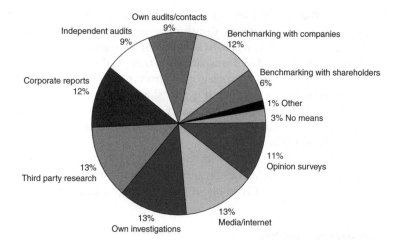

Figure 10.1   Means of assessing corporate social and environmental performance (consumer organizations)

and third-party research. This endorses the impression we got from interviewees – the consumer organization must predominantly base its message on robust research data.

From our interviews it was possible to validate this result and identify three avenues through which consumer organizations influence corporate sustainability performance using processes and tools:

Product testing. According to our interviewees, the most effective mechanism for influencing corporate sustainability performance is through product testing. It is in this area that consumer organizations have the most experience. However, testing is an expensive business and only some of the better-financed institutions can afford to carry it out. All but the wealthiest of consumer organizations outsource testing to scientific institutes. In Germany, however, the testing organization (Stiftung Warentest) is separate from the policy-building consumer organization (Verbraucherzentrale Bundesverband), although very close ties are maintained between the two organizations.

Several consumer organizations have magazines giving information on tested products. It is illustrative of the resource differences between national organizations that Stiftung Warentest publishes a monthly magazine with a distribution of 480,000 paying readers. In contrast, the National Consumer Association in Ireland is registered as a charity and is obliged to distribute its magazine free of charge and with no advertising. This kind of discrepancy makes it extremely difficult for less resource-rich organizations to finance product testing on sustainability criteria, let alone other activities that are considered more important.

Although environmental issues (use of energy, toxic impact and so on) have been part of the testing procedure for some years now, consumer organizations are in a "pilot" mode for social issues. An interesting development is the fact that consumer organizations are increasingly pooling resources for cost efficiency regarding testing in general. There is a lot of sharing of test results between organizations in Europe and this trend is certainly destined to increase according to our interviewees. However, when products are particular to a given country, the products are tested only by that country.

Our research revealed that in 2004 Stiftung Warentest launched a series of three pilot projects which aimed to assess corporate performance in the social arena, linked to salmon, outdoor jackets and detergent. To do this, the organization developed some core criteria and then some product-specific criteria (roughly 50 for each pilot project). The jury is out on whether the testing will lead to increased mainstreaming of testing of social criteria, but our interviewees indicated that interest in this testing had been "reasonable."

Policy initiatives. Consumer organizations lobby primarily for legislation but a few, such as Consumers International, have engaged themselves in groups striving for social standards (such as the forthcoming ISO 26000 social standard).

Interviewees working on international policy initiatives felt that much more work needed to be done in lobbying for more active WTO efforts in the social and environmental arena, although there was some doubt that global solutions can be found for many of the issues. However, the problem area once again is resources. Most of the national consumer organizations in Europe look toward Consumers International to carry out the global and cross-cutting policy work on their behalf. Interviewees clearly viewed the ISO 26000 social standard (which will be available in 2008) as a key solution to a current lack of global social standards for companies. The organization lobbies for national delegation representation at the ISO meetings and several Consumers International members have seats on the ISO advisory committee.

Corporate performance assessment at a national level. Using bilateral activities, consumer organizations in different countries (e.g. the Netherlands and Brazil) may analyze how the behavior of the same industry differs between the two countries. This can primarily be due to differences in legislation but it can also be lack of consistency in the application of standards. Within Europe, organizations can compare corporate claims about sustainability between countries. However, this is a difficult thing to do and in some cases, organizations are working with governments to correct legislation that acts against the interests of consumer information flow.

Few consumer organizations have enough human and financial resources to attend to the individual demands of companies. However, companies increasingly seem to be approaching them for their opinion and views, or for benchmarking their product strategies with them. There were few examples of consumer organizations interfacing directly with individual companies on a one-to-one basis. However, interviewees did see value in talking directly to industry. Organizations reported that they work on direct engagement with companies through various multi-stakeholder platforms such as the Ethical Certification and Labelling forum, the Sustainable Food Laboratory, and so on. Some consumer organizations also engage companies in discussion roundtables at a national governmental level. While such events do not take place very frequently (once or twice a year at most), interviewees saw these forums as opportunities to exchange viewpoints, with companies presenting what they are doing about sustainability, and consumer organizations suggesting how they (the companies) could do better.

Some organizations establish a ranking of companies that are acting in a sustainable and responsible way. For example, if companies have several standards or policies in place, they achieve higher scores than others. However, consumer organizations very much felt that they are dependent on self-reported data and information from companies, which made their assessment vulnerable to criticism.

Organizations such as Konsumentföreningen in Sweden have used longitudinal consumer surveys (regarding organic food, or GMOs) to great effect. By asking the same questions on the same topic every year, they can measure trends in consumer responses. The organization also looks at organic food prices and volumes and monitors these over time.

Overall, the people within consumer organizations who we interviewed felt that, except in the area of product testing, other approaches to corporate sustainability performance still lack scientific rigor.

In order to decide which actions are appropriate to influence companies, most organizations have a fairly informal process. Our survey indicated that the process for deciding on actions is primarily based on experiences made with previous activities (see Figure 10.2). Some organizations we interviewed are clearly in the process of putting into place more systematic processes to help decision-makers choose which strategies to use.

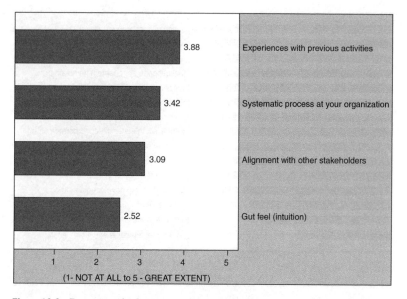

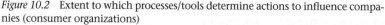

Figure 10.2 Extent to which processes/tools determine actions to influence companies (consumer organizations)

Criteria

Assessment criteria for corporate environmental and social performance are primarily oriented toward formal means by which consumer organizations can reach conclusions. Therefore, according to interviewees, the level of compliance with regulation, and the existence of policies and principles pertaining to social and environmental behavior are the most common basis for assessment. Our survey endorses our interview findings – again, most criteria are in the areas of compliance, accountability and transparency, and actions on social and environmental effects of production (see Figure 10.3). Note that environmental effects is a more important criterion in developed countries, where the membership base of consumer organizations is found, than in developing countries. Conversely, since there is some confidence in social effects of companies in Europe, consumer organizations lend more importance to social effects in developing countries than in developed countries.

In product testing, consumer organizations focus on product performance and have mostly concentrated on environmental impacts that affect sustainability (since the 1980s). Environmental impact testing is now very much a given part of product testing in Europe and has entered the mainstream of product-testing activity. Organizations tend

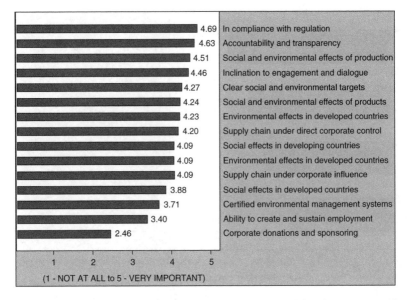

Figure 10.3   Importance of criteria for assessing corporate social and environmental performance (consumer organizations)

to check on whether companies have policies related to sustainability, apply ILO and OECD guidelines, and whether they use management systems such as ISO 14001 or SA 8000. Organizations examine corporate and other reports, and carry out internet reviews about companies. They also sometimes send questionnaires to companies (more the exception than the rule) or use a checklist of questions. Interviewees reported that up to 60 per cent of companies do not even answer their questionnaires (clearly an indication of the relative weight of consumer organization pressure on companies) – and those that do are normally global brands which, according to one interviewee, "recognize that it is better for their image to react." Interviewees commented that smaller companies do not generally react at all to their initiatives.

Health and product safety issues, as well as social issues in developing countries, have now put the production chain on the radar screen of consumer organizations. As yet, however, the criteria for social assessment are largely underdeveloped. Several pilot initiatives have been put in place by the wealthier consumer organizations to develop social indicators, but overall the interviewees' view was that consumer organizations are too small to develop their own approach – however, interviewees appeared to be highly aware of different methods and indicators for measuring sustainability performance, including social, within companies.

Consumer organizations are actively exploring ways in which the consumer can be informed about products without confusing them. Currently, they recognize that the number of labels and certification programs available are indeed confusing and lack the necessary degree of transparency. However, there were few ideas for alternatives other than the introduction of global standards. We came across a handful of examples of other methods considered effective by interviewees, such as the introduction of informative posters in supermarkets, or increased media exposure (particularly TV) to ensure increased consumer awareness. Campaigns to tackle the problem of consumer awareness at the grassroots, such as in primary and secondary schools, are not common.

Organizations were concerned that most companies use sustainability to further their public relations efforts. They cited companies such as Shell and IKEA for having sustainability strategies that go beyond mere public relations, but Enron came up as a typical example of a company that had a "good report but nothing behind it."

Unsurprisingly, our survey indicated that the demand from their immediate members is a primary determinant of consumer organizations' actions, as is the current and future severity of the issues (which is often also based on issue significance). Playing on corporate credibility and image are lesser criteria (see Figure 10.4).

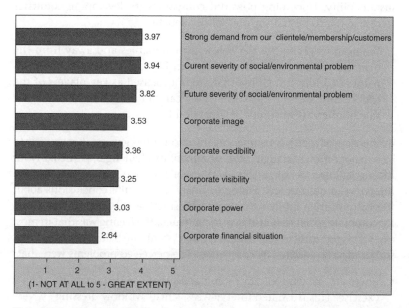

Figure 10.4 Extent to which criteria determine stakeholder actions to influence companies (consumer organizations)

10.3　Expectations and resulting corporate risks and opportunities

The people we spoke to mostly felt that progress in corporate sustainability performance is generally slow, with few new strategic directions, but that it is important that, on the whole, companies are moving in a positive direction. However, consumer organizations did not appear to have high expectations of companies in either the social area, in particular, or the environmental area. Existing standards and legislation mainly define the expectation. Several interviewees commented that they were happy that companies are at least "doing a bit" in these areas.

The Brent Spar episode with Shell and the Nike child labor scandals were often cited as reasons why branded companies see economic value in being proactive. Interviewees felt that branded companies are moving far quicker than companies that are further up the value chain. In their view, small and medium-sized enterprises are "practically doing nothing" beyond compliance in the social and environmental arena. Hard discounters (described as "a closed shop") were also perceived as presenting significant barriers to sustainable consumption. Several organizations have tried and failed to engage the hard discounters in providing information about products or even in taking part in the dialogue about sustainability. Upcoming powerful companies in developing countries were also felt to be "falling out" of the debate:

> We need to get to the tier below big companies and away from the dialogue on big companies in Western Europe. There are huge companies in India and China that are not focused as key players of the CSR debate. I don't think that these can fall off the radar screen for much longer. (Consumer organization K)

In the view of many consumer organization interviewees, this was felt to be a major problem fraught with sustainability challenges, particularly for the agriculture, textiles, toys and mobile phone production sectors. Interviewees did not feel willing to reach any definite conclusions about the status of their influence on corporate sustainability performance. But, for corporate social responsibility in particular, the feeling was that in most cases "it is too early to tell" and that new systems are being developed that still need to be adopted by companies. The perceived problems were that:

- There are, as yet, too many companies that use sustainability as a PR exercise. This frustrated interviewees, since "window dressing" is very quickly identified and seen for what it is, resulting in companies losing credibility.

- A far better understanding by their organizations and by companies of corporate sustainability management is necessary before any conclusions can be reached.
- More attention certainly needs to be given to social issues.
- There is scant motivation for companies to move more quickly, since "leaders tend not to be rewarded and laggards are not punished."
- There is a lot of confusion among consumers about the different systems, standards, guidelines and norms that companies use particularly to assess their supply chains.
- Companies are generally against new standards and legislation.

Overall, interviewees were convinced that "the consumer voice" is not being listened to by companies. Shareholders are perceived by consumer organizations to be the major stakeholders for companies, and interviewees definitely felt that more of a balanced approach is required in the short to medium term. Consumer distrust and skepticism of companies was apparent in cases cited by several interviewees. One interviewee cited the case of a supermarket chain that replaced free plastic bags with paper bags (to be paid for), which led to a public perception that the supermarket was simply trying to "cash in" to earn more money rather than the intended objective (that the chain be perceived as a first mover in environmental action).

Where companies have sustainability strategies, their organizations were largely perceived as unaligned to these strategies. In particular, marketing and product service departments were seen as falling out of the sustainability alignment model:

> All those glossy brochures ... and the consumer is still totally confused about what companies are doing about sustainability. The problem is that those interfacing with customers filter out the indicators that companies are doing something. The consumer is left with little to no information. Glossy brochures benefit employees, but not consumers. (Consumer organization A)

One interviewee proposed his perceived solution:

> A better link has to be made between what companies have in reports and those building the brand. Consumers are not interested in reports, but they are interested in brands. At the brand level, there should be people working with the issues and trying to link them to the brand. (Consumer organization J)

Most interviewees felt that the key for companies is to provide more transparency to their consumers, and that it is extremely likely that pressure from civil society for more transparency will continue and increase. However, interviewees realized that this is a major challenge for companies:

> There are secrets in trade that dictate that companies are not transparent on certain issues (so that their competition does not get comparative advantage). This means that there is a lack of transparency that affects social responsibility. (Consumer organization F)

Many interviewees did not empathize with the current perceived reticence within companies to have imposed standards and legislative solutions that would, in their view, "level the playing field." In addition, interviewees felt that a change of attitude to "listening to consumers" would benefit companies in that they would be more aware of consumers' needs and their competitive environment:

> Companies base themselves too much on "buying" criteria, and then the trends escape them. (Consumer organization E)

Interviewees felt that many of the sustainability issues companies are dealing with are "bigger" than the companies themselves (such as problems with AIDS and obesity) and that increasingly companies will have to call on tools like multi-stakeholder dialogues and partnerships in order to resolve and mitigate the issues that are economically relevant to them.

In general, most interviewees felt that companies should "do something" and that the very fact they are moving at all is creating synergies and opportunities that otherwise would not have been identified. The advice of interviewees for laggard companies was that they should at least set the pendulum in motion, getting independent advice as to how they might go about incorporating sustainability into their strategies, or appointing a coordinator internally to take responsibility for pushing this agenda by reviewing the value chain, helping to identify and prioritize issues, and then choosing those that the company could focus on.

Companies were largely seen as being reticent about adopting a sustainable approach to doing business. The reason for this, according to our interviewees, was simply that there are no economic benefits perceived by companies. However, our interviewees also pointed out that the consumer is rapidly changing and that companies would do well to recognize this fact:

> Products today are not very different to 20 years ago. What has changed is the public. Years ago, the main preoccupation was "How

do I buy a washing machine?" There was more concern with basics to make life easier. Now these basic products inspire consumer confidence and there is a shift in concerns particularly to food products for example; this is a very interesting subject for the public to read about as it affects them personally. A lot is changing and will change, particularly in the food area. (Consumer organization B)

Our interviewees also felt strongly that sustainability could be used as a differentiation factor by companies and that this potential is currently not being exploited. For example, there was a concern that retail stores, when faced with intense competition from hard discounters, tend to underestimate the option they have – rather than joining the price wars – of "marketing the best" and giving more shelf space to organic and sustainable products as a clear differentiation factor over the discounters.

Our survey indicates that, overall, consumer organizations are much more satisfied with corporate compliance with regulation and the presence of social and environmental systems than, say, companies' performance as regards their influence on the supply chain, environmental and social effects of their activities in developing countries or, indeed, their degree of transparency (see Figure 10.5).

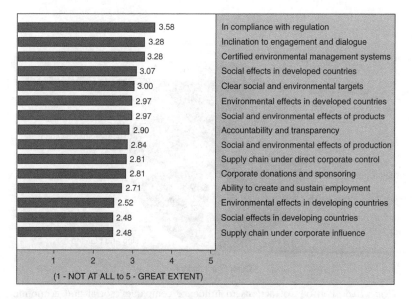

Value	Category
3.58	In compliance with regulation
3.28	Inclination to engagement and dialogue
3.28	Certified environmental management systems
3.07	Social effects in developed countries
3.00	Clear social and environmental targets
2.97	Environmental effects in developed countries
2.97	Social and environmental effects of products
2.90	Accountability and transparency
2.84	Social and environmental effects of production
2.81	Supply chain under direct corporate control
2.81	Corporate donations and sponsoring
2.71	Ability to create and sustain employment
2.52	Environmental effects in developing countries
2.48	Social effects in developing countries
2.48	Supply chain under corporate influence

(1 - NOT AT ALL to 5 - GREAT EXTENT)

Figure 10.5 Level of satisfaction of consumer organizations with corporate environmental and social performance

10.4   Current stakeholder strategies

Actions and their effectiveness

Our survey indicated that the main actions that consumer organizations engage in to influence companies' environmental and social performance are, firstly, engaging with companies, and, secondly, praising and blaming. Lobbying for additional regulation and legislation, standards and guidelines and labeling and certification schemes altogether make up 33 per cent of corporate activity. Praising and blaming is carried out through objective testing mechanisms, since interviews revealed that organizations do not see themselves as activists in the traditional "NGO" sense (see Figure 10.6).

Consumer organizations in Europe vary a great deal in terms of their size and level of professionalism (ranging from skeletal organizations operating with volunteers to full-blown professionally structured operations). Therefore we could identify no common set of processes in place to allow them to decide on appropriate actions at a national level. The issues they select as targets pertain to the very current interests of the consumer: GMOs, organic food, child labor, human rights, transport (of bottled water, for example).

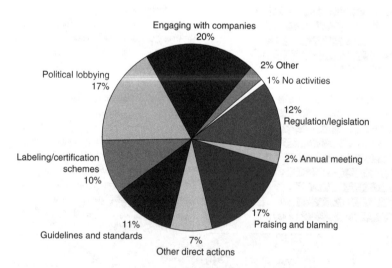

Figure 10.6 Portfolio of actions to influence companies' social and economic performance (consumer organizations)

However, on a European and international level, there are more defined processes. Consumers International coordinates international policy issues and BEUC (Bureau Européen des Unions de Consommateurs) coordinates national members at a European level. At a European level, a CSR working group meets two to three times per year to select topics, discuss methodology and formulate working groups (representatives of groups tend to volunteer from different national organizations) around selected topics. In this way, costs are shared and results can be jointly published and more widely disseminated. In smaller organizations, the board sets targets, but individuals may come up with ideas that, through informal discussions with decision-makers in a "bottom-up" process, may be pushed through to implementation. In larger organizations, matrix structures enable flexible approaches to issues and strategies are well worked out; Conservation International, for example, works on a three-year strategy. Other organizations establish priority areas with standing working groups that meet twice a year. Overall, sustainable development is dealt with rather more horizontally than vertically within organizations in order to capitalize on the (sometimes-scant) resources available.

While influence in the environmental arena is not seen as a big area of concern for products produced in Europe due to now-strict European legislation and standards, interviewees nevertheless felt that attention to environmental matters has greatly fluctuated over time depending on different factors, such as political interest, price of energy and impending legislation. Also, with the increasing outsourcing of manufacturing to Southeast Asia, interviewees felt a lot of transparency has been lost on environmental criteria and that the importance of social criteria has taken on a new dimension. Many interviewees perceived the success or otherwise of their activities in the area of corporate social responsibility in particular as very difficult to evaluate since they have only been involved with it during the past five years.

In 1999 VKI, the Austrian consumer organization, carried out a project called "The Ethics of Consumption," followed by a conference on the subject, financed by the European Commission, in 2000. This helped to stir interest in environmental and social consumer issues within the hitherto passive consumer organizations around Europe. This was the beginning of a process that prompted the Nordic organizations (Denmark, Finland, Norway, Sweden and Iceland) to collaborate and to publish a jointly financed CSR test for the first time (on jeans); the results were published in early 2002. Since then, there have been several examples of jointly financed CSR testing of products or simply a sharing of information about products:

> Before, only the wealthy organizations could afford to pay for CSR surveys and what we call "ethic" testing (those that have many subscribers to their magazines, e.g. Germany, Britain and the Netherlands). We published our first so-called ethic test in October 2000 – we financed it ourselves, but it was very expensive to do it alone. Sharing resources is the best solution. (Consumer organization B)

A "CSR working group" was founded at a European level in November 2002, which facilitated the sharing of resources for CSR surveys and testing. Several representatives of consumer organizations that we spoke to expressed their concern at the fact that much of their activity depended on the reigning political climate within the country. In some countries, the finances of consumer organizations partially depend on government and this contribution is heavily influenced by governmental interest in sustainability issues. There was not much faith in governmental capacities to instigate change in the status quo:

> The public expectation is much higher than real practice. Consumers basically expect of their government that products not ethically produced should be stopped at the border. However, the expectations of government regarding companies are decreasing – it takes a scandal to shake things up. (Consumer organization I)

Consumer organizations do not see themselves as forcing companies to take particular actions, but rather as a reliable source of consumer information based on a solid research base (perceived as just as powerful as activism). Indeed, this was seen as being the main strength of the consumer organization by interviewees. Some saw NGOs, such as Greenpeace, usurping their role to some extent (Greenpeace has also carried out some product testing).

Overall, interviewees also pointed out the urgency for companies to be "doing something" in the short term:

> If we raise awareness and nothing can be done, people turn away as we are introducing these concepts gradually to our members. Some say that we are going too fast. (Consumer organization I)

Interviewees at consumer organizations felt that although the sharing of resources among European organizations has led to very positive effects, their own shortcomings are due to lack of resources:

> Every week, companies contact us to participate in a dialogue on these issues. Unfortunately, we do not have the resources to meet these demands. The demands are increasing, which is indicative of increasing interest in these issues. (Consumer organization C)

However, interviewees felt that until there are better tools for knowing the nature of the company they are interfacing with, increased direct dialogue will probably not be forthcoming. As one interviewee put it:

> We do not want to be linked to bad companies. (Consumer organization B)

However, dialogue with companies on more neutral multi-stakeholder platforms was deemed to be very effective and necessary.

The number of product tests based on social criteria still remains extremely low – out of the 140 product tests that are carried out by Stiftung Warentest in any one year, only three to four are CSR tests and even these are being carried out on a pilot basis. In order to assess whether the CSR tests are influencing consumer behavior, the experts we spoke to felt that similar tests have to be carried out every year over a five-year period. Consumer organizations have observed that, customarily, if the testing is consistent over the years, it does start to affect consumer behavior. This was the case with environmental tests that were initiated in the mid-1980s:

> Companies now expect that some of our tests will be on environmental and safety aspects and they prepare for this. We mainly looked at products from the time they were used and disposed of. Now the proposition is to go into social issues in the supply chain and there is the same kind of discussion that we had about environment in the mid-1980s. (Consumer organization H)

Also, consumer organizations fully realize that only the better-off consumers can afford to make choices based on social and environmental criteria and that the audience reached by their published magazines is sometimes not representative of populations as a whole. However, the "reach" of consumer magazines produced by consumer organizations is increasing.

Survey respondents viewed regulation first and foremost as the most effective action to influence companies, followed by "praising and

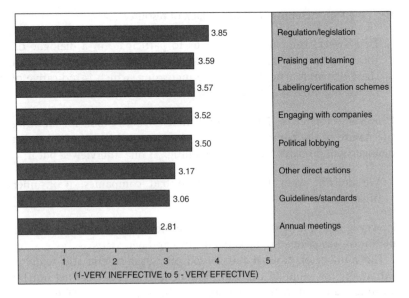

3.85	Regulation/legislation
3.59	Praising and blaming
3.57	Labeling/certification schemes
3.52	Engaging with companies
3.50	Political lobbying
3.17	Other direct actions
3.06	Guidelines/standards
2.81	Annual meetings

(1-VERY INEFFECTIVE to 5 - VERY EFFECTIVE)

Figure 10.7   Perceived effectiveness of actions in influencing companies' social and environmental performance – regardless of whether used by the individual stakeholder or not (consumer organizations)

blaming," labeling and certification schemes and engaging with companies (see Figure 10.7). One can surmise, therefore, that pressure from consumer organizations to legislate is likely to continue and even increase (this was endorsed by interviewees). Indeed, consumer organizations are actually less convinced that guidelines and standards are appropriate means of action to influence corporate sustainability performance, although labeling and certification schemes appear to have more of their confidence.

Determinants of effectiveness

Interviewees' perceptions of factors contributing to success with their actions to influence environmental and social performance were as follows:

- Extensive consumer reach.
- Effective media work (particularly television shows/appearances).
- The visibility and increased brand recognition sought after by major companies, making them increasingly better targets for campaigning.
- The democratic set-ups and consensus-building frameworks of most consumer organizations imply that strategies are coherent and are supported by staff.

- Longevity and continuity of staff. Many of the people we spoke to at national organizations were loyal and dedicated staff who had been with their organizations for many years.
- While having few resources was regarded as a drawback, the fact that most organizations are small, nimble and able to move quickly without many bureaucratic hurdles was regarded as an advantage by many interviewees.
- In addition, in smaller countries, consumer organization players move in a political and corporate environment that allows people to know each other well and to reach mutual understandings about concepts and actions. An interviewee commented, "We work in a multi-layer fashion."
- A handful of charismatic and visionary leaders within the consumer organizations were perceived as having promoted great steps forward in the sustainability agenda; in general, passion about the topic goes a long way in consumer organizations toward achieving action.
- But, above all, the fact that policies and actions are grounded in solid and robust research.

Interviewees commented on a number of obstacles that, conversely, jeopardized their efforts:

- Primarily, a lack of financial and human resource capacity.
- The vagueness of the concept of social responsibility (CSR).
- The slow nature of mindset change within companies and lack of alignment behind existing strategies.
- The disconcerting contradiction between what the consumer reports as an interest and concern for environmental and social issues and his actual behavior. Consumer organizations conclude that without clear labeling and standards, the consumer will continue to "vote with his wallet."
- The many existing eco-labels that confuse the consumer; an absence of clear labeling options.
- The absence of transparent standards allowing consumers to make informed consumer choices.
- The unwillingness of companies and sometimes whole sectors to participate in testing efforts.
- The sheer number of issues that the consumer organization has to look at, which is a major drain on resources and jeopardizes their potential to influence the global arena on social and environmental issues.

Our survey gave us a perspective on consumer organization interviewees' perceived reaction of companies to their actions (see Figure 10.8). Clearly, global and branded companies have more of a tendency to engage in dialogue. However, consumer organizations also perceived that companies have a tendency to increase PR and lobbying efforts or act defensively rather than proactively change business processes. Indeed, many interviewees expressed their frustration with superficial corporate PR strategies that do little to change the status quo. We conclude that the influence of consumer organizations on companies appears to be relatively constrained.

The reason companies might rush to PR strategies is apparent in consumer organizations' views of the drivers of corporate success that are most affected by their actions. In the view of our survey respondents, customer loyalty, corporate reputation and brand value all stand to be most sharply affected by consumer organizations' actions; this is where consumer organizations can have most impact. Note, however, that access to markets and capital, and indeed to the talent that makes up their workforce is, in the view of the respondents, hardly affected (see Figure 10.9).

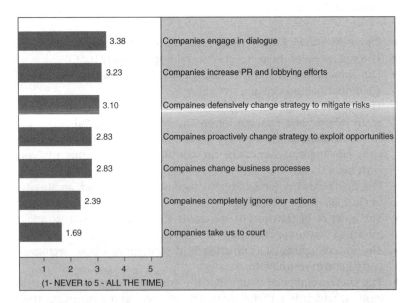

Figure 10.8 Frequency of corporate reactions to stakeholder action (consumer organizations)

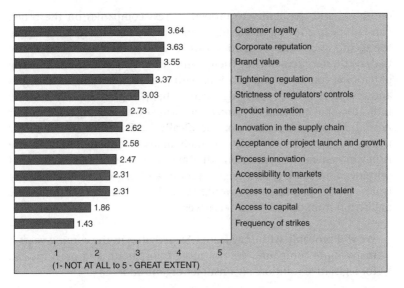

Figure 10.9 Extent to which stakeholder actions affect corporate value drivers (consumer organizations)

10.5 Future trends

While many of the current strategies and approaches of consumer organizations are likely to remain in place, it is not clear whether the momentum of testing the social impacts of production will increase significantly in the future. Interviewees felt that it will largely depend on consumer interest in these matters. At the time of writing, surveys have indicated that there is an "average" consumer interest in the pilot CSR testing program being carried out by Stiftung Warentest in Germany. The jury is still out on whether the tests will be repeated. The problems outlined reveal that the testing is often, of necessity, based on subjective criteria, whereas it is possible to be more objective with other criteria of product testing. Surveys carried out by VKI in 2000 and 2004 showed that more than 70 per cent of the Austrian population want information about the social and environmental performance of companies and feel that consumers can influence companies' behavior in these areas. Interviewees from that organization confirmed that they observe increasing demands for such criteria to be applied in testing.

In addition, efforts to enter into dialogue directly with companies are clearly avenues that require further attention from the consumer organizations, although this does seem to be dependent on resources on the one hand and the ability to properly assess companies on the other. Pan-European efforts and sharing of information are likely to dominate the agenda as consumer organizations get used to their newfound ability to draw on resources outside their own national organizations. Merging of national consumer organizations with a related marrying of synergies and resources is also clearly destined to happen gradually. There were indicators that consumer organizations will also be looking internally at how they can restructure, not specifically to deal with sustainability issues, but in order to deal with their many fragmented and diverse issues in general. Organizations that are better positioned to focus on priorities are also likely to strengthen the attention given to sustainability issues. However, companies would do well to listen to the following prediction from one of our interviewees:

> We will probably withdraw from CSR activities in the coming years if many more companies are not more transparent, and press instead for legislative solutions. (Consumer organization C)

The danger for companies is that because of scant resources, consumer organizations will revert to pressing for more legislation – an easier and less resource-intensive option than trying to cut through the tangled web of differing standards, norms, approaches and actions.

Consumer organizations broadly support global standards such as ISO and expect that a process will put criteria in place to make verification of corporate sustainability performance easier, and facilitate communication of corporate sustainability performance to the consumer.

> We will work more on the ISO standards; in my view, this is a possible solution to the huge number of existing codes, norms and guidelines. The ISO standards are promising to become the "de facto" standard among industries. (Consumer organization K)

The trend to move vast amounts of the manufacturing bases in Europe to China and India, for example, is regarded by consumer organizations as a considerable threat to already achieved standards within Europe. The tensions created on the environmental and social fronts are clearly illustrated in this interviewee comment:

> In China, environmental standards are in existence, but are not enforced. We cannot lower environmental standards in Europe as we are "suffocating" already. On the social side in China, labor rights are

also in place but are not enforced. Unions are only staged unions. Practiced standards are lower, yet companies are moving business to China wholesale. We have to find ways of dealing with these dilemmas. Companies are only imposing environmental and CSR management systems on the first step upwards in the supply chain. And yet the wages that Chinese people get are less than 1 percent of the final price of a product! (Consumer organization I)

Also, it was clear from our interviews that there are issues related to public mindset and sustainable consumption that are not necessarily within corporate control – the comment was made by several interviewees that global companies cannot answer every concern. No matter how good companies' corporate sustainability performance is, some of those we interviewed felt that for a sustainable world, the consumer will ultimately have to change behavior, by, for example, opting for more locally produced products and in this way limiting gross transport eco-inefficiencies. However, our interviewees felt that the likelihood of such mindsets changing in the near future is slim.

10.6 Conclusion

Consumer organizations on an international level appear to have reached a conclusion on their main dilemma of lack of resources: They are convinced that the development of ISO standards of social responsibility is a more cost-effective way to get companies to engage in corporate sustainability action, particularly in the social arena. The push for corporate sustainability performance from consumers appears to be increasing, but is still relatively weak. Overall, consumer organizations are not entirely convinced of their own strength vis à vis the consumer and particularly with regard to environmental and social issues:

I think that consumer organizations are not as mighty as they themselves think they are. Consumerism was a strong movement 20 years ago. Now it has lost momentum. (Consumer organization F)

As consumer organizations respond to their consumer clientele and this clientele only, a lot depends on how the consumer moves in the coming years in this domain. Currently, interviewees stated, consumers in Europe do not have these issues foremost on their agenda since employment and cheap products are their main concerns.

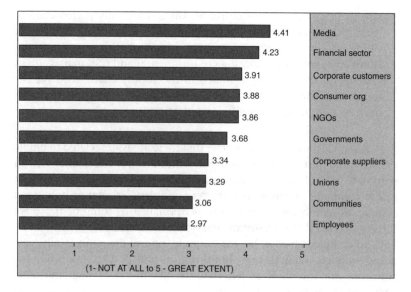

Figure 10.10   Extent to which stakeholders are able to influence corporate behavior (consumer organizations)

However, interviewees indicated that the consumer simply assumes that companies are doing the right thing. The consumer looks toward governments and legislators to stop goods at the borders of their countries should they not be produced in an environmentally and socially acceptable manner. In the absence of clear and transparent labeling, the consumer, according to most interviewees, can hardly be held responsible for making unsustainable choices. The focus, they feel, must be on governments and companies for now, and once the consumer is in a position to choose, the focus can be more fully on consumer behavior.

According to our survey, consumer organizations tend to view firstly the media and then the financial sector as the most influential stakeholders over corporate behavior. Customers are in third place. Clearly, the stakeholders that are of most economic relevance are the most influential. However, they viewed themselves in a very close fourth place almost on a par with NGOs (see Figure 10.10), ahead of government and considerably ahead of communities and employees.

Our interview research indicated that consumer organizations have far from exhausted their potential. They currently appear to be rallying forces and becoming more of a presence, and this seems to have been a particular feature of the last five years. However, political and economic climates in Europe do not seem to point toward an accelerated or significant strengthening of their sphere of influence as regards social and environmental performance of companies in the near future.

11
Media: Indifferent Observers of Corporate Sustainability

Simon Tywuschik

This chapter presents empirical evidence collected from the media through 32 semi-structured interviews (average duration of 60 minutes each) and 30 self-completion questionnaires. We greatly acknowledge the participation of journalists of major European TV stations, radio stations, print media and the internet (names of institutions not displayed to respect respondents' wishes for confidentiality). The participating organizations were chosen by such criteria as their background and relative importance and type to provide a comprehensive and balanced view on Europe's media. The 32 interviews were conducted with media in the following countries: UK (9 interviews), Germany (8), Spain (5), France (4), Benelux (3) and Scandinavia (3). We always interviewed the journalist in charge of sustainability. In some cases, this position coincides with that of the chief editor.

We developed a framework distinguishing four strategies media can assume in the context of corporate sustainability (see Table 11.1).

This framework is based on the level of analysis and the frequency of publication. For example, a strategic sustainability approach is characterized by regular coverage of corporate sustainability and in-depth analysis.

Next to a more generic approach, the framework also features the two types of mass communication (internet news, news agencies) and media with a niche approach (magazines with special reports, dailies, weeklies with special supplements).

The focus of our investigation was media with a (1) strategic focus, (2) generic focus and (3) media with a niche strategy in sustainability. Mass communication media were excluded from our interviews, as overall they lacked detailed corporate sustainability coverage. Our self-completion questionnaire targeted journalists in business-to-business (B2B) media and, to a lesser extent, in consumer media.

Table 11.1 Types of strategic orientation in corporate sustainability coverage

		Level of Analysis	
		General	*In-depth*
Frequency of Publication	**Regular**	Mass Communication	Strategic Approach
	Irregular	Generic Approach	Niche Approach

The chapter is structured as follows: First, we provide general background information about the stakeholder. In section 11.2, we describe the stakeholder's approach to corporate sustainability (mission, incentives and motives, processes and tools, criteria and expectations). In section 11.3, we describe our key findings on current stakeholder strategies, their actions and effectiveness as well as success factors and obstacles. In section 11.4, we elaborate on future trends. We conclude the chapter in section 11.5 by highlighting the key findings and implications.

11.1 Stakeholder background

Media can be defined as an institution that mediates viewpoints and information. It can be segmented along various criteria, such as the range of subjects it covers, criteria of assessment, its reach, its mission, popularity or technological platform. Media are monitored by institutions and organizations on various administrative levels (EU, national and federal) in order to ensure neutrality and plurality in contents. In Western European countries, the media are widely accessible. More than 90 per cent of the population has access to television and radio and the consumption of print media is relatively high. The access and frequency of use varies by country due to differences in cultural, political and technological conditions. For instance, internet use is significantly higher in Scandinavia than in Southern Europe. In the following, we will provide a brief overview on print media (dailies, magazines) and electronic media (TV, radio and internet).

Print media

Print media are comprised of newspapers and magazines. Newspapers contain news, information and advertising and they are usually printed on low-cost paper. They cover areas of general or special interest and are most often published daily or weekly, such as the *Financial Times* or *The Times* (both UK, dailies) or *Die Zeit* (weekly, Germany). In contrast, magazines are periodical publications containing a variety of articles, financed by advertising and purchased by readers.

One can also distinguish between:

- Consumer titles targeting a specific *societal group* defined by age, interest, and business titles (or business-to-business titles), targeting a specific *professional group*, defined by position and function.
- General-interest titles, which appeal to a broad spectrum of readers and highly specialist titles covering particular themes or interests.

Consumer magazines are focused on the public and are usually available through retail outlets and increasingly on the internet. They range from general-interest to highly specialist titles. A subset of consumer magazines is the customer magazine, a publication similar in format and style to a consumer magazine but issued by a corporation. Such magazines are usually free to the reader; the quantity of advertising that they carry varies greatly; and their circulations range from very small to very large – in some countries, customer magazines have among the highest-circulation of all magazines. The other broad category of magazines is the business magazine, sometimes called a trade magazine or B2B magazine. These publications carry news and other information relevant to a particular profession or industry. Some are sold through retail outlets – such as *Forbes* and *Business Week* – and are in many respects similar to the current-affairs-oriented consumer magazines.

TV, radio and internet

The TV and radio stations in Western Europe are embedded in a dualistic structure between government and the free market as their shareholders.

- The leading *private* media companies (publishers and broadcasters) active in Western Europe are Bertelsmann, Time Warner, Reed Elsevier, Axel Springer, The News Corporation and Pearson.[1]
- The main *public* broadcasters (TV and radio) are BBC (UK), ARD (Germany), TVE (Spain) and France Television (France).

Segmentation along program types relevant for the subject of corporate sustainability can be established by differentiating between (1) environmental and knowledge, (2) politics and economics, (3) news, (4) lifestyle and service and (5) talk show programs. Programs outside this scope, such as (6) entertainment, (7) movies or (8) fictions, are not relevant for the subject of corporate sustainability. Again, one can distinguish between general and special interest channels. While general interest stations cover various aspects of societal, political and economic affairs, special interest stations focus on certain well-defined areas. In the context of electronic media, we define the internet as a worldwide network of independent networks, serving communication, information and other activities.

Overall, we discovered that few journalists specialize in corporate sustainability in Europe. We also observed that media companies such as *The Guardian* (Print Media, UK) or *BBC* (Television, UK) engage themselves – as corporations – in corporate sustainability by, for example, issuing their own corporate sustainability reports.

11.2   Approach to corporate sustainability

Mission

The principal mission of media is to report and inform the public on the most pressing issues by interacting with companies or institutions. We note that across different types of media (internet, TV, radio and print media), corporate sustainability, as a subject, is located in different departments, such as finance, management, environment, economics or political editorials. It is often combined with the core subjects of those departments to ensure relevance to the individual target audience. For example, the subject of sustainable investments is discussed in various contexts of financial, ethical, social and ecological standards. Coverage of corporate sustainability as the core and only topic is rather unusual.

The majority of print media covers corporate sustainability as a side issue in the economics, business or management section. This points to a generic rather than strategic approach:

> The mission of our magazine is the presentation of relevant topics for our readers, which are business people or investors. There is no debate about the basic principles of the market economy: We do not have a direct mission in social and environmental reporting, but cover these issues when of relevance for the readership. (B2B title, General Interest, UK)

> We are neither defensive nor offensive, but entirely objective. In general, we write what we think is right. For sustainability, this means that companies should take their responsibility. We look at companies where they are, object, ask critical questions and report and comment on them. (Consumer title, General Interest, Finland)

However, we also discovered dailies and periodicals that act more strategically in terms of corporate sustainability, although such coverage remains a niche (in-depth but sporadic):

> We are examining if companies are improving their production, procurement and products, looking at energy and chemical companies especially. Topic-wise global warming is particularly relevant: Here we observe how companies deal with it. My background is as an environmental consultant and I also have a master in environmental economics. I inform the readership on environmental progress in the industry, regulation and identifying trends. (B2B title, Specific Interest, London, UK)

> Our readership is accountancy-related people, so corporate sustainability is of importance to us. (B2B title, Specific Interest, UK).

> Energy risk, energy market and electricity generation by coal, gas and oil are our topics. Recently the magazine has become interested in green issues. (B2B title, Specific Interest, UK)

A strategic approach tends to reflect a different mission, such as challenging the social and environmental performance of companies:

> Our core mission is to inform and criticize on the corporate sustainability practice and situation of global companies (B2B title, Specific Interest, UK).

Similar to print media, electronic media also frequently link corporate sustainability to other – more mainstream – topics such as business and finance, environment and science. They do not pursue a strategic mission on corporate sustainability:

> The reason for our coverage of corporate sustainability is that we principally think that a discussion on location-bound investment factors is important. We investigate, to what extent sustainability is a driver for investments in Germany. We look at sustainability from an economic-political perspective. (Public TV station, General Interest, Germany)

> We, as an editorial, provide sustainability material for different programs, such as political, economical, environmental and news programs. (Public TV station, General Interest, Germany)

Coverage of corporate environmental performance appears to occur more frequently in public channels. Employment-related issues are often discussed in the context of politics and economics. Clearly, the frequency, the quality and the focus of corporate sustainability coverage is also dependent on the country. It appears to be most frequent in the UK. Our interviews also suggest that print media often assign independent sustainability experts (freelancers) to cover sustainability in their editions. There are advantages to this strategy:

1. Corporate sustainability is far from being part of the mainstream. However, in case of a peak in the public attention – the editorial team can decide to put a special edition on the market, without changing its long-term focus and mission.
2. Freelance journalists have a high level of expertise and ensure an adequate level of quality necessary for up market print media.

We conclude that media have no direct mission with regard to corporate sustainability. They only cover corporate social and environmental performance when it is of relevance to their target group.

Incentives and motives

The main motive for reporting on corporate sustainability and related social and environmental issues is to provide the target audience with relevant information. Particularly B2B media, with both a special and general interest, track ongoing developments to ensure comprehensive coverage of corporate sustainability as a business topic.

Media develop appropriate formats and sections to satisfy their readers' need for information. General interest media from the B2B segment include corporate sustainability if it is in line with their actual mission.

> Our incentive is to improve financial performance for our readers, hence social and environmental performance might be of relevance. (B2B, General Interest, UK)

> Our readership is interested in how companies manage those [social and environmental] issues, so we inform them on how companies deal with the issues; we serve our readers. (B2B, General Interest, UK and Germany)

Similarly, special interest B2B magazines (in our sample, e.g. insurance, energy, chemical and accounting) report on corporate sustainability in the context of the industry or topic under consideration. Coverage occurs if corporate sustainability overlaps with the special interest focus:

> Also where people can save money with environmental doing, we look at compliance risk (B2B magazine, Special Interest, UK).

Our incentive is to inform our clientele on new risks, damages and potential costs. In this context, we analyze also social and environmental risks. (B2B, Special Interest, London, UK)

Our incentive is to inform about best practices in corporate sustainability management. (B2B, General Interest, UK)

Consumer magazines with a general interest focus (such as high-circulation newspapers) have a slightly different incentive to report on corporate sustainability. Given their multi-focal orientation, corporate sustainability is considered a "connector" between political and economic issues.

Corporate sustainability must really be dealt with, as "business is not an island." Stakeholder value is representing the society better than do shareholders and customers. (Freelancer journalist in Sustainability, UK)

Sustainability is an element necessary to improve our societies. (Consumer title, General Interest, UK)

Concerning TV and radio, a highly relevant factor for coverage of corporate sustainability is the government and its involvement in public TV and radio stations across Europe. Governments set certain guidelines and standards on programs, which leads to a more regular coverage of corporate sustainability on TV and radio:

We have a mission to outline the societal conversation in the exact proportion in our program: Unemployment, business relocation and sustainability are such topics, we try to deal with the worries and questions of our audience. (Public TV station, General Interest, Germany)

In TV, specialized programs often deal with sustainability topics of wide general interest such as unemployment, pollution or general environmental topics. Pure corporate sustainability formats are rare.

In conclusion, media attempts to satisfy the presumed interest of its target groups, which is rather low overall when it comes to corporate sustainability. This means that coverage of corporate sustainability tends to increase during times of high public awareness (corporate scandals, environmental accidents).

Processes and tools relating to corporate sustainability

Overall, processes and tools are determined by general guidelines for editorial processes, as well as on style and content. They are set by internal house guidelines and form a certain basic layer for journalists to fulfill their daily tasks. Furthermore, media must also comply with regulatory requirements and, to some degree, certain professional and ethical standards.

Assessing corporate performance. To obtain necessary information, journalists rely on a certain set of tools. They start usually with desk research, investigating the background of the specific subject and then they conduct interviews and collect further information through personal contacts. Here we note that journalists often work along established networks of contacts in academia, industry and stakeholders, particularly NGOs and financial institutions. We observed a positive relationship between the educational background of the interviewee and the complexity of the toolset applied and between the toolset and the analytic level of the content.

The choice of processes and methods is strongly linked to the context, in which issues are elaborated on: certain data and internet sources may deliver sufficient information for the journalist and make any use of other tools superfluous. In other situations, a more in-depth investigation on corporate behavior and its effects may require a direct engagement with other stakeholders, experts or corporations.

> Direct engagement with companies is always possible (personal interviews and local investigation) when producing reports. I've experienced some companies that are proactive, and others that show less inclination to engagement and dialogue. The companies, which tend to be very proactive, are rather large companies. (B2B, Special Interest, UK)

> I read all the financial and the corporate sustainability reports of the Dutch listed companies. I speak a lot with NGOs and thus get a lot of information from the outside. I think interviews are best suited for a sound assessment. (Consumer title, General Interest, Netherlands)

The use of external experts is particularly essential when it comes to new and complex issues:

> The more complex the issue, the more third party involvement is necessary. (B2B magazine, Special Interest, UK)

Our quantitative data align with the insights we gained in the interviews. The most widely used sources to assess corporate social and environmental performance are the media/internet, annual and sustainability reports and third party research (e.g. NGO studies and expertise) (Figure 11.1).

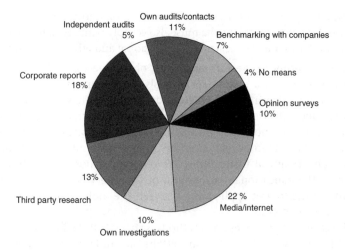

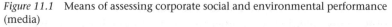

Figure 11.1   Means of assessing corporate social and environmental performance (media)

In light of the marginal relevance of corporate sustainability to media's mission, it is not surprising that overall low-cost tools such as the media/internet and corporate reports are the dominant tools. However, we also ascertain that some journalists and media specializing in the area of corporate sustainability have more advanced sets of tools:

> We use sustainability standards, which are on the market. We also examine the reputation level of the corporation, ask NGOs, industry and financial analysts and try to find sector-based sustainability measures. In addition, we rely on tools from WWF and other organizations (e.g. labels). (B2B, Special Interest, UK)

Determining actions to influence companies.   Decisions to cover issue A rather than B are generally based on past experiences and intuition.

> Journalists and journalism tend to be rather intuitive. (B2B, General Interest, UK)

> The fundamentals are always the same, there are not many systems or procedures to follow, no general applicable standards. (B2B, Special Interest, Scandinavia)

As Figure 11.2 shows, our quantitative data deviate slightly from these findings: However, the surprisingly high mean value of systematic

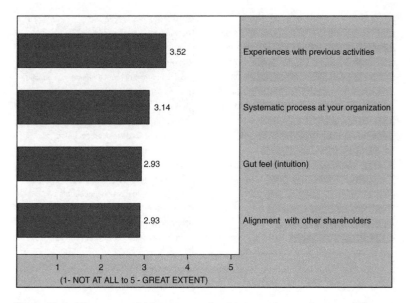

Figure 11.2 Extent to which processes/tools determine actions to influence companies (media)

processes is most likely due to a self-presentation bias (i.e. respondents do not want to be perceived as unsystematic).

Criteria

Assessing corporate performance. Our interviews clearly show that the employment-related aspects of corporate performance are currently most relevant to media, such as the ability of corporations to globalize their operations without sacrificing home production and employment levels. In the environmental domain, the most pressing issue was climate change. Other criteria mentioned were resource depletion, destruction of nature and education.

Overall, the most important issues, particularly the social ones, are located in developed countries. This is not surprising since this is where media's target audience is. Furthermore, our interviews pointed to significant dynamics in issues and corporate sustainability management:

> Insurance companies tend to cover the topic in detail when it causes companies damage; however, risk is a moving target, changing form and size. (B2B, Special Interest, UK)

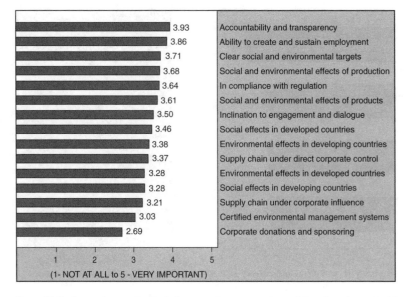

Value	Criterion
3.93	Accountability and transparency
3.86	Ability to create and sustain employment
3.71	Clear social and environmental targets
3.68	Social and environmental effects of production
3.64	In compliance with regulation
3.61	Social and environmental effects of products
3.50	Inclination to engagement and dialogue
3.46	Social effects in developed countries
3.38	Environmental effects in developing countries
3.37	Supply chain under direct corporate control
3.28	Environmental effects in developed countries
3.28	Social effects in developing countries
3.21	Supply chain under corporate influence
3.03	Certified environmental management systems
2.69	Corporate donations and sponsoring

1 2 3 4 5
(1- NOT AT ALL to 5 - VERY IMPORTANT)

Figure 11.3 Importance of criteria for assessing corporate social and environmental performance (media)

Our quantitative data confirm our findings from the interviews: When asked to rate the importance of criteria for the assessment of corporate social and environmental performance, media professionals emphasized the importance of the accountability and transparency of corporations and their ability to create and sustain employment (see Figure 11.3).

It is plausible that accountability and transparency as well as clear target setting have relatively high mean scores, since both make life easy for journalists and the media: The more open companies are, the more accessible information is. Furthermore, it is easier to report on companies' social and environmental targets (on which progress may be reported on company websites) than to assess corporate performance "on the ground."

Criteria determining actions. Once a certain social or environmental issue is on the media's agenda, editorial teams or an individual journalist carry out an assessment using certain criteria, such as novelty and relevance to the target audience. The relevance to the target audience is determined by the current level of public awareness, reference to certain regions and countries, company size and issue type (scope of the problem and potential for improvement).

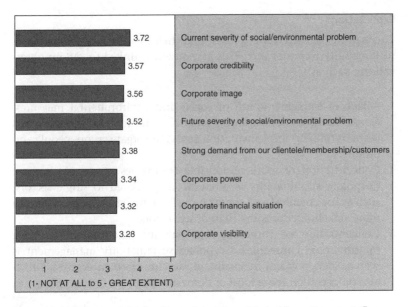

3.72	Current severity of social/environmental problem
3.57	Corporate credibility
3.56	Corporate image
3.52	Future severity of social/environmental problem
3.38	Strong demand from our clientele/membership/customers
3.34	Corporate power
3.32	Corporate financial situation
3.28	Corporate visibility

1 2 3 4 5
(1- NOT AT ALL to 5 - GREAT EXTENT)

Figure 11.4 Extent to which criteria determine stakeholder actions to influence companies (media)

> Factors influencing the decision for or against a certain story are big names, big numbers, government policy [Reason: impact on the whole industry] or shocking findings. (B2B, Special Interest, UK)

Our quantitative data do not point to one dominant criterion that determines the media's decision to cover one topic rather than another (see Figure 11.4). It appears that corporate characteristics such as size and credibility that capture the audience's attention are roughly as important as the severity of the issue.

Although data should be interpreted cautiously due to the small sample size, two additional findings are interesting:

1. The current issue is more important than the future one: This shows that media's focus is on real-time coverage and short-term effects.
2. Issue severity determines decisions more strongly than audience demand. This could suggest that media push news and information about issues *into* the market rather than reacting to their audiences' demand. This also reflects the existing strong dynamics in the media world.

Expectations

The majority of interviewees stated that their expectations for corporate sustainability were not met. This assessment is linked to certain observations, such as:

1. A lack of implementation of social and environmental measures: Corporations communicate social and environmental achievements without (proper) implementation across the organization, people and products.
2. Concentration of more responsible companies on certain sectors: Corporate sustainability is often strongly related to single sectors, such as the chemical and energy industry, which have been subject to more stakeholder pressure than other sectors.
3. Concentration of corporate sustainability management in large multinational companies: Corporate sustainability management is seen as less prevalent in small and medium-sized enterprises, which also reflects their more local or domestic focus.

The single most important reason for interviewees' dissatisfaction with corporate sustainability performance was the attempt by some corporations to get a free ride on the sustainability image without any implementation on the operational level. Journalists strongly criticized this kind of "green-washing," as it undermined – in their opinion – the credibility of future efforts in corporate sustainability, and the corresponding coverage.

We also observe greater skepticism about corporate sustainability among journalists with a B2B/general interest focus, as they point to a trade-off between corporate sustainability management and profit maximization. Journalists with a B2B/special interest focus appear to be relatively satisfied:

> Given my profession and focus on accounting, I believe that the vast majority of companies are doing well. CSR becomes increasingly more important and is taken up rather by big companies. (B2B magazine, Special Interest, UK)

Our interviews also point to the difficulty of a conclusive overall assessment (as corporate performance can diverge substantially – even within the same industry) and the fact that corporate sustainability is far from being mainstreamed (even if it may be a growing niche).

Our quantitative survey (see Figure 11.5) shows respondents' highest levels of satisfaction with corporate regulatory compliance, adoption of

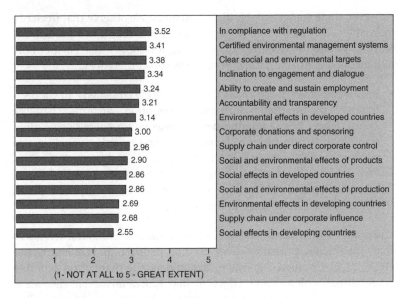

Figure 11.5 Satisfaction with corporate social and environmental performance (media)

environmental management systems and target setting, which appears to reflect the existence of relatively high social and environmental standards in Europe.

Our respondents were least satisfied with corporate behavior in developing countries, i.e. social and environmental effects in those countries and a lack of supply chain in general. These are also precisely the areas (apart from employment-related issues in a Europe struggling for regional competitiveness) that have had most extensive coverage in recent years.

11.3   Current stakeholder strategies

Actions and their effectiveness

Portfolio of actions and effectiveness. Compared to other stakeholders, the media's portfolio of actions is rather limited. The majority of our respondents stated that they do not engage in any substantial activities beyond distributing information they consider relevant. At the most, they comment and put forward suggestions:

> Our actions are writing articles and highlighting problems. We try to put forward suggestions on how things should work and how things might develop. (B2B magazine, Special Interest, UK)

However, there are several significant nuances: We observe that freelance journalists also engage in other activities such as teaching and textbook writing, public discussions or consulting for companies. Furthermore B2B media organize sustainability awards and conferences.

- In November 2005, the *Financial Times London* launched – in cooperation with the International Finance Corporation – an annual banking award. *Energy Risk*, a London-based magazine for energy generation, trading and consumption, launched several awards, including two concerning CSM (on emission trading and renewable energy).
- The Ethical Corporation organizes sustainability summits, where corporations and NGOs can, for example, exchange on their targets and missions, and engage in partnerships.

The results of our quantitative survey show – in line with our interviews – that the media primarily tend to use praising and blaming (see Figure 11.6). Compared to other stakeholders, the share of no activities is substantial, which clearly reflects media's lack of mission in the area of corporate sustainability, i.e. it jumps onto the bandwagon if a compelling issue emerges. We attribute the 13 per cent of engagement to actions such as interviews during investigations, the use of informants and

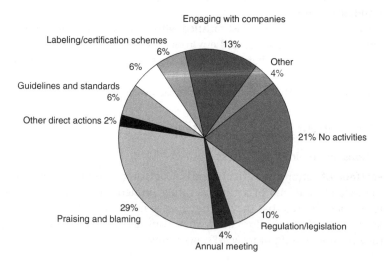

Figure 11.6 Portfolio of actions to influence companies' social and environmental performance (media)

"whistleblowers" (employees exposing their own company by providing third parties with necessary information).

In terms of the effectiveness of actions to influence companies (independently of whether used or not by the individual stakeholder), again we could not detect one clear dominant action. Regulation/legislation is ranked highest (see Figure 11.7).

However, our interviewees pointed to the more nuanced view on this action by journalists. They maintain that the multinational corporations: (1) can actively influence the course of regulation by political lobbying; and (2) are not really challenged by new social and environmental regulation. They also claim that regulation bears certain challenges. In light of enforcement and the effects on corporate competitiveness, social regulation is more difficult to implement and hence less effective:

> In the social area, regulation is difficult to implement and to assess. My impression is that regulation is not really effective and rather counterproductive here. (B2B title, Special Interest, Germany)
>
> For the small and medium-sized companies, regulation is too bureaucratic; overall regulation is effective with environmental issues and industry. (Consumer title, General Interest, Germany)

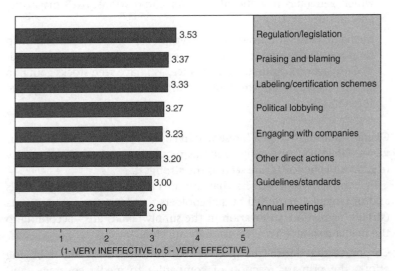

3.53	Regulation/legislation
3.37	Praising and blaming
3.33	Labeling/certification schemes
3.27	Political lobbying
3.23	Engaging with companies
3.20	Other direct actions
3.00	Guidelines/standards
2.90	Annual meetings

1   2   3   4   5
(1- VERY INEFFECTIVE to 5 - VERY EFFECTIVE)

Figure 11.7 Perceived effectiveness of actions in influencing companies' social and environmental performance – regardless of whether used by the individual stakeholder or not (media)

Effect on corporate value drivers. The interviewees clearly pointed to reputation, customer loyalty and brand value as those that are most effectively targeted by media:

> The possible risks from my work for corporations are: 1) financial risks, 2) share price risk, 3) less investment opportunity, 4) less access to funding and 5) reputation risks. The last one is a huge one and can be linked to the ability to recruit people that are highly relevant in businesses, such as accounting. (B2B magazine, Special Interest, UK)

> Negative coverage can change peoples' [consumers, shareholders] perception, implying a falling share price and different buying behaviors. (B2B magazine, Special Interest, UK)

Although the primary effects on companies are negative, interviewees also point to some opportunities that can arise from positive media coverage:

> We report also on best practices in the market. Our reporting helps to improve their [corporate reporting] environmental performance which generates free and nice PR for corporations. (B2B magazine, Special Interest, UK)

> Media increases the awareness for certain corporations. This can help to increase sales, and it is nice PR. I am pretty convinced of our positive impact on corporate performance, as I have seen stocks going up in my career as an effect of my articles. (B2B magazine, Special Interest, UK)

Overall, quantitative data (presented in Figure 11.8) align with our interviews. Effects on intangibles such as reputation and customer loyalty (e.g. possible boycotts) are seen as the strongest.

In contrast, value drivers that are affected on a longer-term basis and/or largely determined by stakeholders that have their own agenda (strikes, regulation, innovation in the supply chain) are – according to the media respondents – less strongly affected.

Corporate reactions. Our interviewees considered PR and lobbying efforts the primary reaction of companies to media coverage (and other activities). They also suggested that corporations (1) should limit

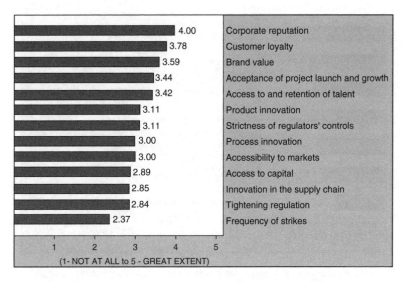

Value	Driver
4.00	Corporate reputation
3.78	Customer loyalty
3.59	Brand value
3.44	Acceptance of project launch and growth
3.42	Access to and retention of talent
3.11	Product innovation
3.11	Strictness of regulators' controls
3.00	Process innovation
3.00	Accessibility to markets
2.89	Access to capital
2.85	Innovation in the supply chain
2.84	Tightening regulation
2.37	Frequency of strikes

(1- NOT AT ALL to 5 - GREAT EXTENT)

Figure 11.8 Extent to which stakeholder actions affect corporate value drivers (media)

their PR efforts, (2) allow for engagement that is more real and (3) change their behavior.

> Less talk, more consideration how it can be part of the business, less rhetoric and ethical marketing. The increase of ethical marketing and ethical advertisement is troubling. (B2B magazine, General Interest, UK/Germany)

Our quantitative data also point to major PR- and lobbying-based reactions of companies (see Figure 11.9).

Except litigation, the remaining items roughly have the same mean frequency, which overall appears to reflect media's perception of a corporate sector that is not very proactive.

Finally, we asked media for a self-assessment of their effectiveness – relative to other stakeholders – in influencing corporate behavior. As Figure 11.10 shows, they consider themselves the most influential stakeholder, followed by four with roughly the same influence, namely financial institutions, consumer organizations, governments, and corporate customers, which all represent (or are closely connected – in the case of consumer organizations) transactional stakeholders.

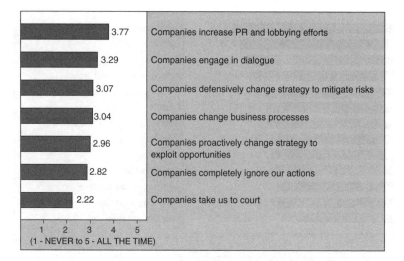

Figure 11.9   Frequency of corporate reactions to stakeholder action (media)

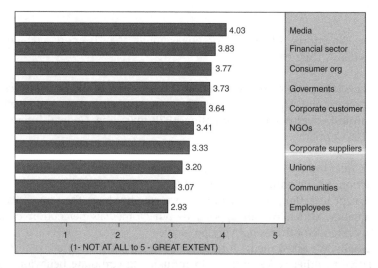

Figure 11.10   Extent to which stakeholders are able to influence corporate behavior (media)

The media's self-assessment of its influence on companies is in line with the ratings in the total sample. Nevertheless, interviewees tended to be more modest and placed media with the three most influential stakeholders – financial institutions, consumers (and consumer organizations) and governments.

11.4   Future trends

Few journalists see any significant future changes concerning the actions of media in the field of corporate sustainability. To some extent, they expect modifications in the way information is gathered, analyzed and presented:

> I believe that future developments will concern the way we present issues. We [sustainability reporters] will probably try to communicate sustainability from a much broader perspective by including more stakeholders' opinions and contrast it with the corporate perspective on the issues. (Consumer magazine, General Interest, Spain)

We see three principal factors driving development of corporate sustainability coverage in the media in the future, namely technological innovation, increased public sensitivity to corporate sustainability and greater stakeholder influence as well as the creation of more appropriate formats for covering corporate sustainability by media.

Technological innovation. Technology (e.g. digitalization, mobile and wireless technologies) is continuously changing media in terms of how the sender and the receiver interact, how the content is provided and what information needs the audience has. Clearly, the digitalization of media is blurring geographic borders and distinctive elements of each media type.

A contemporary example for innovation in media is blogging. A blog is a website in which items are posted on a regular basis and displayed in reverse chronological order. Blogs have made it possible for each individual to become essentially part of the media by publishing information on certain events or situations. Sustainability blogs can be used by (freelance) journalists as well as non-journalists to share opinions and viewpoints on corporate sustainability management, concerning all sectors, countries, criteria and dimensions.

Especially due to the internet, media as a platform becomes more accessible and open to third parties, leading to (1) a more decentralized media structure, (2) wider supply of information to the public and (3) an increase in perspectives on sustainability.

Public sensitivity and stakeholder influence. We also expect a continued (but not rapid) shift from a shareholder to a stakeholder perspective.

> The stakeholder thinking has increased, before it was rather a pure shareholder thinking. (B2B, Special Interest, Germany)

It is also possible that certain media will increase public sensitivity to corporate sustainability by focusing more on strategic and analytical content. This could go hand in hand with greater demand for corporate sustainability information because of the paradigm of shareholder value and incongruent social and environmental standards across the globe (in particular, the social impacts of globalization).

> Awareness of societal problems is increasing since 4–5 years, whereas awareness of environmental problems has peaked in the 80s and is decreasing ever since. (B2B, General Interest, Germany)

Today B2B titles clearly focus on shareholders and tend to ignore stakeholder themes and issues. However, they are on a learning curve concerning corporate sustainability, and some are adopting a more inclusive and holistic coverage in the specific context of their readership. Consumer titles have taken a more balanced shareholder–stakeholder view for some time now. The focus of coverage has moved from shareholder value, growth and profitability to a more balanced coverage that takes into account the social and environmental implications of economic actions (e.g. emissions, climate change, outsourcing and unemployment).

More appropriate media formats.   As mentioned above, print and electronic media are already covering corporate sustainability in various forms, yet with little strategic orientation and resources. They are in search of formats and structures that fit the complex topic of sustainability better. The electronic media aim to include sustainability in current programs and ensure appropriate (complete, informative) and successful (audience, circulation) coverage. Sustainability awards and conferences organized by the print media underpin efforts of some players in the market to occupy (and possibly grow) the niche of corporate sustainability. Obviously, this always requires interest and buy-in from the audience.

11.5   Conclusion

Overall, we ascertain a rather pragmatic, observant and opportunistic approach of the media to corporate sustainability, largely determined by the novelty and relevance of the issue for the target audience. Although media's mission is confined to describing, explaining and evaluating situations and events triggered by other stakeholders, its potential influence on companies is significant. This applies particularly to the effects on intangibles such as reputation, image and customer loyalty. The group of journalists "falling for" corporate PR in sustainability is small and decreasing, partly because external experts are increasingly covering sustainability issues across the media.

Based on our interviews, the following recommendations to mitigate risk and exploit opportunities associated with corporate sustainability can be presented:

• Companies are advised to be more transparent: A proactive and honest communications strategy is considered less risky than an attempt to conceal incidents. Stakeholder platforms and effective communication departments (that are in tune with stakeholders) are considered highly important.

• Companies are advised to more unreservedly analyze opportunities of social and environmental innovation, and adopt a more proactive approach to corporate sustainability thus avoiding regulatory and public pressure.

In general, journalists reporting on corporate sustainability tend to know which leading companies take significant measures. Moreover, a few specialized sustainability journalists are opinion leaders in their countries, "benchmarking" corporations and their behavior in their publications. These individuals tend to be more systematic and analytical than the "average" journalist and often have a corresponding academic (business administration, environmental management) and professional background (industry, NGO, government). We also observe that these experts go beyond classical journalistic activities by organizing conferences and establishing award schemes.

We observe that the quality of corporate sustainability coverage (e.g. more in-depth analyses) in B2B media has increased. This trend is also mirrored in an increase of coverage in consumer titles focusing on economic conditions and social (rather than environmental) problems, and the two key issues of climate change and unemployment.

Note

1   Datamonitor, *Global Publishing*, Industry Profile (December 2005).

12

Corporate Customers and Suppliers: How Companies Influence Other Companies On Corporate Sustainability

Aileen Ionescu-Somers

This chapter presents the empirical results of research conducted on corporate customers and suppliers in the context of our IMD cross-stakeholder study. We define

- the role of the "corporate customer" to be that of the corporation as a customer of other companies (B2B relationships)
- the role of the "corporate supplier" to be that of the corporation as a supplier of other companies (again in B2B relationships).

In total, we conducted 52 interviews: 35 with managers in the supply chain of the companies (purchasing and procurement officers) and 17 with the sales and marketing officers of these companies. In this way, we covered both upstream and downstream spheres of influence of corporations within their value chains. In addition, we analyzed 94 self-completion questionnaires in total: 37 from "corporate customers" and 57 from "corporate suppliers."

The following companies participated in the interview research: Aarhaus United, ABB, BASF, British Nuclear Group (Spent Fuel Services), Du Pont de Nemours, Hartmann, Hilti, Lafarge, Mesalitto, M-Real, Nestlé, Philip Morris International, RWE, Scottish & Newcastle, Shell, Sulzer, Unilever and a few other global companies that shall remain anonymous.

The chapter is structured as follows: In section 12.1 we provide some background on corporate customers and suppliers (without a specific focus on corporate sustainability). In section 12.2 we provide information about the stakeholders' approach to sustainability (mission, incentives and motives, processes and tools, criteria and expectations). Section 12.3 contains our key findings on current stakeholder strategies, their actions and effectiveness as well as corporate risks and opportunities. In section 12.4 we elaborate on future trends, and in section 12.5 we conclude by highlighting the key findings and implications.

12.1 Stakeholder background

In a global business environment, corporate value chains have become increasingly complex. Whereas, in the past, companies primarily concerned themselves with what went on "inside the factory gates," no company today could claim that this approach would suffice. Companies are affected by sustainability issues that occur either upstream or downstream of their own operations and often stakeholders expect them to act upon these issues as part of a "brand promise." Global companies, therefore, increasingly have social and environmental responsibility for the actions of their suppliers and even their customers. The purpose of this chapter is to assess how far up or down the chain companies go to influence their suppliers and customers and promote sustainable performance, and how corporate players view the effectiveness of their own actions. We plan to examine these two very different dynamics here.

12.2 Approach to corporate sustainability

Mission

Our research revealed that corporate customers are convinced of their mission: Generally ensuring appropriate environmental and social behavior of suppliers by setting standards and enforcing them where necessary. On a micro level, managers we spoke to perceived that they are working mainly toward eco-efficiency or social performance benefits that have been spelt out for them. However, on a macro level, some managers felt that for corporations in a volatile global environment in which competitiveness drives significant societal change, the role of suppliers as regards social and environmental performance is considerably less well defined.

Since a good deal of what companies do in terms of supplier assessment is related to regulatory concerns, the corporate customer expects supplying companies to at least be in compliance with EHS regulations. Most global companies practice zero tolerance where health and safety accidents are concerned and expect their direct suppliers to do the same. Several companies we included in our research ask their suppliers whether they have business principles related to corporate sustainability, environmental or social policies, an EMS (Environmental Management System), and/or if they apply ISO 14001 or SA 8000. Sometimes additional criteria are requested, but in general these requests, tend to be industry-specific.

In contrast to the corporate customer, the role of the corporate supplier is significantly less proactive in terms of influencing customer social and environmental performance. The responses from marketing and sales people demonstrated to us that, except in cases where there is a pronounced product responsibility down to the end-user (toxic or dangerous products, recycling/take back rules and regulations, product packaging), the corporate supplier is unlikely to be proactive about influencing customers' social and environmental behavior in other ways. However, the marketing and sales managers we spoke to did see a role for instructing and educating customers about the environmental features of their company's products.

Industry leaders felt that to lead by example is an important part of their role to influence both customers and suppliers more indirectly.

Incentives and motives

It was clear from our interviews and questionnaires that companies have a significant incentive to protect their reputation and brands from social

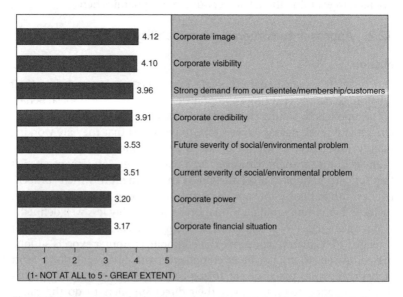

4.12	Corporate image
4.10	Corporate visibility
3.96	Strong demand from our clientele/membership/customers
3.91	Corporate credibility
3.53	Future severity of social/environmental problem
3.51	Current severity of social/environmental problem
3.20	Corporate power
3.17	Corporate financial situation

1 2 3 4 5
(1- NOT AT ALL to 5 - GREAT EXTENT)

Figure 12.1   Extent to which criteria determine stakeholder actions to influence companies (corporate customers and suppliers)

and environmental risks: When we asked respondents which criteria influence the actions they take to affect the social and environmental performance of their suppliers, corporate image and visibility took first place (see Figure 12.1).

Interestingly, the actual current or future severity of the problem itself was significantly less important.

Social and environmental risks created by supplier behavior are clearly part of the overall risk management scheme of all companies, but global companies in the limelight are particularly under pressure in this regard. For example, because of their brands, they tend to attract the attention of NGOs and society stakeholders as a whole, and managers felt that in this respect, "expectations have changed." It was their view that, because of these changes, companies must strive to avoid environmental or social issues and that global companies should be proactive and take a leadership role where possible.

Managers saw their own customer demands as a significant propeller of companies' activities with suppliers in social and environmental areas. As one interviewee remarked:

> Our customers expect it from us (the question is would we do it if they did not – I hope so!?) – Customers often want to see evidence themselves. I have to show them the things that we ask suppliers. If they see hard data – they believe it. When we look at the billions of dollars we spend overall, half is outside our company – therefore our suppliers have to act in a responsible way. (Corporate customer A)

Suppliers receive questionnaires, are provided with guidelines or (more rarely for major leading global companies) are subject to audit by their customers. Managers were convinced that the end consumer is not really the key promoting agent – although most managers recognized that there is a growing niche of consumers who "do care." Several managers we spoke to felt that consumers are difficult to "read," since many simply assume that global companies, with global operations and reputations, are "doing the right thing" in their supply chains. As a result, when a scandal breaks out (often provoked and augmented by the media), there is often a shocked public reaction because "things are not as they perceived them to be."

In quite a few cases, companies are devoting more attention to social and environmental issues with suppliers than in previous years. This is often the result of supplier manufacturing bases moving from Western Europe to Eastern Europe and South East Asia, in particular China. Interviewees felt that standards and the enforcement of standards in

Eastern Europe are lagging substantially behind Western Europe. Managers were clearly uncomfortable with China's human rights record and its effect on the workplace, and also with its record of non-enforcement of environmental legislation. Cross-industry interviews bore witness to the fact that manufacturing industries are moving wholesale out of Europe toward Asia. Clearly, such moves are motivated by several competitive economic factors, which in some cases can perhaps be closely related to social and environmental criteria, as is reflected in the following statement from one manager:

> Companies are profit-oriented. If environmental regulations in one part of the world are stricter, then they tend to move to areas where they are less strict. In China, this can vary from province to province. It tends to be stricter in the coastal areas, moving inland to less stringent areas. Because of the huge unemployment problems, companies are welcome even if this causes problems for the environment. (Corporate customer B)

Time and again, we spoke to managers who felt that Europe has lost its competitive edge, and in some industries, this is due to what was perceived as an over-legislated economic environment in the EU (including environmental legislation), as well as the sheer costs of social systems which are overly burdening industry in some countries (France was the most cited example). Managers' perceptions were that some countries in Europe seriously need to look at these factors in order to recreate an economic environment conducive to economic growth. The lack of cohesiveness between commonly accepted standards and the degree of enforcement of standards also appears to be a factor. However, some managers felt the following question should be posed: Should the global legislative environment (through the WTO and GATT) be raising the bar and leveling the global playing field rather than Europe stepping back on hard-won social and environmental standards? Clearly, managers were much more confident about the behavior of their suppliers in Europe, and they attributed this to the fact that legislation, standards and enforcement are of a high standard.

Given the perceived risks to their brands and reputations, the move to Eastern Europe and Asia has prompted companies to look a lot more closely at the social and environmental standards they impose on their suppliers. Many companies we included in the research had been used to working with suppliers in Western Europe which, in turn, worked with other suppliers in Western Europe. However, the past five years have given way to a completely different picture and companies are clearly uncomfortable with the social and environmental risks associated with such moves.

Systems that worked within the previous scenario are no longer deemed to be adequate protection in the new scenario where even existing social and environmental legislation is not enforced in developing countries. Companies are, therefore, moving to protect themselves and to recreate a "stable base of suppliers," as one manager put it, but in a global sphere of influence. Most managers saw a clear business case for ensuring that the supply base remains as solidly anchored as before.

Supplying companies have less incentive to push for better social and environmental behavior on the part of their customers. Managers were clear about the reasons:

- Power goes up the supply chain, not down. (Corporate supplier K)
- He who pays the piper calls the tune – pressure goes up the supply chain, not down. (Corporate supplier D)
- There is no room for that – my job is to manage, run and grow the business. From day to day, other than aspects of good management, I do not have space for these issues. (Corporate supplier B)

When asked whether corporate suppliers should be more proactive about influencing customer behavior, marketing and sales managers tended to take the view that the corporate incentive is to do business, not reduce business (and they clearly thought that insisting on more standards from customers would do this) and that there is simply no business case for going further than legislated product responsibility. If there is a product-related issue where risk to corporate image is high, it is evident that supplying companies are proactive and generally get cooperation from customers because the customer also perceives this risk.

Supplying companies embrace a passive role of awaiting requirements from customers and reacting to them. Suppliers clearly take customer expectations seriously when it comes to environmental and social standards, and act on them where feasible.

Processes and tools

Taking a proactive stance regarding supplier social and environmental behavior is often enhanced by an observed event with other companies and industries. For example, the Nike media splash which exposed the use of child labor in its supply chain was quoted repeatedly by interviewees.

This event, and Shell's clash with Greenpeace over Brent Spar, were the ones that most influenced the upgrading of environmental and social issues to the business risk agenda in some cases.

We conclude from our interviews that global companies are careful about who they do business with. Long-term relationships dominate the agenda. Procurement people like to know who they are dealing with and several companies we spoke to have a grading system ranging from "preferred" suppliers (which supply key components, ingredients or parts of their products) to their less important suppliers (such as the suppliers of paper clips). Environmental and (less often) social criteria are part of supplier qualifying processes. This checklist focuses on two things: (1) viability as a business partner (mainly a financial and technical check) and (2) how the company does business (including ethical, social and environmental criteria to varying degrees).

Companies have begun to ask supplying companies to sign off on their corporate business principles. For example, we learned from our interviewees at Unilever that the company has extended its own code of business principles to include its business partners. Thus, it has taken the unprecedented step of writing a letter to all of its thousands of direct suppliers requesting positive assurance on their corporate social responsibility (CSR) policies and codes. Unilever established an objective of obtaining an overview of the responses by the end of 2005 and to initiate risk assessments on individual suppliers where positive assurance was not complete in the short term. The company's intention is to establish a global approach to its supply base, including risk assessment as a key part of the process. The company describes the process as "nonnegotiable." We noted that companies that have fewer suppliers are often more advanced in terms of supply chain control over social and environmental aspects; in a complex supply chain, such as that of the food industry, gaining overview is almost an impossible route to take.

Several managers made the point that it would make more sense to have an industry sustainability guideline for suppliers. In some industries, where companies source from the same suppliers all the time, managers felt it would make sense. The food industry is one such example, where hundreds of thousands of suppliers are used for sourcing by a handful of major global companies.

A number of companies – Lafarge, Unilever and Nestlé are examples – have initiated pilot projects with suppliers with a view to testing the introduction of new sustainability guidelines or criteria and new ways of working with suppliers. Some of these pilots were intended to hit the mainstream eventually, but as yet none have.

Our survey further clarified the means by which companies assess suppliers (see Figure 12.2). We learned during our interviews that the principal means, corporate audits carried out on suppliers, are primarily internal audits not carried out by third parties. Moreover, most companies have no intention of entrusting supplier audit to third parties since managers felt that this would mean a loss of control on key factors that influence both their familiarity with suppliers and operations in general. A great deal of benchmarking with other companies, as well as other company investigations, guide corporate efforts to audit and monitor suppliers.

Supplying companies tend to put in place mechanisms to monitor what their customers expect of them, and may even appoint a manager with that delegated responsibility. Beyond that, the tools used to influence customer behavior are mainly product-related. For example, DaimlerChrysler has a training workshop for lorry drivers to instruct them in a more eco-friendly use of its vehicles. Some companies invite customers to internal workshops organized to highlight the importance of environmental considerations in packaging. In addition, new products have to jump a number of environmental hurdles before they are marketed or sold. There are even some progressive companies, notably in the energy industry, which are working on changing customer mindsets about their products. Their new philosophy is to provide a service along with their product to ensure a more sustainable use of it in the long term (dematerialization). This has led to more supplier/customer partnerships, where the supplier works on a product solution with sustainability benefits that are proactively promoted by the supplier.

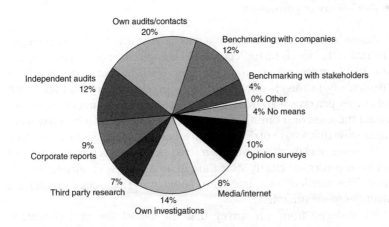

Figure 12.2 Means of assessing corporate social and environmental performance (corporate customers and suppliers)

Criteria

The criteria that companies use to assess their suppliers are industry- and sometimes company-specific. The need to apply legislation and the level of perceived corporate exposure to supplier behavior were primary drivers for criteria selected. The level of spending with an individual supplier often dictates the level of attention it gets in terms of overall scrutiny (but also including environmental and social risk factors). In addition, the level of risk implied by the product was another reason for increased scrutiny. While many criteria were based on legislative requirements, companies have clearly begun to include some "beyond compliance" criteria where there are obvious gaps, such as in the area of child labor. The following are examples of the sustainability principles outlined in Unilever's letter to suppliers:

- Compliance with national laws/regulations
- Respect for human rights
- Application of local regulations in wages /working hours
- No use of forced or child labor
- Importance of criteria for assessing corporate social and environmental performance
- Respect for workers' right of association
- Safe and healthy working conditions for employees
- Operations carried out with care for the environment and in compliance with environmental regulations
- Products/services delivered to required quality and safety standards
- No bribery or corruption

Across industries, environmental criteria appear to be the most clearly defined as this area is highly legislated in Europe. Managers often criticized the highly regulated environment they work in and some managers (particularly in the chemical industry) were clearly very frustrated with what they perceive as an overregulated European environment, even criticizing the sense or meaning of some of the regulations. Quite a few managers sense that a wave of deregulation is bound to come in the short term.

However, social criteria were perceived as much less formally defined and companies are clearly struggling more with new challenges in this area. The problem that managers raised was that social criteria are mainly not measurable.

We deduced from our survey that the availability of a systematic process to ensure supplier compliance with regulation is what guides customers' assessment criteria, as does the knowledge of suppliers, built up over time through accountability and transparency (see Figure 12.3). Supplier compliance with regulation is an essential prerequisite for companies to do business with them.

According to our survey (see Figure 12.4), "gut feel" was the least influential factor for selecting actions to influence companies.

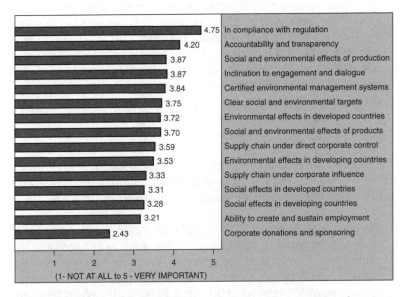

Figure 12.3 Importance of criteria for assessing corporate social and environmental performance (corporate customers and suppliers)

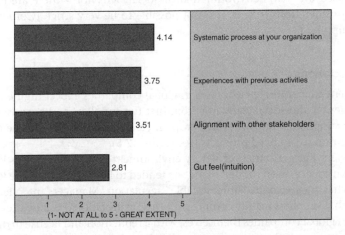

Figure 12.4 Extent to which processes/tools determine actions to influence companies (corporate customers and suppliers)

Indeed, most managers we interviewed feel uncomfortable with using "gut feel" and welcome the guidance of a formal process. As one manager commented:

> For "beyond compliance," we want suppliers to be comparable to the level used in our own production plants. For the moment, it is not exactly the same. And in some countries, it is not possible to come even close. There is a cut-off point between what is acceptable and what is not, but it is an individual, almost personal assessment that is not always easy to make. The guidelines that we are currently developing will make the difference between the personal decision and the cut-off point. The knowledge built up over time in experiences with previous suppliers is the major influencing factor in selection of criteria for assessing suppliers. (Corporate customer B)

The feedback we received suggests that corporate suppliers do not tend to assess customers per se – the criteria they use are very much based on risks surrounding products. One marketing manager put it in a nutshell:

> We do not assess our customers and that would only be possible if there is a potential to build a competitive edge or create value. We cannot treat downstream like upstream. We try to influence the regulators to push people to behave in a sustainable way, for example. We also provide examples of behaviors to push this. When times are difficult, it is not easy to tell a company that we will not supply them based on "bad" environmental or social behavior – there are legal considerations to this. It is not possible to be very strict. (Corporate supplier F)

Expectations

In general, corporate customers in global companies expect high environmental and social standards from first-tier suppliers and are satisfied that supplying companies in Europe meet expectations in Europe and for European sourced products (see Figure 12.5).

Again, Europe's strict regulatory environment contributes to this level of confidence, even though managers tended to be critical about the level of what they view as "unreasonable" regulation. Managers interviewed felt that suppliers mainly comply with their expectations because they are often global companies themselves, with a reputation and license to operate to consider. Customers that are global companies generate substantial

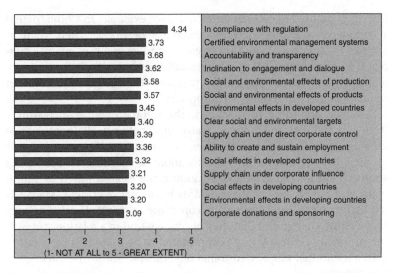

Value	Category
4.34	In compliance with regulation
3.73	Certified environmental management systems
3.68	Accountability and transparency
3.62	Inclination to engagement and dialogue
3.58	Social and environmental effects of production
3.57	Social and environmental effects of products
3.45	Environmental effects in developed countries
3.40	Clear social and environmental targets
3.39	Supply chain under direct corporate control
3.36	Ability to create and sustain employment
3.32	Social effects in developed countries
3.21	Supply chain under corporate influence
3.20	Social effects in developing countries
3.20	Environmental effects in developing countries
3.09	Corporate donations and sponsoring

(1- NOT AT ALL to 5 - GREAT EXTENT)

Figure 12.5 Satisfaction with corporate social and environmental performance (corporate customers and suppliers)

business for suppliers – they have considerable economic "clout," and can make a real economic difference to the financial sustainability of the supplying company's business. This increases the rate of success for heavyweight corporate customers in trying to influence their suppliers.

The survey indicated that there is less confidence in suppliers' social and environmental performance in developing countries, and in the supply chain, which companies can only influence (as opposed to control). As previously mentioned, managers felt that moving manufacturing bases to Eastern Europe and Asia encompassed many risks, particularly Asia. The fact that their suppliers also tend to do so was perceived as potentially risky by their customers:

The major companies have done a lot. The problem is with the many small ones. Few of them care. It is important for main suppliers to take responsibility – if the chain is broken and there is a leakage in the chain, I would get worried (especially for chemicals and raw materials). Outsourcing is not always positive – companies think that you can get away with more by outsourcing. This is a risky business in a corporate environment where CEOs survive on a quarterly basis. To change raw materials, for example, takes a long time – we need, therefore, to be very careful about our initial selection. (Corporate customer H)

Managers pointed to cultural differences: For example, in China there is a completely different view or perception of worker safety than in Europe. From factory layouts to hygiene in toilet facilities, many examples were cited in our interviews of situations where developing country managers and employees simply perceive risk, danger and value of human life quite differently to Europeans.

However, according to managers, the trend to source increasingly from Asia and Eastern Europe is clearly set to continue. Rather than dismissing supplying companies in these countries, global companies see it in their best economic interests to adopt a coaching or mentoring approach for an initial period, including the establishment of action plans and targets for certain standards to be met over time. Managers felt that such coaching approaches constitute the most effective strategy for ensuring change and that they ultimately lead to a relationship with the supplying company that is considered to be more of a partnership than a traditional supplier/customer relationship. But as one interviewee pointed out:

> There is a fine line between coaching and deciding that we should not work with them. (Corporate customer C)

Managers reported that they have been surprised by the speed and openness of most Chinese companies to make changes and become transparent. However, they also felt that audits and continuous assessment are fundamentally important for identifying problem areas early and addressing them.

In the interviews, marketing and sales managers of supplying companies reiterated that they do not have high expectations of their customers, except in the treatment and use of dangerous or toxic products. One company replied that it did have very high expectations (a company with high product risk through to end users). However, the interviewee at that company expressed the "How far do you go?" dilemma:

> We do not want to be associated with a company that does not share our values. We measure our contractors and ask them about these issues in the same way as we do for ourselves. We track safety incidents for example. We try as much as we can to sell to responsible companies – with the bigger global companies there is a degree of confidence. However, we also sell to distributors and the question then is – how far should one go? (Corporate customer E)

12.3   Current stakeholder strategies

Actions and their effectiveness

Several companies involved in our research are starting to make active attempts to increase and/or be more stringent with the level of assessment of suppliers on environmental and particularly social criteria. Clearly, companies that have been under pressure for some time are more advanced with their strategies. These companies have become more open about these aspects of their operations, mainly because of customer pressure and the need to respond to the demands of certain consumers.

The portfolio of actions used by corporate customers to assess suppliers mainly includes the application of guidelines and standards, and engaging with companies. Assuring that regulations are addressed is also essential, as mentioned earlier (see Figure 12.6). Companies in Europe do not tend to engage much in political lobbying, although managers held the view that this is probably much higher up on the agenda in US companies.

Global companies are currently concentrating on assessing and influencing first-tier suppliers and we have mentioned the diverse range of techniques and approaches being applied. While their long-term expectation is that the supplying company will subsequently put pressure on its own suppliers (in a "knock-on" effect), we have deduced from our research that "cradle to grave" transparency is still a dream for most

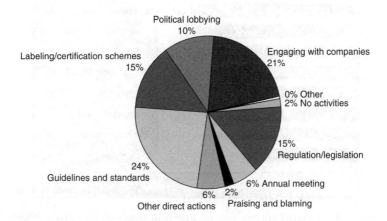

Figure 12.6   Portfolio of actions to influence companies' social and environmental performance (corporate customers and suppliers)

industries, even those that have worked hard on this. Managers had varying views depending on the industry and number of suppliers in the value chain:

> We are on top of our direct suppliers in terms of their sustainability performance – we know them – but where the sub-suppliers are concerned, we are still in the jungle. We will never pretend that we have 100 percent control, but the aim should be there. We aim to have what we call reasonable control. We should know about the second line of suppliers. Yes, the first and second line of supply is necessary and should be in line with our code of conduct. Feasibly, we could go to 90 to 95 per cent. (Corporate customer E)

> The question for us is how far do we want to go into our supply chain? We want to come up with a proactive response to new developments such as GRI and we are taking a cautious approach. (Corporate customer K)

> It is impossible to have 100 percent coverage of the supply chain in terms of environmental and social performance. We have to draw the line and say that at a certain stage we have to stop. (Corporate customer E)

Our survey indicated managers' perceptions of what actions are most effective at influencing companies' social and environmental behavior (see Figure 12.7). Clearly, regulation and legislation stands out as the

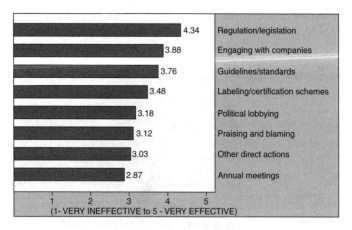

Figure 12.7 Perceived effectiveness of actions in influencing companies' social and environmental performance – regardless of whether used by the individual stakeholder or not (corporate customers and suppliers)

single most effective mechanism. Engaging directly with companies and ensuring the application of guidelines and standards are close runners-up.

Some industries are going further than first tier, for example the food industry (prompted by extreme consumer pressure for traceability in products). The reason for this is primarily because of risk criteria linked to the product:

> The actions of procurement people are different depending on whether you are looking at raw materials directly processed from agriculture, or packaging materials for example. For the raw materials, the issue is clearly taken into consideration, but when it comes to solid board, rigid plastic or flexible packaging, the issue is rarely addressed with the suppliers. (Corporate customer I)

Most managers interviewed appeared to think that the idea of "cradle to grave" transparency is a "pipe dream" because of the sheer expense involved and the number of suppliers they deal with (in one case more than 100,000 suppliers). However, more than one manager pointed out that companies should still strive for this:

> We are not there yet, and we will never be. If we are, then we should stand aside because it will mean that we are stagnating. (Corporate customer H)

Companies are reducing the number of suppliers they deal with globally in order to exert more control and build closer relationships, thus allowing for more familiarity with supplier operations and activities, and giving increased overview.

Marketing and sales managers appeared to be more aware than procurement managers and purchasing officers of the potential of labeling and certification schemes as an influencing action (see Figure 12.8 and Figure 12.9).

We also asked managers about the reactions of suppliers to the pressures they exert. The corporate customer perception is not surprising – there is a strong business case for suppliers to engage in dialogue and/or change business processes. Weighing up risks and opportunities is also clearly a part of putting together defense strategies in order to assure continued business relations (see Figure 12.10).

Interviewees appeared to be convinced that the corporate customer has a significant influence on supplying companies. However, the

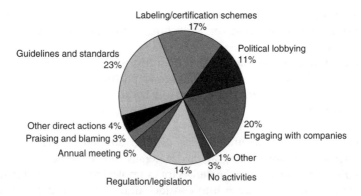

Figure 12.8 Portfolio of actions to influence companies' social and environmental performance (corporate suppliers only)

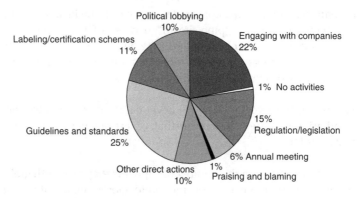

Figure 12.9 Portfolio of actions to influence companies' social and environmental performance (corporate customers only)

results of our survey show that the level of conviction is not very pronounced either – naturally, suppliers look to economic gain first and foremost. One interviewee commented:

I keep trying to convince companies that there is benefit in doing things, but it is difficult particularly if there is a fixed price contract – some companies have ongoing contracts and they tend to say – "This is not in the contract!" If there is new legislation, they might choose to implement it differently to how we would like them to (it would be the bare minimum, whereas we want them to go beyond the letter of the law). It boils down to whether they get something out of it or not. (Corporate customer C)

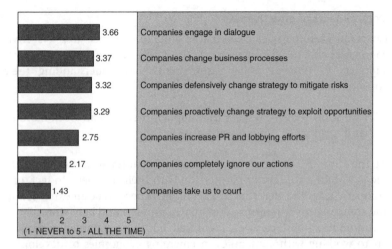

Figure 12.10 Frequency of corporate reactions to stakeholder action (corporate customers only)

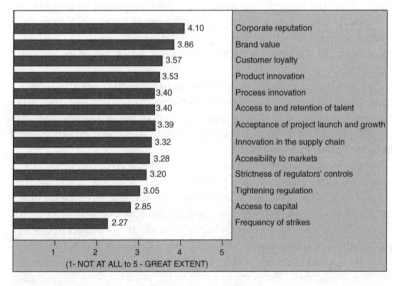

Figure 12.11 Extent to which stakeholder actions affect corporate value drivers (corporate customers and suppliers)

Both procurement managers and marketing and sales managers saw that the actions of their company affects several drivers of corporate success, mainly corporate reputation, brand value and acceptance of project launch and growth (see Figure 12.11).

Determinants of effectiveness

Corporate customers perceived that in order to influence suppliers' environmental and social behavior, a consultative process – speaking with suppliers to transmit their requirements and understanding their concerns and needs – is a key success factor:

> If we show that we respect the supplier, then we can work hand in hand together. (Corporate customer F)

At the time of our interviews, several companies were beginning to move toward a concept of partnership with their suppliers. In fact, one company takes the view that its key suppliers need to be an extension of the company itself in terms of approach, mindset and behavior.

A number of obstacles were identified, but these pertained in particular to working with companies in emerging economies or developing countries. Developing the capacity to apply standards does not happen overnight and many such companies are still struggling with technical issues. The cost of applying standards is also somewhat of an obstacle, but global companies are often prepared to pay to have similar standards everywhere rather than being perceived as inconsistent, with the resulting risks that such a public perception would bring to corporate reputation.

As regards Asia, cultural issues were again brought up as an obstacle – it is often difficult for European managers to understand the Asian approach and because of very different approaches, it is sometimes not possible to obtain a clear view on a supplier's social and environmental behavior in order to assess it.

In general, marketing and sales managers felt that customers should seek synergies, share standards and guidelines more, and that above all they should streamline their demands. Faced with multiple buyers with different requirements and monitoring, auditing and remediation processes, the corporate supplier can be quickly out of their depth. Managers in the supply chain were afraid that, as the numbers of audits to ensure that guidelines are applied increase (as they are likely to), supplying companies will become inundated; this seems to point to the need for the rationalization of expectations. In the food industry, for example, a full 10 per cent of farmer time is spent on audits – this is viewed by managers in the industry as truly excessive. However, the challenge is immense:

> Even though we are trying to limit the number of audits performed at our supplier's sites, there are still too many repeats internally. This by

itself allows you to size the challenge if we want to address it from an industry perspective. We are now part of a thinking group that is defining how we can develop and implement a third party audit system that could be acceptable to all food industries in Europe. (Corporate customer I)

Marketing and sales managers pointed out that often companies are asked to comply with requirements that make little sense; the way out of this conundrum, as they saw it, is clearly to use more communication mechanisms. Several managers mentioned cases where they had succeeded in reversing decisions by simply talking and asking questions about the expectations as well as being proactive in coming up with new solutions.

Corporate risks and opportunities

The major opportunity for suppliers in meeting their customers' social and environmental demands was the assurance of their own financial sustainability. Very few examples were found in our research of suppliers that had refused to meet social and environmental standards demanded by a global company. Global companies are well aware of "where the power sits" and managers stated that suppliers have an "open and shut business case" to comply with their requirements. Cases were cited to us of decisions taken to drop a supplier because of unacceptable social or environmental behavior, but in most cases, suppliers simply comply with requests. Decisions to drop customers for similar reasons were, however, practically non-existent. Nevertheless, when suppliers are asked to meet a previously unmet requirement, the question of cost is often raised – and this is a major sticking point for price-sensitive procurement departments, although some companies did state that they accept an increased price depending on the level of risk.

Some of the managers we interviewed pointed out that influencing suppliers' environmental and social standards is a real opportunity to get local companies in developing countries up to more acceptable standards and to change cultural and corporate mindsets fundamentally. Several managers mentioned that once standards are translated to Chinese factories on a "non-negotiable" basis, the learning is rapid, acceptance is full and the enforcement is almost better than in Europe. One manager commented:

Companies nearly always improve social standards when they move into a country. Environmental standards seem to follow afterwards. Is it realistic to treat social and environmental expectations as equal? Maybe there is a hierarchy of needs here that cannot be ignored. (Consumer organization I)

Depending on their experience, some managers praised Asian suppliers, in particular, but also Eastern Europeans for their flexibility and willingness to meet criteria and standards, and they criticized companies in Western Europe for a certain complacency and smug attitude that, they felt, is affecting European competitiveness overall. However, this complacency does not appear to rub off on environmental and social performance, which is highly regulated in Europe in any case.

Managers had noticed that key branded Asian companies have recognised the differentiation benefits they can reap by living up to high environmental and social standards and that many of these companies are more attractive as suppliers to other global companies as a result of working with their companies.

12.4　Future trends

All companies included in our research are either working on, or have recently worked on, enhancing the environmental and social demands they are putting on their supplying companies. This is a trend that most managers felt is likely to continue; increasing consumer pressure will be transmitted through corporate customers up into the value chain. On the one hand, managers felt that it is likely that legislative demands on them will increase, but not necessarily accelerate significantly over the next five to ten years. Most managers suggested that there will be a steady increase in both legislation and external pressure over time and that while companies would be well advised to prepare to respond to this, there is no immediate urgency either except in cases cited where the manufacturing base is being reallocated (and this urgency applies only to global companies).

In addition, on a macro level, the emergence of China and India as formidable trade competitors to the European Union and United States is likely to continue to bring pressure to bear on European institutions and national governments to review expensive social frameworks and revise their social and environmental legislation.

Clearly, some industries will move faster than others in considering homogeneous approaches to supplier assessment (for example, the food industry). It was also clear that, conscious of their risks, companies will probably further rationalize their supplier bases, focusing on fewer suppliers and thus be able to cultivate closer relationships and more competent, process-based assessments in the future.

However, marketing and sales managers at supplying companies stated that they are unlikely to become more proactive in terms of their customers' behavior. It did seem, though, that managers at leading companies perceived that pioneer efforts in using sustainability to enhance consumer benefits in the marketing of certain products might eventually have a knock-on effect on corporate customers and consumers. In addition, some managers thought that as suppliers are becoming more "savvy" about sustainability, they are starting or will start to take on more of a leadership role themselves.

12.5 Conclusion

As we interviewed and researched, it became clear that social and environmental issues are part of a tension in global competitiveness between developed and developing countries. Clearly, poorer environmental and social standards in developing countries help to make them more competitive compared with more developed countries that have higher, and therefore more costly, standards. We identified the beginnings of a resulting "pull" on Europe to expect less ambitious standards, to deregulate, to review its social framework and policies. Managers were asking a key question – should social and environmental standards ultimately become a trade barrier?

In addition, the extremely diverse range of criteria and systems applied to social and environmental expectations of suppliers seems to point to the need for more cohesiveness. The Global Reporting Initiative (GRI) guidelines go some way to resolving this dilemma – but a social guideline such as the ISO 26000, currently being developed (to be finalized in 2008), should help to get social issues on the same measurable and transparent par as environmental issues as a result of ISO 14001. However, many managers felt that such standards do not ensure that a company behaves in a sustainable manner, and that there is no way around the certainties established through long-term partnerships or relationships and a more process-oriented approach.

Should corporate customers go beyond assessing the first tier of suppliers and, if so, how far should they go? This question is clearly being posed in most global companies, but managers appeared to think that this is an impossible goal, but nevertheless a goal to be kept in view. We

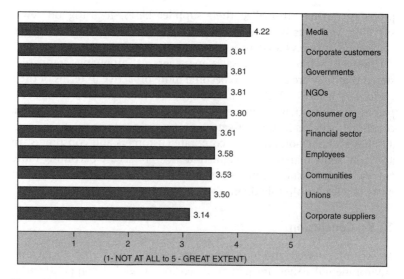

Figure 12.12   Extent to which stakeholders are able to influence corporate behavior (corporate customers only)

suspect that managers think this because they know that they will have more pressure to go further up the supply chain in the future. However, this is such an expensive and resource intensive activity, that the business case for doing so must be robust.

The fact that corporate customers are combing through their suppliers and rationalizing their supply bases may pose a threat for small and medium-sized enterprises (SMEs). Given the need to increase the number of small and medium-sized enterprises in order to meet the Millennium Goals related to poverty, this might not necessarily be good news for SMEs. Will reducing and streamlining suppliers mean that only big suppliers are taken into account, depriving smaller suppliers of markets?

In our discussions with managers, we identified room for more proactive and collaborative marketing and product development initiatives involving sustainability concepts between corporate suppliers and customers, with sometimes even the supplier taking the initiative. While it seems that companies are only starting to think about the social and environmental behavior of their customers beyond risk management of dangerous or harmful products, the question remains as to whether there is potential for a more influencing role for corporate suppliers – for instance, will the time come when companies will refuse customers because of their environmental or social behavior? It certainly seems unlikely that this will materialize in the short to medium term.

Companies clearly have a very strong potential to influence other companies – mainly upstream, where their power to influence is unquestionable. Managers perceived that the influencing role of the corporate customer is greater than that of governments and NGOs. However, the media was deemed to be the most influential stakeholder. Interestingly, they also rated corporate customer influence as more or less on a par with governments (see Figure 12.12).

Nevertheless, managers generally felt that public expectations surpass what companies could ever actually deliver. As one manager commented:

There are huge needs that cannot be met by any single company. We have the ability to minimize problems short term. Ultimately, these are very long-term issues. (Corporate customer A)

13
Unions: On the Backseat of Corporate Sustainability

Oliver Salzmann and Jens Prinzhorn

This section presents empirical evidence collected from unions through 19 semi-structured interviews (60 minutes average duration) and 36 self-completion questionnaires. We gladly acknowledge the participation of CEF-CGC (France), Comisiones Oberas (Spain), Danish Confederation of Trade Unions (Denmark), DKK (Denmark), General Federation of Free Trade Unions (UK), Gewerkschaft der Privatangestellten (Austria), International Confederation of Free Trade Unions (International), IGBCE (Germany), the Norwegian Confederation of Trade Union (Norway), Landsorganisationen i Sverige (Sweden), Metal (Sweden), Oesterreichischer Gewerkschaftsbund (Austria), SACO (Sweden), UNIA (Switzerland).

In section 13.1, we provide some background on unions (without a specific focus on corporate sustainability). In section 13.2, we provide information about the mission of unions and their approach to sustainability (mission, incentives and motives, processes and tools, criteria and expectations). Section 13.3 features our key findings on unions' stakeholder strategies, their actions and effectiveness as well as success factors and obstacles. In section 13.4, we elaborate on future trends. We conclude the chapter by highlighting the key findings and implications.

13.1   Stakeholder background

In Europe, unions have been central actors in both the political and economic field through their affiliation with the political labor movement in most Western European countries. Although it is arguable that unions will continue to remain powerful in the future, the widespread impression is that their importance has declined in the last two decades.[1]

Union membership in most OECD countries is declining, principally due to structural changes in the labor market and rising unemployment. Whereas the latter may ease off in the future, the former factor is likely to have a persistent downward pressure on levels of unionization. Unions have lost members in their traditionally strong sectors (manufacturing and public) due to falling employment rates. They have been unable to compensate for this trend for two primary reasons: First, emerging new groups of workers in service and small companies exhibit a lower propensity to unionize. Second, an increasing proportion of workers go into "non-standard employment" (part-timers and temporary workers).

It is important to note that unionization varies significantly across nations due to a variety of institutional and political factors such as union access to the workplace, union involvement in the provision and administration of unemployment insurance and the centralization of collective bargaining. In countries where all three factors are (or were) present, unions appear to have fought off most of the aforementioned downward effect on membership.[2]

So far, internationalization of trade and European integration have not brought any significant convergence in union presence. In particular, the latter has somewhat ambivalent implications for unions: On the one hand, a firm's dominant position in the European market can be associated with windfall profits and "thus potentially rich awards to powerful unions." On the other hand, a firm's strong international basis and its ability to switch location undermine the bargaining position of unions. The following general trends can be expected in the future:[3]

1. Formal bargaining at more decentralized levels (firm, workplace) in most – but not all – Western European countries, which will also coincide with more informal coordination through consensual norms and guidelines. Such "social pacts" may involve both governments and employers.
2. Continuing decline in membership that may slow down if unemployment levels decrease again.
3. Growing importance of non-standard work (part-time, temporary) and the need for pay systems that are tailored to individual situations: This will make central bargaining and national coordination increasingly difficult.
4. There may be a new role for unions as service providers and bargaining agents in local contexts. They will need to strike a balance between "employer demands for productive efficiency" and the legitimate desire of employees to cope with the stress of modern working life.

5. Restructuring is likely to continue. The resulting "conglomerate unions" will be more likely to deal with cost pressure. They will also need to manage significant internal diversity.

Approach to corporate sustainability

Mission

We note that the positions of unions on corporate sustainability are sector- and country-specific. Agendas (chemical workers vs musicians, local/regional vs global industry) and bargaining power ("militant" French vs "Thatchered" British unions) can differ significantly.

The most important issues for unions are linked to their traditional area of competence: employment, wages, working time, freedom of association, occupational health and safety. Hence, the social dimension is traditionally stronger than the environmental one. Unions are calling for more consistency in corporate behavior, a level playing field across developing and developed countries (in terms of labor conditions in particular) and a long-term perspective without today's strong focus on shareholder value:

> The same company may launch a project for handicapped people and at the same time attempt to prevent an election of a work council. (Union B)

Overall, corporate sustainability does not play a significant role in unions and their federations:

> We have no declared goal in the field of corporate social responsibility (CSR), but of course, we look out for the rights of our members. (Union C)

In some cases, we have detected a rather defensive and skeptical attitude toward corporate sustainability, because it is perceived as a corporate means of strengthening bargaining positions and preventing regulation ("it softens our negotiating position" – Union H).

> We have a nuanced view on CSR: It is neither inherently bad, nor good. And, it is not a substitute for regulation and collective bargaining. (Union K)

Compared to their [unions'] involvement in corporate governance, unions "overslept" the emergence of CSR: Obviously they are now skeptical, and prefer regulation. (Union N)

However, a few unions exhibited a more progressive and sophisticated viewpoint by advocating more sustainable business models, systematic inclusion of stakeholders and adoption of the UN global compact. Some are even considering the use of their pension funds for shareholder activism.

Incentives and motives

The low significance of corporate sustainability to unions (beyond the issues mentioned above) clearly reflects the interests of their key clientele (employees and works councils):

Employees are primarily concerned about their job security, pay and safety; CSR is of minor importance. (Union D)

There is pressure from governments and union members to get more involved in CSR-related themes. However, we see CSR as a topic raised by companies. (Union H)

Our underlying intention is to focus on topics that are of interest to employees. (Union B)

The clientele of unions is very diverse. Federations of unions need to align the different demands of their affiliated unions. Unions rely on building consensus among their individual members:

We [union headquarters] fight for long-term objectives, whereas individual employees may have their own short-term kind of agenda, e.g. working longer hours to increase their pay. (Union A)

Alignment of interest can be particularly challenging after a merger. For example, the German VER.DI incorporates five, formerly individual, unions, which makes a top-down approach impossible and the development of common agendas very difficult. Hence, it is important to keep track of the membership's needs: This is achieved through decentralized networks (company groups, regional groups) that ensure contact with employees in companies. To ensure alignment with the memberships' demands, surveys are conducted to prepare for collective agreements. Overall, positions are established through democratic bottom-up processes (per region/sector) as it is essential to have the support of the membership in order to generate the necessary advantage for bargaining.

Processes and tools

Assessing corporate performance. Our interviewees suggested that the assessment of corporate performance primarily occurs through networks of members and works councils (in the case of unions). They also suggested that company documents and third-party data are used when assessing corporate performance, including rating agencies, ILO, OECD and the media. In one case, a checklist for works council members was being developed to assess the effects of management decisions on multiple dimensions of social and environmental performance.

Although there is little systematic and continuous assessment of corporate social and environmental performance, unions claim to have a relatively accurate perception of performance levels:

> Trade unionists know more about their company than NGOs, because they have immediate internal insights. (Union K)

Nevertheless, more systematic assessment is needed, and will most likely be put on the agenda of unions. Overall, the quantitative data (presented in Figure 13.1) align strongly with our interviews.

We ascertain that the dominant assessment means (corporate reports, opinion surveys, media/internet and own investigations) reflect the

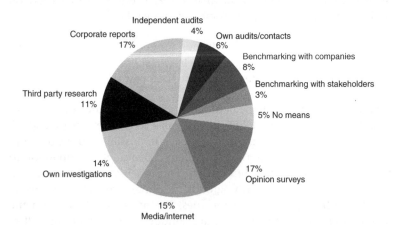

Figure 13.1 Means of assessing corporate social and environmental performance (unions)

reliance of unions on their network (to ensure alignment with the views and interests of their members) and other inexpensive sources (e.g. media, corporate reports). In Germany, for example, assessment also occurs at the supervisory board level, which includes union representation.

Determining actions to influence companies. As interests and demands are diverse and conflicting, strategic decisions are sometimes difficult to make. Democratic bottom-up processes are necessary to obtain a coherent position.

Once policy decisions are made, senior staff at unions and federations have a significant amount of managerial discretion. They rely on support and information from individual unions and companies.

Decisions for or against certain actions are made primarily based on experiences and systematic processes such as target setting and performance measurement. As Figure 13.2 illustrates, respondents also aim to align with other stakeholders.

Criteria

Assessing corporate performance. The criteria for assessing corporate social and environmental performance are contingent upon industry and country. Our interviewees suggested that assessment criteria include

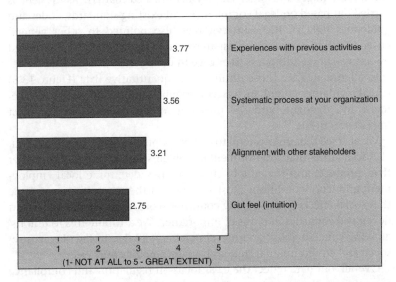

3.77	Experiences with previous activities
3.56	Systematic process at your organization
3.21	Alignment with other stakeholders
2.75	Gut feel (intuition)

1   2   3   4   5
(1- NOT AT ALL to 5 - GREAT EXTENT)

Figure 13.2 Extent to which factors determine actions to influence companies (unions)

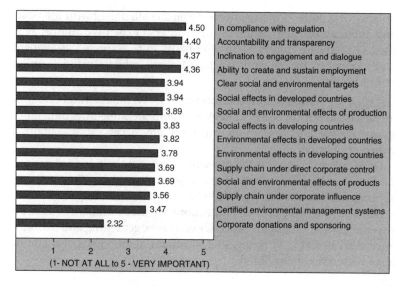

Figure 13.3 Importance of criteria for assessing corporate social and environmental performance (unions)

performance levels on the issues mentioned above, in particular on labor conditions, wages and other employment-related matters. Assessment is carried out based on legal compliance and existing standards, codes and guidelines (OECD, ILO). Interviewees also pointed to other general criteria such as corporate transparency (e.g. readiness to be monitored by unions) and willingness to engage in dialogue.

In alignment with those findings, our quantitative data (Figure 13.3) reveal regulatory compliance, accountability and transparency, engagement and dialogue, and the provision of employment as the most important criteria.

We also see that unions tend to – as one would expect – focus more on: (1) social rather than environmental problems; and (2) production rather than products and the supply chain, as they determine local employment and labor conditions most strongly. Furthermore, it is remarkable that social effects in developing countries score relatively the same as in developed countries in terms of importance. We attribute this to unions' growing concern about an unlevel playing field due to low (less costly) social and environmental standards in developing countries.

Overall, our data reflect the clear focus on regulation and compliance as well as on the opportunity to engage with companies, which underlines the significance of sustaining local employment and coping with shrinking bargaining power.

Determining actions to influence companies. According to our interviewees, decision-making criteria include:

- The severity and urgency of the problem.
- Support from the membership. (Can it be mobilized for the issues under consideration?)
- Existing "rules of the game" determined by legislation or collective agreements, corporate attitudes (confrontational vs cooperative).
- Level of public awareness and political support (as significant moderating factors) and expected benefits.
- The win–win potential, for parties under consideration (unions, companies, communities).

The win–win situation may occur between the company and the union or between two unions at different locations (e.g. when attempting to create a level playing field across developed and developing countries in terms of labor standards).

Our quantitative data align with our qualitative findings as follows. Corporate characteristics (e.g. visibility, power and financial situation) appear to be less important than the severity of issues and memberships' demands (Figure 13.4).

We suggest that this reflects the unions' inability to select actions opportunistically, i.e. when positive moderating factors are strong (see

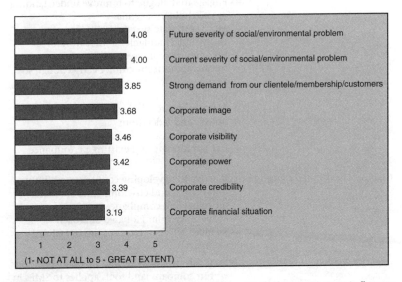

Figure 13.4 Extent to which criteria determine stakeholder actions to influence companies (unions)

section 13.3). Most of the time, they are only able to react to corporate actions (e.g. downsizing, relocation, outsourcing). This is presumably for two complementary reasons: (1) lack of bargaining power and (2) lack of knowledge and positioning on their part, which makes it difficult to be more proactive and "crafty" when building their own case.

Table 13.1   Unions' expectations (based on interviews)

Category	Concrete examples, rationale
"Classical" expectations	— Allow for workers' participation — Do not focus on figures only — Provide decent wages — Comply with ILO standards — Improve working conditions — Close gap between top and bottom management through more open communication, listen to your employees — Let top management "grow up" in your company — Introduce and clearly communicate code of conduct — Top management commitment
Transparency and dialogue	— Improve contact with community and particularly the mayor — Engage in dialogue to improve understanding of stakeholders' agenda — Make corporate sustainability reporting more easily understandable, so that workforce becomes more interested — Inform about restructuring early enough so that less confrontational approach is still possible — Actively and regularly communicate with unions and federations — Be more precise, communicate targets — Use appropriate and existing performance indicator
Change behavior on the ground	— If active in developing countries (exhibiting lower social and environmental standards), move beyond compliance — Move away from PR-based approach — Be more active in terms of the UN Global Compact
Capacity building	— Establish structures (create adequate positions within company)and tools applies to SMEs in particular

Expectations

Interviewees voiced various concrete expectations of companies, which we broadly assign to the four categories described in Table 13.1.
Most interviewees indicated that their expectations were not met, the moderating factors being current legislation and existing collective agreements. Companies are seen as being largely compliance-oriented reacting merely to outside pressure and focusing on short-term profits and shareholder value. Interviewees also reported a lot of corporate rhetoric ("CSR reporting is largely corporate PR"), and few changes "on the ground."

> Companies have a long way to go. In this country, they are reporting on social and environmental performance – which is now mandatory – but reporting is not the same as action. (Union D)

Corporate social and environmental performance is seen to vary a lot across different industries, within the same industry and between different forms of ownership: For example, interviewees were more satisfied with local and family businesses than with multinationals, which appears to reflect a more sensitive and local approach of the former and the strong bargaining power of the latter.
Our quantitative data (Figure 13.5) do not show any high levels of dissatisfaction on the key items discussed above (regulatory compliance, engagement and accountability).

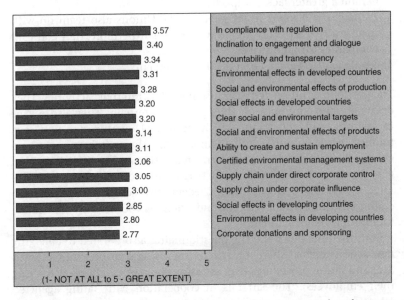

Value	Item
3.57	In compliance with regulation
3.40	Inclination to engagement and dialogue
3.34	Accountability and transparency
3.31	Environmental effects in developed countries
3.28	Social and environmental effects of production
3.20	Social effects in developed countries
3.20	Clear social and environmental targets
3.14	Social and environmental effects of products
3.11	Ability to create and sustain employment
3.06	Certified environmental management systems
3.05	Supply chain under direct corporate control
3.00	Supply chain under corporate influence
2.85	Social effects in developing countries
2.80	Environmental effects in developing countries
2.77	Corporate donations and sponsoring

(1- NOT AT ALL to 5 - GREAT EXTENT)

Figure 13.5 Satisfaction with corporate social and environmental performance (unions)

Hence, we conclude that (1) unions in Europe are aware of the current economic pressure companies face and that (2) higher levels of satisfaction would be possible if companies were considered more proactive.

13.3 Current stakeholder strategies

Actions and their effectiveness

Our data point to four main actions unions carry out to influence companies. They include the following (see also Figure 13.6):

1. *Political lobbying*: Unions influence policies through participation and consultation – at the European, national, regional and local level, and through members who are active politicians. Political lobbying is also carried out at the intergovernmental level (e.g. UNCTAD, ILO) and in developing and emerging countries where unions "use" their domestic ministries as intermediates to raise social standards in particular.

2. *Engaging with companies* (e.g. dialogue, partnerships): Unions engage through discussions with managers ("We can use other means of communication through media, but we prefer face-to-face discussions.") – and the supervisory board. Furthermore, they consult and coach managers and companies – particularly SMEs, since they exhibit a greater lack of capacities.

3. *Praising and blaming in the public arena*: Unions also team up with media or NGOs to raise public awareness. Furthermore, they confront companies through strikes.

4. *Regulation/legislation*, i.e. collective agreements.

The portfolio of union activities also includes "internal" activities: They document and communicate their position internally. They also engage in training and education, which occurs: (1) within a union (e.g. training works councils and members, as "the members make and change the company"); (2) between a federation and an affiliated union (e.g. the union is coached on wage bargaining, occupational health and safety); and (3) between unions/federations across countries: most commonly unions in developing and emerging countries are trained on, for example, labor standards.

Both the interviews and the questionnaires also pointed to emerging new actions such as shareholder activism (using pension funds as leverage) and rating procedures (e.g. assessing companies' efforts at training their employees). The latter is in cooperation with rating agencies.

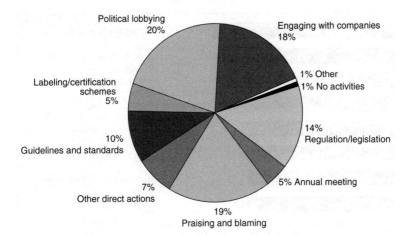

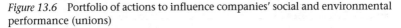

Figure 13.6   Portfolio of actions to influence companies' social and environmental performance (unions)

Obviously, federations (particularly international federations) are more active at political lobbying, whereas individual unions tend to engage more directly with companies.

Figure 13.7 on the general effectiveness of actions also reflects – in alignment with the evidence presented above – unions' preference for regulation and legislation to influence companies. The significant role of political lobbying (to determine future legislation – ranked in fourth place) is also plausible in this respect. Concomitantly, in light of globalization and the imperative of regional competitiveness, respondents see engagement and praising and blaming as the most effective "second-best" alternatives.

Quantitative data on companies' reactions to unions' initiatives are somewhat ambivalent (Figure 13.8). The most common corporate reaction appears to be engagement in dialogue (this result is most likely positively biased), followed by increased PR and lobbying efforts and proactive strategic change. Concomitantly, merely ignoring the actions of unions cannot be ruled out either.

Overall, responses appear to reflect, reasonably well, unions' limited bargaining power, as engagement does not necessarily mean that companies actually compromise, particularly if one takes into consideration that they are also viewed as: (1) increasing PR; and (2) changing strategies proactively. The latter result is particularly telling, as it suggests that companies are actually doing more than they are "forced" to do.

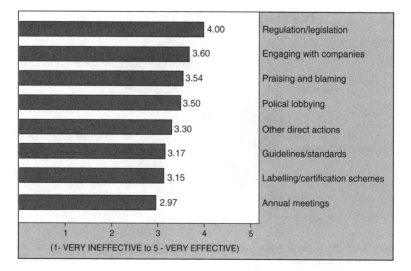

4.00	Regulation/legislation
3.60	Engaging with companies
3.54	Praising and blaming
3.50	Polical lobbying
3.30	Other direct actions
3.17	Guidelines/standards
3.15	Labelling/certification schemes
2.97	Annual meetings

1 2 3 4 5
(1- VERY INEFFECTIVE to 5 - VERY EFFECTIVE)

Figure 13.7 Perceived effectiveness of actions in influencing companies' social and environmental performance – regardless of whether used by the individual stakeholder or not (unions)

3.24	Companies engage in dialogue
3.12	Companies increase PR and lobbying efforts
2.97	Companies proactively change strategy to exploit opportunities
2.79	Companies defensively change strategy to mitigate risks
2.68	Companies change business processes
2.64	Companies completely ignore our actions
1.79	Companies take us to court

1 2 3 4 5
(1- NEVER to 5 - ALL THE TIME)

Figure 13.8 Frequency of corporate reactions to stakeholder action (unions)

Overall, unions appear to adopt a more cooperative than confrontational approach, particularly when interacting with powerful MNEs. Nevertheless, interviewees also stressed the need for both "carrot and stick," i.e. willingness to engage *and* the bargaining power resulting

from a large membership that can be mobilized:

> It would be naïve to think that negotiations with companies would be effective – without our ability to mobilize our members. (Union B)

Our interviews also pointed to some industry- and country-specific differences across Europe, which reflect the existing variation in political systems and industry structure (local industries such as power generation face greater bargaining power from unions) – often due to historical developments. In France, for example, communication between unions and companies is seen to be more serious due to the relatively strong and "militant" role of French unions.

Leading unions assess their own effectiveness based on a system of objectives. Performance is tracked in terms of membership development, changes in employment and the characteristics of collective agreements reached. It is difficult to assess seriously the overall effectiveness of activities, as their success is contingent upon various and often-situational factors (see next section). However, we are able to draw two broad conclusions:

1. Compared to federations, unions are in a better position to influence companies due to their direct contact with them.

   > Unions can be most influential at the local workplace level. Federations find it more difficult as they are "one or two stages removed." (Union D)

2. Cooperative approaches tend to be more effective than confrontational approaches, if the corporate attitude and the nature of the issues allow for this. In light of globalization and the pressure to sustain regional competitiveness, this finding likely reflects the limited bargaining power of unions.

Based on our quantitative data (Figure 13.9), we note that – surprisingly – the frequency of strikes only plays a secondary role, and is clearly dominated by effects on corporate reputation, strictness of regulators' controls and access to/retention of talent.

We suggest that this points to a growing awareness among unions that intangibles have become increasingly important to companies. It is also in line with unions' portfolio of actions, which is dominated by political lobbying, praising and blaming, engagement and only features a minor share of direct actions, i.e. strikes. Overall, unions see

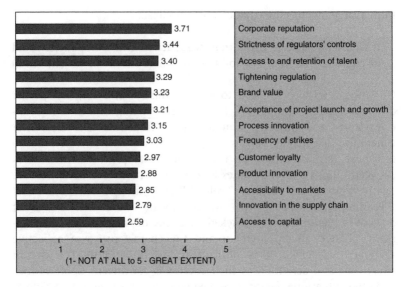

3.71	Corporate reputation
3.44	Strictness of regulators' controls
3.40	Access to and retention of talent
3.29	Tightening regulation
3.23	Brand value
3.21	Acceptance of project launch and growth
3.15	Process innovation
3.03	Frequency of strikes
2.97	Customer loyalty
2.88	Product innovation
2.85	Accessibility to markets
2.79	Innovation in the supply chain
2.59	Access to capital

1   2   3   4   5
(1- NOT AT ALL to 5 - GREAT EXTENT)

Figure 13.9 Extent to which stakeholder actions affect corporate value drivers (unions)

themselves in a rather difficult position, due to their limited bargaining power.

> There are no real risks for companies. We mainly intend to cooperate. However, risks can occur for laggard companies. (Union F)

Determinants of effectiveness

We identified various factors that determine the effectiveness of actions carried out to influence corporate social or environmental performance (see Table 13.2 below).

13.4   Future trends

Trends are largely determined by globalization and pressure to improve local and regional competitiveness as well as corporate credibility and trust. Based on the interviews, the following developments can be expected:

1. More capacity building among unions to assess corporate performance (e.g. corporate credibility) and to make corresponding decisions.

Table 13.2   Determinants of effectiveness

Determinant	Further remarks
Moderating/situational factors	
Timeliness of action	The timelier the action, the less confrontational the atmosphere between union and company.
Support from third parties	— Public — Political community — NGOs — Media — Multi-stakeholder alliance However, in many instances, communities and governments are viewed as unsupportive; local and national positions are not aligned.
Regional competitiveness	The more competitive the region, the less inclined the company is to leave.
Close personal contacts at top level	Applies to contacts between unions and companies as well as between unions (works councils, members, federations etc.). The closer the contact, the greater the trust.
Market opportunities	The greater the opportunities, the greater the incentive for companies to compromise.
Existing international guidelines and certification schemes	Providing a reference point for negotiaons.
Complexity	Great variation in cultural and economic conditions across countries. Differences in issues make single global agreements difficult to draw up, e.g.women's rights in Arabic countries (Union H).
Union-related factors	
Membership	Scale and interest: Can membership be mobilized? In many countries, union membership is in decline.
Lack of resources: time and money	Declining membership and support.
Existing networks	Networks on the national and international level facilitate information exchange and are claimed to strengthen bargaining power. In reality, however, solidarity among employees and locations is limited, which makes unions vulnerable to being played against each other.

Continued

Table 13.2   Continued

Determinant	Further remarks
Company-related factors	
Company size	The greater the company size, the more jobs are at stake. This boosts the company's bargaining power.
Corporate attitude	Companies have increasingly focused on short-term profits and shareholder value. Interviewees criticize the ignorance of MNEs in particular: They are testing our strength (in terms collective agreements and legislation). (Union M) There is too much rhetoric, too little willingness to act. (Union I)
Local ties of company	SMEs and family businesses more locally rooted, and willing to engage: When dealing with SMEs, one can achieve a lot at the local level. Union D)
Top management awareness and commitment	Today's CEOs are less interested and less in touch with local communities. Furthermore, their remuneration is share price-based.
Corporate transparency	Companies exhibit a lack of communication, which also manifests itself through a "cliquey" atmosphere at top management level (supervisory boards).

2. Unions are likely to sustain (and increase) their expertise in their traditional areas (labor conditions, occupational health and safety, etc.). Some of them are also likely to make a stronger connection between those areas and corporate sustainability. However, we doubt that the importance of corporate sustainability as a whole will increase substantially in unions, as they rely on greater involvement from individual employees and the associated funding they provide. Their attention will remain focused on employment.

3. There is a tendency to engage in more dialogue and cooperation. In particular, international networks with other unions and federations, NGOs and governments are going to be strengthened further. However, substantial coordination costs will have to be incurred.

4. Efforts to sustain and strengthen influence: There are certain fears among unions that corporate sustainability could undermine unionism and regulation. Most aim to prevent and compensate for deregulation (see quote below). Political lobbying will continue to play a significant role. Some consider strengthening new areas of activism through, for example, pension fund investments.

> If governments stop providing certain social services in the future, we will try to get those issues included in our collective agreements. (Union L)

Interviewees have witnessed a continuing trend away from a "naturally" socially responsible "patron" (due to his close and historically grown ties with the local community) to a "hard-nosed" CEO with a strong international background. They consider a rebound in this respect toward more sensitive leadership and corporate culture unlikely.

In the context of globalization and stalling economic growth in Europe, most unions expect to continue to have a difficult job in Europe and to fight for their legitimation. Unions' role as a co-legislator may continue to suffer due to declining membership. Serious social and political conflicts may also occur, if governments feel compelled to enforce wage restraint. However, we also note a certain renaissance of unionism in some countries such as Switzerland, in which the membership of unions is partly growing again.

13.5 Conclusion

The agendas and activities of unions are clearly driven by globalization and the constant pressure for regional competitiveness: Their efforts are clearly geared toward wage bargaining and sustaining employment levels. They also largely reflect a somewhat reactive and skeptical attitude toward corporate sustainability: corporate sustainability is often perceived as a corporate means of forestalling legislation. However, a few leading unions are taking a more sophisticated and active approach to corporate sustainability management: They assess corporate performance more holistically and link their traditional areas of interests to corporate sustainability.

Overall, our evidence suggests that:

1. Most unions are still at the beginning of their learning curve on corporate sustainability.

2. Many lack the criteria, tools and processes to assess corporate social and environmental performance more accurately.
3. They strongly rely on political lobbying, engagement and praising and blaming to influence companies and are met with corporate willingness to engage in dialogue but little readiness to act.

It is uncertain to what extent further capacity building on corporate sustainability in unions would actually contribute to higher levels of social and environmental performance in Europe. Given Europe's high social and environmental standards, win–win situations are difficult to find, in which corporate social and/or environmental performance can be further improved without compromising financial performance.

Hence, the most obvious strategy – even if primarily to sustain regional competitiveness (and employment) – is the creation of an international level playing field through political lobbying and partnerships with other unions. However, this route is also associated with several significant obstacles: developing countries' lower awareness of social and environmental issues (in both governments and unions), their imperative of economic growth (e.g. China in particular) as well as the lack of employee representation in many developing countries.

Notes

1   T. Boeri, A. Brugiavini, and L. Calmfors (eds), *The Role of Unions in the Twenty-First Century* (Oxford: Oxford University Press, 2001).
2   Ibid.
3   Ibid.

Appendix 1: Interview Guidelines

Opener

Briefly emphasize the need for and relevance of this study. A cross-stakeholder study of this scope has never been carried out and so far only rather superficial opinion surveys are available.

Establish common basis. Companies undertake various kinds of social and environmental initiatives for different reasons, including the satisfaction of stakeholder demands. We are interested in

- the aspects of corporate social and environmental performance that you/your organizations are interested in
- the activities you engage in to influence corporate performance in those areas
- the resulting risks or opportunities for companies

A. Assessment of corporate social and environmental performance

Questions	Notes for interviewer/Recommended focus
A1. Mission and drivers (for stakeholders' interest in companies' social and environmental performance)	
1. What is your **mission** in terms of companies' social and environmental performance?	• *Essential to cover this question, since not part of the questionnaire*
2. What are your **incentives/motives** to improve companies' social and environmental performance?	• *Environmental and social issues of importance (NB)* • *Internal motives and organizational interests (e.g. funding, (educational) background of the members/staff to be satisfied, target audience of activities?)* • *Declared goals of organization*

Questions	Notes for interviewer/Recommended focus
A2. Criteria and processes/tools (for assessing companies' social and environmental performance)	

3. Do you **assess** companies' social and environmental **performance?**	
4. If, yes, what **criteria** do you use to assess it?	• *E.g. compliance with regulation, accountability and transparency, ability to create employment, corporate sponsoring*
5. What **means** do you use to assess it?	• *E.g. surveying opinions of clientele, media screening/internet search, benchmarking, third party research*
6. Please provide a **real-life example** of a company you interact with – what challenges did you encounter and how did you deal with them?	• ***Most importantly revisit this question also in the context of section B and C*** • ***Be aware of time constaints when asking this question*** • *Interviewee should be precise and limit his anwer to the three most important points* • *Possibility for interviewee to mention a "best-case" example as well as a "worst-case" example* • *Emphasize the confidentiality of the research, if interviewee hesitates to give an example*

A3. Outcome of the assessment	
7. To what extent are your **expectations** currently being met by companies?	• *Should be possible to get a time perspective here, i.e. how expectations and corporate performance changed over time*
8. What **conclusions** have you drawn from assessing companies' social and environmental performance?	• ***Essential to cover this question, since not part of questionnaire*** • *How drastically does the organization need to change corporate social and environmental performance to satisfy its clientele/target audience? What strategy is appropriate?*

A4. Recommendations to meet stakeholder demands	
9. What **should companies do** differently in order to meet your demands?	• ***Essential to cover this question, since not part of questionnaire***

Questions	Notes for interviewer/Recommended focus
10. What **specific steps** would you recommend?	• *Essential to cover this question, since not part of questionnaire*

B. Stakeholders' activities to influence corporate performance

B1. Actions in the present and future

11. Which **actions** do you undertake presently to influence companies' social and environmental performance?	• *Depending on stakeholder: regulation/legislation, other direct actions (e.g. boycotts, imposing standards and guidelines), political lobbying, partnerships* • *What are the actions geared toward: confrontation or engagement?*
12. Which of those actions are **most effective** at influencing companies' social and environmental performance?	
13. Do you expect the nature of your **actions** to **change** significantly in the future (5–10 years)?	• *Essential to cover this question, since not part of questionnaire*
14. If yes, **in what way** and why?	• *Essential to cover this question, since not part of questionnaire*

B2. Factors determining actions

15. Which **processes** do you go through when determining the actions you take to influence companies' social and environmental performance?	• *E.g. intuition, alignment with other stakeholders, systematic process (target setting, etc.)*
16. What **criteria** determine the actions you undertake to influence companies' social and environmental performance?	• *E.g. companies' power, visibility, demand from clientele and membership, companies' image and credibility*

B3. Outcome of activities

17. How **successful** have your activities been until today?	
18. What were the **success factors**?	• *Essential to cover this question, since not part of questionnaire*
19. What where **stumbling blocks**?	• *Essential to cover this question, since not part of questionnaire*
20. Do you expect your success rate to **change in the future**?	• *Essential to cover this question, since not part of questionnaire*

Questions	Notes for interviewer/Recommended focus
21. If yes, **in what way** and why?	• *Essential to cover this question, since not part of questionnaire*

C.   Implications and recommendations for companies

C1. Risks and opportunities for companies

22. What **risks** do companies incur, if they do not respond to your actions or take on a proactive role?	• *E.g. changes in accessibility to markets, strictness of regulators' controls, brand value, acceptance of project launch and growth, customer loyalty* • *To what extent is superior performance rewarded, to what extent are laggards "punished"?*
23. What **opportunities** exist for companies, if they respond to your actions or take on a proactive role?	
24. How **convinced** are you that your actions are really having an impact on companies?	• *Cite IMD research on the importance of stakeholders if appropriate: External pressure on companies to improve social and environmental performance is marginal*

C2. Stakeholders, recommendations to mitigate the risks and exploit opportunities

25. If you were to put yourself "into the shoes" of companies, what would you do to **mitigate or even avoid the risks** mentioned above (question 22)?	• *Essential to cover this question, since not part of questionnaire*
26. If you were to put yourself "into the shoes" of companies, what would you do to **exploit the opportunities** mentioned above (question 23)?	• *Essential to cover this question, since not part of questionnaire*

Appendix 2: Self-completion Questionnaire

IMD   IMD, Forum for Corporate Sustainability Management, P.O. Box 915, Chemin de Bellerive 32, 1001 Lausanne, Switzerland   *Forum for* **CSM**
E-mail: Oliver.Salzmann@imd.ch

Dear Respondent,

Companies have a significant potential to engage in activities that improve their social and environmental performance (e.g. protecting human rights, reducing emissions).

We aim to examine how different stakeholder groups relevant to business
- perceive the effectiveness of these activities and
- engage in activities to improve companies' social and environmental performance.

We will send you the research results when this study is completed, should you so wish. An online version of this questionnaire can be found at www.imd.ch/go/stakeholder

Please simply indicate your personal opinion and perception in response to the following questions. We guarantee strict confidentiality.

1. Which of the following **means** does your organization use to **assess** companies' social and environmental performance (Please mark all that apply)?

☐ No means	☐ Independent audits
☐ Opinion surveys of our clientele/membership/target audience	☐ Own audits and contacts
☐ Media screening/internet searches	☐ Benchmarking company performance with other companies
☐ Own investigations (e.g. testing environmental quality, surveillance of corporate activities and their effects)	☐ Benchmarking with the position of other stakeholder groups
☐ Third party research	☐ Other, please specify:
☐ Analysis of corporate reports	

2. How important are the following **criteria** to your organization **when assessing** companies' social and environmental performance?

① = Not at all to ⑤ = Very important

In compliance with regulation	①	②	③	④	⑤
Inclination to engagement and dialogue	①	②	③	④	⑤
Accountability and transparency	①	②	③	④	⑤
Certified environmental management systems	①	②	③	④	⑤
Ability to create and sustain employment	①	②	③	④	⑤
Clear environmental and social targets	①	②	③	④	⑤
Corporate donations, sponsoring	①	②	③	④	⑤
Social and environmental effects of products	①	②	③	④	⑤
Social and environmental effects of production	①	②	③	④	⑤
Social and environmental effects of the supply chain within direct corporate control	①	②	③	④	⑤
Social and environmental effects of the supply chain that companies can only influence	①	②	③	④	⑤
Social effects in developing countries	①	②	③	④	⑤
Environmental effects in developing countries	①	②	③	④	⑤
Social effects in developed countries	①	②	③	④	⑤
Environmental effects in developed countries	①	②	③	④	⑤
Other, please specify:	①	②	③	④	⑤

IMD, Forum for Corporate Sustainability Management, P.O. Box 915, Chemin de Bellerive 32, 1001 Lausanne, Switzerland
E-mail: Oliver.Salzmann@imd.ch

3. To what extent are your **expectations** about the following facets of corporate social and environmental performance met?

① = Not at all to ⑤ = Great extent

In compliance with regulation	①	②	③	④	⑤
Inclination to engagement and dialogue	①	②	③	④	⑤
Accountability and transparency	①	②	③	④	⑤
Certified environmental management systems	①	②	③	④	⑤
Ability to create and sustain employment	①	②	③	④	⑤
Clear environmental and social targets	①	②	③	④	⑤
Corporate donations, sponsoring	①	②	③	④	⑤
Social environmental effects of products	①	②	③	④	⑤
Social and environmental effects of production	①	②	③	④	⑤
Social and environmental effects of the supply chain within direct corporate control	①	②	③	④	⑤
Social and environmental effects of the supply chain that the companies can only influence	①	②	③	④	⑤
Social effects in developing countries	①	②	③	④	⑤
Environmental effects in developing countries	①	②	③	④	⑤
Social effects in developed countries	①	②	③	④	⑤
Environmental effects in developed countries	①	②	③	④	⑤
Other, please specify:	①	②	③	④	⑤

4. Which **actions** does your organization engage in to **influence** companies' social and environmental performance (Please mark all that apply.)?

☐ No activities at all	☐ Providing guidelines and standards for companies
☐ Regulation/legislation	☐ Providing labeling or certification schemes
☐ Direct actions at annual meeting (e.g. shareholder resolution)	☐ Political lobbying
☐ Praising and blaming in the public arena	☐ Engaging with companies (e.g. dialogue, partnership)
☐ Other direct actions (boycott, imposing standards, etc.)	☐ Other, please specify:

5. How effective are the following **actions at influencing** companies' social and environmental performance – **independently** of whether they are used by your organization or not?

① = Very ineffective to ⑤ = Very effective

Regulation/legislation	①	②	③	④	⑤
Direct actions at annual meeting (e.g. shareholder resolution)	①	②	③	④	⑤
Praising and blaming in the public arena	①	②	③	④	⑤
Other direct actions (e.g. boycott, imposing standards)	①	②	③	④	⑤
Providing guidelines and standards for companies	①	②	③	④	⑤
Providing labeling or certification schemes	①	②	③	④	⑤
Political lobbying	①	②	③	④	⑤
Engaging with companies (e.g. dialogue, partnership)	①	②	③	④	⑤
Other, please specify:	①	②	③	④	⑤

IMD   IMD, Forum for Corporate Sustainability Management, P.O. Box 915, Chemin de Bellerive 32, 1001 Lausanne, Switzerland
E-mail: Oliver.Salzmann@imd.ch   *Forum for* **CSM**

6. To what extent do the following **factors** determine the **actions** your organization takes to **influence** companies' social and environmental performance?

① = Not at all to ⑤ = Great extent

"Gut feel" (intuition)	①	②	③	④	⑤
Experiences made with previous activities	①	②	③	④	⑤
Alignment with other stakeholders	①	②	③	④	⑤
Systematic process at your organization (target setting, performance measurement)	①	②	③	④	⑤
Other, please specify:	①	②	③	④	⑤

7. To what extent do the following **criteria** determine the **actions** you take to **influence** companies' social and environmental performance?

① = Not at all to ⑤ = Great extent

Strong demand from our clientele/membership/customers	①	②	③	④	⑤
Corporate visibility (recognition of brand and company name)	①	②	③	④	⑤
Corporate power (relationship with government, ability to create employment)	①	②	③	④	⑤
Corporate financial situation	①	②	③	④	⑤
Corporate credibility	①	②	③	④	⑤
Corporate image	①	②	③	④	⑤
Current severity of social/environmental problem	①	②	③	④	⑤
Future severity of social/environmental problem	①	②	③	④	⑤
Other, please specify:	①	②	③	④	⑤

8. The following list describes possible **reactions of companies** to the activities your organization undertakes to improve companies' social and environmental performance. Please rate the reactions in terms of how often they occur.

① = Never to ⑤ = All the time

Companies completely ignore our actions	①	②	③	④	⑤
Companies bring us to court	①	②	③	④	⑤
Companies increase PR and lobbying efforts	①	②	③	④	⑤
Companies engage in dialogue	①	②	③	④	⑤
Companies change business processes	①	②	③	④	⑤
Companies defensively change strategy to mitigate risks	①	②	③	④	⑤
Companies proactively change strategy to exploit opportunities	①	②	③	④	⑤
Other, please specify:	①	②	③	④	⑤

9. To what extent do the **actions** your organization takes to improve corporate social and environmental performance **affect** the following **drivers of corporate success**?

① = Not at all to ⑤ = Great extent

Corporate reputation	①	②	③	④	⑤
Brand value	①	②	③	④	⑤
Acceptance of project launch and growth	①	②	③	④	⑤
Strictness of regulators' controls	①	②	③	④	⑤
Tightening regulation	①	②	③	④	⑤
Customer loyalty	①	②	③	④	⑤

IMD, Forum for Corporate Sustainability Management, P.O. Box 915, Chemin de Bellerive 22, 1001 Lausanne, Switzerland
E-mail: Oliver.Salzmann@imd.ch

	①	②	③	④	⑤
Frequency of strikes	①	②	③	④	⑤
Accessibility to markets	①	②	③	④	⑤
Access-to-capital	①	②	③	④	⑤
Innovation in the supply chain	①	②	③	④	⑤
Process innovation	①	②	③	④	⑤
Product innovation	①	②	③	④	⑤
Access to and retention of talent	①	②	③	④	⑤
Other, please specify:	①	②	③	④	⑤

10. Please indicate the extent to which the following groups are able to **influence corporate behavior.**

① = Not at all to ⑤ = Great extent

	①	②	③	④	⑤
Unions	①	②	③	④	⑤
Consumer associations/organizations	①	②	③	④	⑤
Public pressure groups (e.g. conservation and human rights organizations, citizens' initiatives)	①	②	③	④	⑤
Media	①	②	③	④	⑤
Financial institutions (e.g. banks, (re)insurers, stock exchanges, rating agencies)	①	②	③	④	⑤
Employees	①	②	③	④	⑤
Communities/local authorities	①	②	③	④	⑤
Regulators/politicians	①	②	③	④	⑤
Companies as suppliers of other companies	①	②	③	④	⑤
Companies as customers of other companies	①	②	③	④	⑤

A. Please indicate the **stakeholder group** you represent (Mark only one box):

☐ Manager in sales and marketing	☐ Manager in the following functions ONLY: purchasing, supply chain, procurement
☐ Public pressure group	☐ Regulator/politician
☐ Community/local authority	☐ Financial institution (e.g. bank, (re)insurer, stock exchange, rating agency)
☐ Media	☐ Union
☐ Consumer association/organization	☐ Other, please specify:

☐   I am working at the global or European office/headquarters of my organization or working with an institution of the European Union.

B. Please indicate your country location:_____

Thank you for completing this survey. If you would like to receive the results of this survey, please provide us with your e-mail address.

My e-mail address is: _____

Please fax your completed questionnaire to CSM on +41 21 618 0641 or mail it to:

CSM
IMD - International Institute for Management Development
P.O. Box 915
Chemin de Bellerive 32
1001 Lausanne
Switzerland

Index